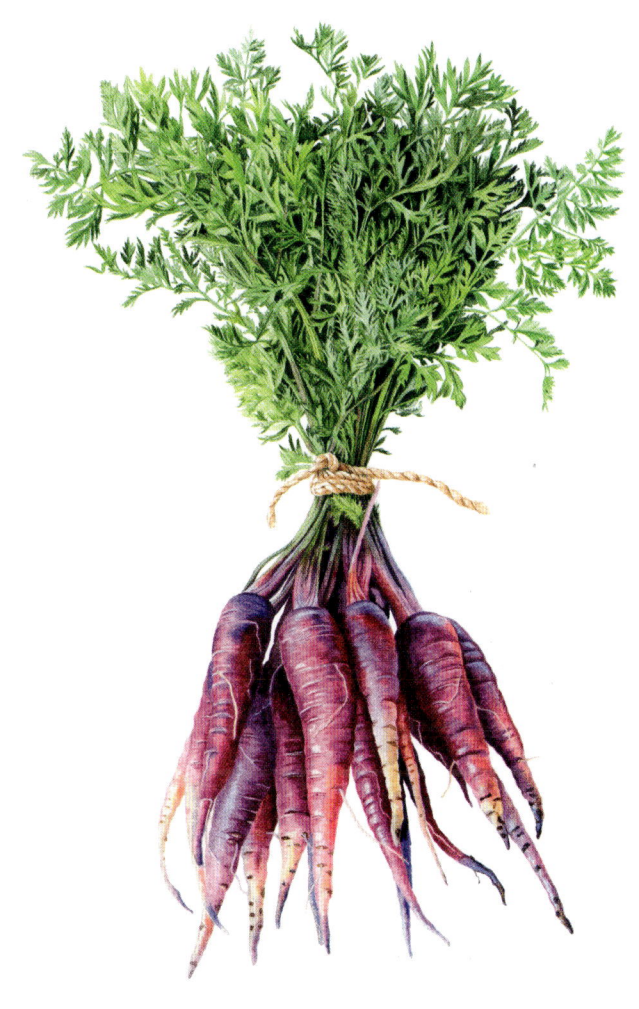

NEW IDEAS IN
BOTANICAL
PAINTING

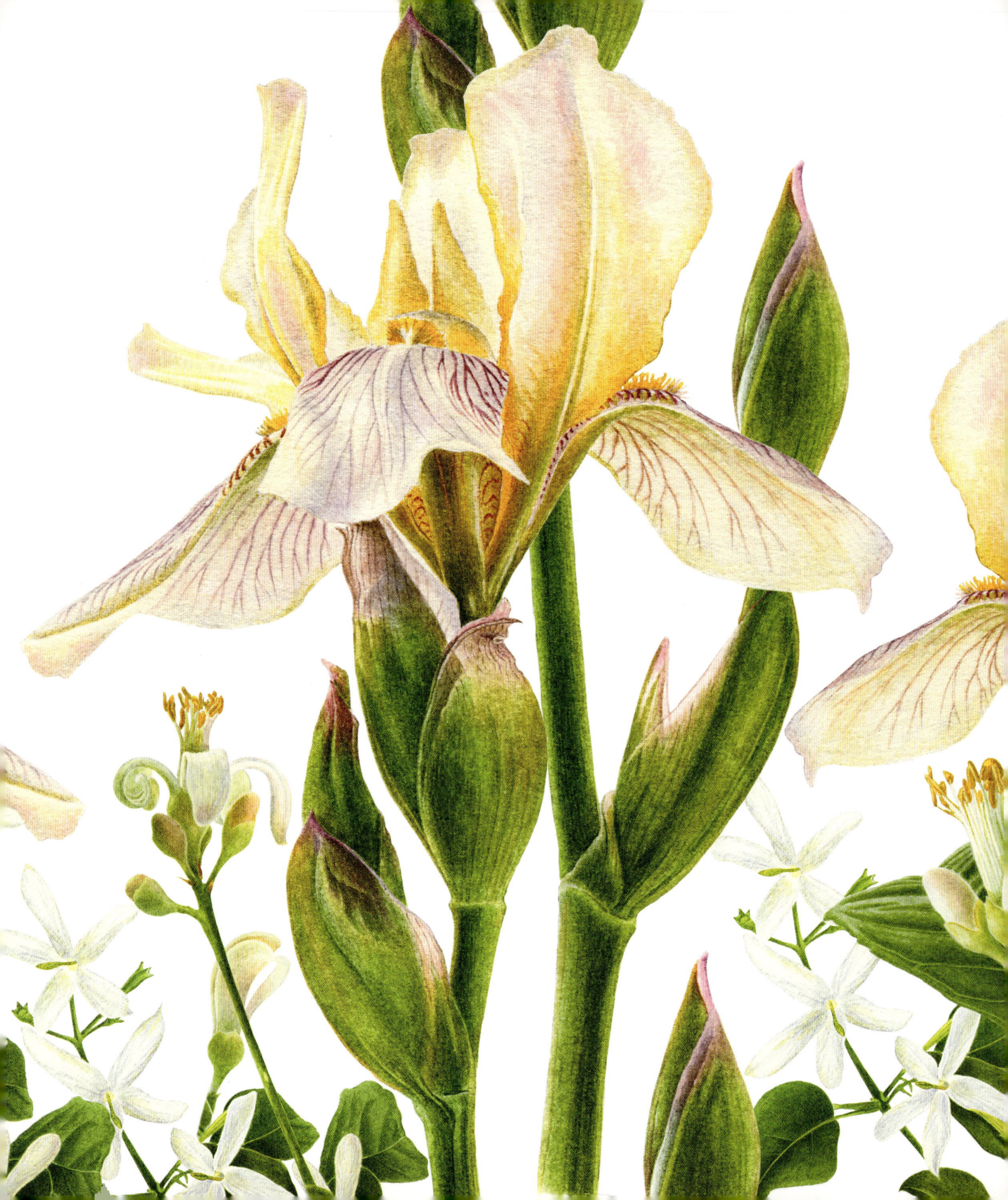

NEW IDEAS IN BOTANICAL PAINTING

Composition and Colour

Carolyn Jenkins with Helen Birch

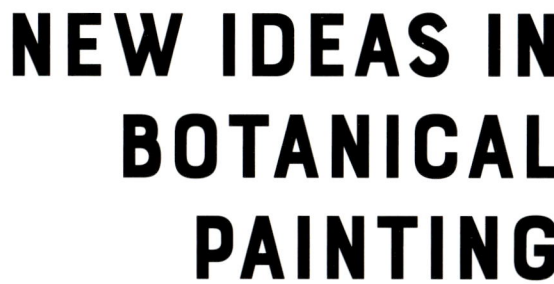

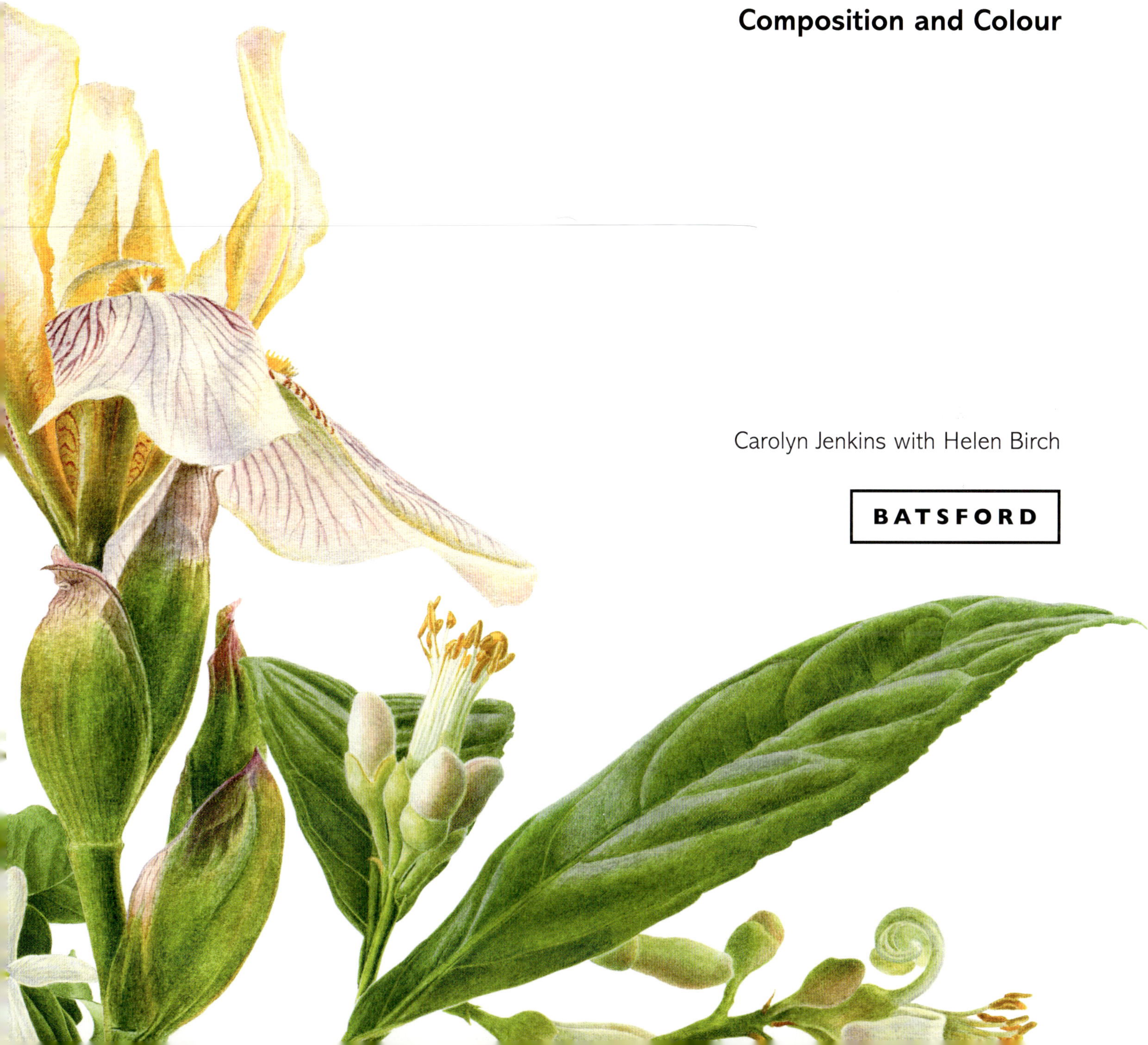

Dedications

Carolyn Jenkins
To my sister, Nathalie, who taught me to love plants and who inspired me to begin my botanical painting journey.

Helen Birch
For my cousin, Caroline, for her especial spirit, strength and love.

First published in the United Kingdom in 2022 by
B.T. Batsford Ltd
43 Great Ormond Street
London WC1N 3HZ
An imprint of B.T. Batsford Holdings Limited

ISBN: 9781849946629

A CIP catalogue record for this book is available from the British Library.

30 29 28 27 26 25 24 23 22
10 9 8 7 6 5 4 3 2 1

Reproduction by Rival Colour Ltd
Printed and bound by Toppan Leefung Ltd, China

This book can be ordered direct from the publisher at the website www.batsford.com, or try your local bookshop.

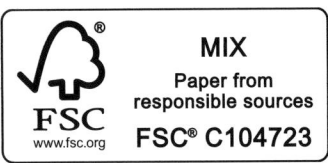

Page 1 Purple carrots (*Daucus carota*).

Page 2-3 Iris, jasmine and neroli. The warm sunlight shining through the translucent petals of this tall bearded iris highlighted a delicate haze of fine purple veins running through the margins of the petals.

Right *Delphinium* 'Faust'.

Next page Jasmin, peony and ylang-ylang.

CONTENTS

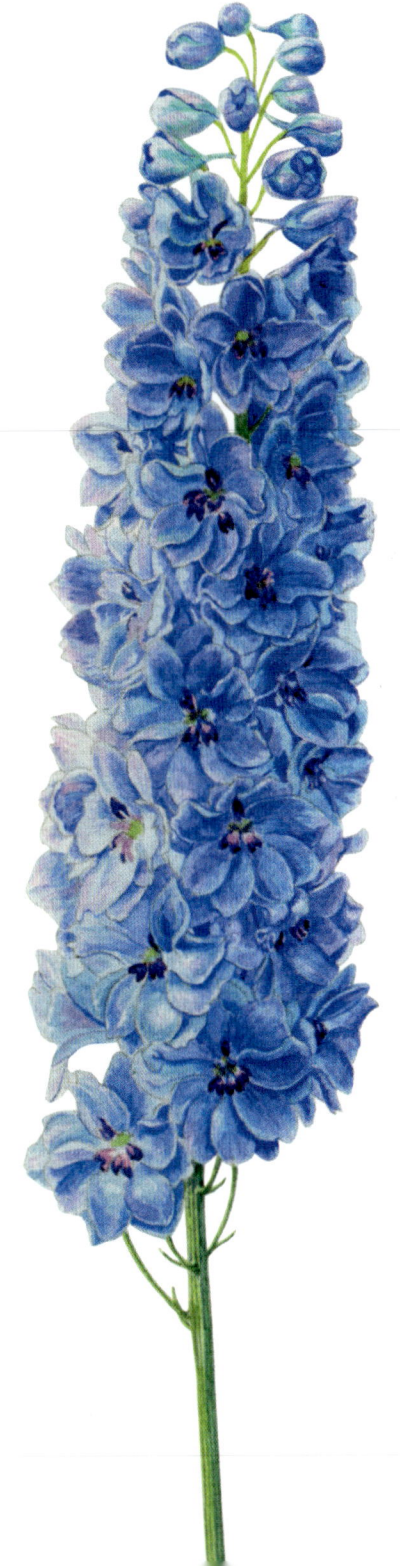

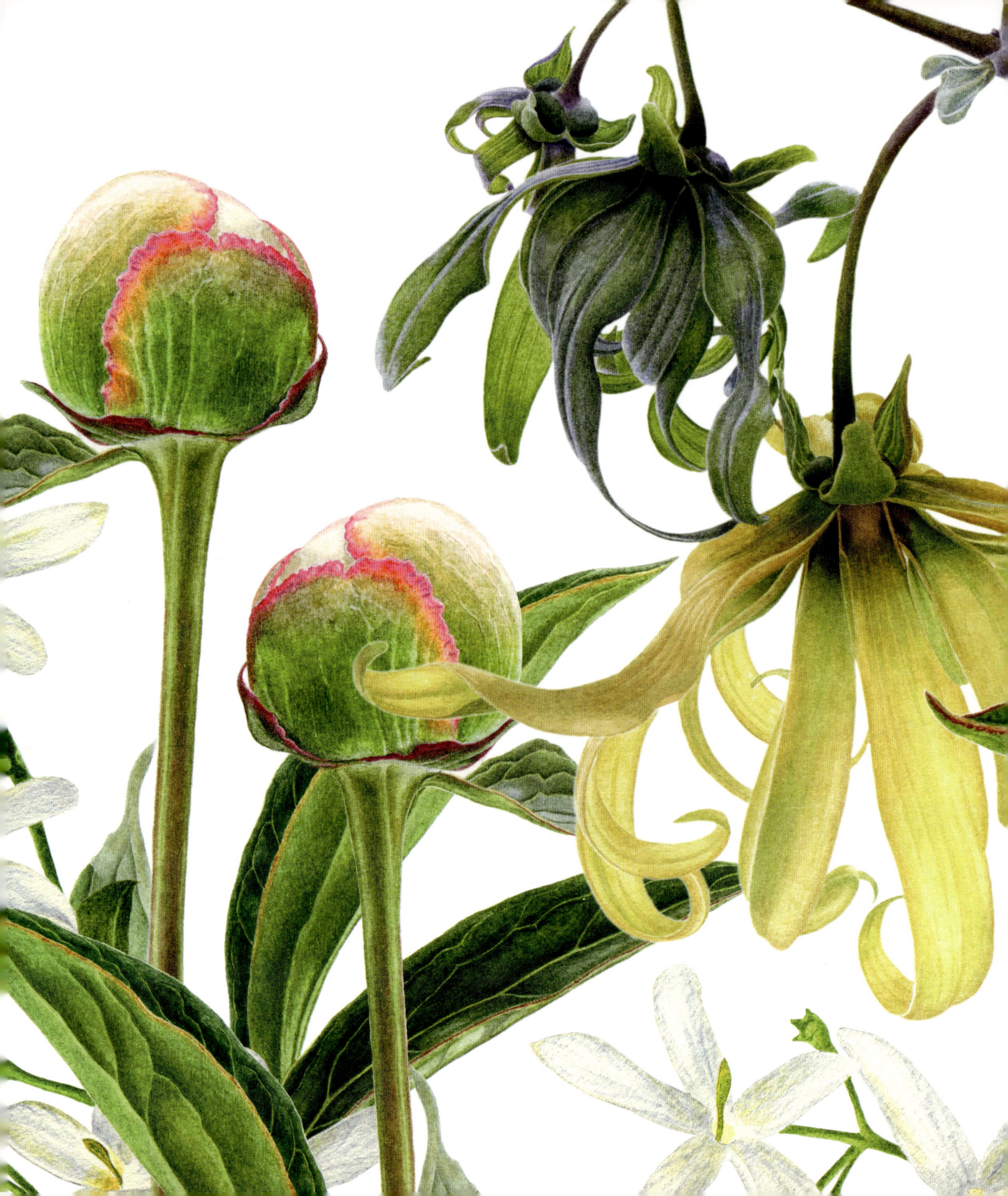

INTRODUCTION

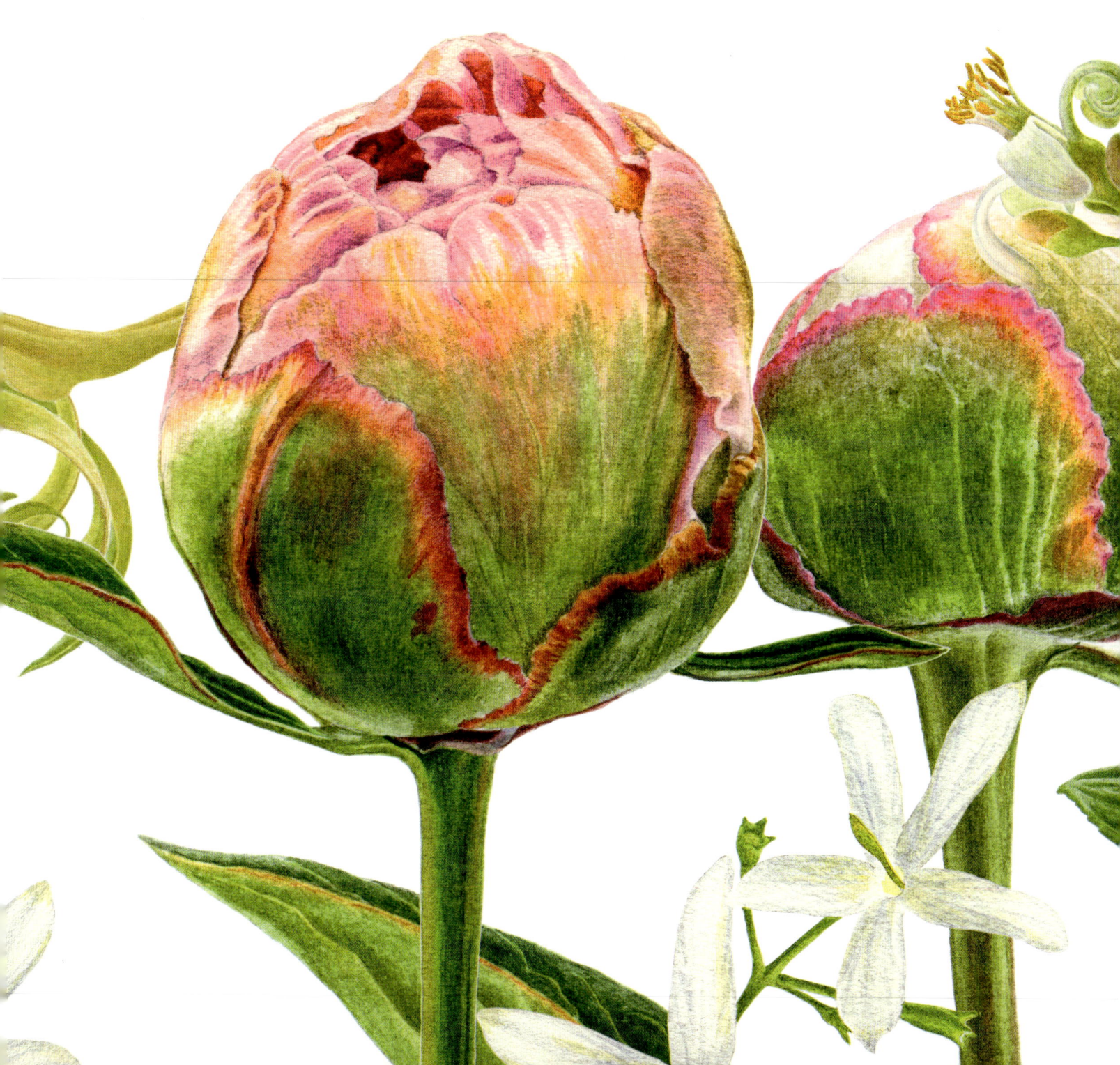

INTRODUCTION

Some people know what they want to do in life, but for me it took many years to hone in on what I love best.

Although almost all of the painting I do now is botanical, it hasn't always been the case. This focus has developed over at least 20 years as I've realized what I'm most interested in and hopefully best at. I've developed into a botanical specialist only after exploring and experiencing various other subject matters – through education, employment, adult training courses and family influence.

I feel lucky to have come from an artistic family. My father was a graphic designer and lecturer at the Royal College of Art. I'm sure that my interest in graphic compositions has come from the influence of my father's work. An upbringing in this creative environment has undoubtedly been a contributing factor to what I do now.

There was always a diverse assortment of art materials to experiment with at home, loads of wonderful art books and a large collection of paintings on the walls. I used to spend hours designing my own magazines and comics and entering artistic competitions – I remember winning a prize and a coveted *Blue Peter* badge in a competition!

In addition to my father being artistic, my great-aunt Joan Warburton was a painter and my great-uncle Peter O'Malley a ceramicist – and their son Liam O'Malley was a painter too. We frequently stayed with them; they were all extremely talented and a lot of fun. I know that one of the reasons I have ended up being a botanical painter is to do with my great-aunt's influence and our visits to her home. I was enthralled by the work my aunt did, her garden and particularly her paintings of plants, flowers, fruit and vegetables. She was always working, produced hundreds of paintings in oil, gouache and watercolour, and was constantly planting new and interesting things in the garden to paint. My aunt would show me what she was working on and let me have a go with her paints. Her husband, Peter, also a hugely talented artist and a senior tutor of ceramics at the Royal College of Art, had a studio and kiln at the bottom of the garden where he would let me try out throwing pots and experimenting with glazes.

I was very lucky as a child to be so encouraged and be able to have all of these artistic experiences.

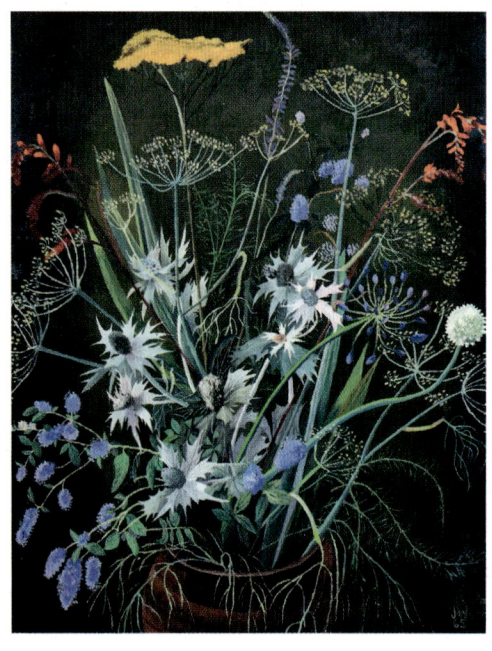

Above *Summer Flowers* (1962) by Joan Warburton. Oil painting, 61 x 76cm (24 x 30in).

Right Cornflower (*Centaurea cyanus*). A mixed-media portrait in watercolour and coloured pencil.

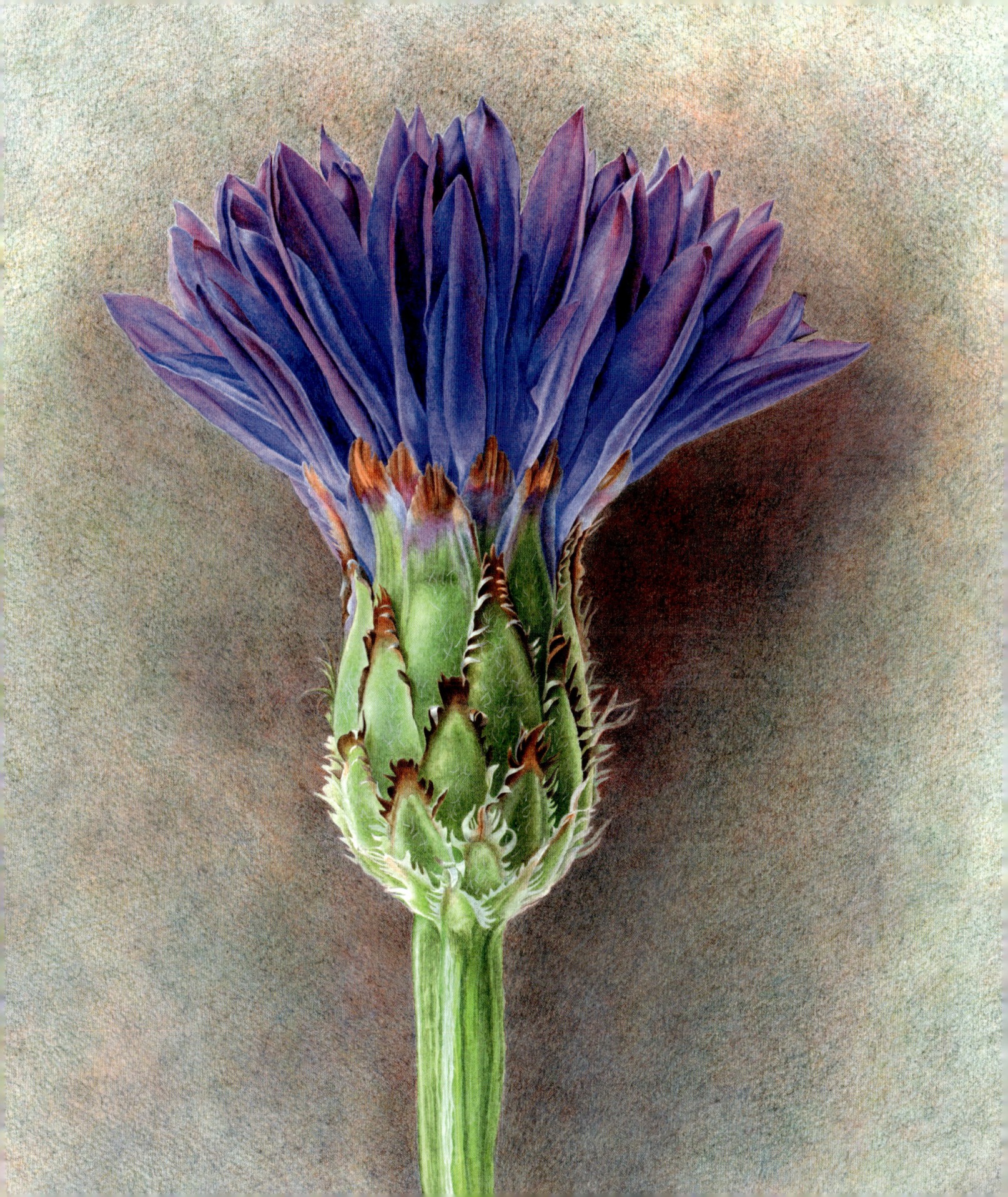

My Love of Plants

I've always been equally interested in plants and painting, and feel very lucky that these interests – gardening and botanical art – have come together in the way they have.

Working on this book has helped me to think about my dual roles as an illustrator and gardener and how they fit together. They weren't always so clearly defined, but the foundations for both were laid down early.

I am fascinated by the morphology of things, especially the form, shape, colour and structure of plants. I have always been interested in finding out about flowers, taking them apart to see how their component parts fit together and wanting to know more about how plants and flowers actually grow. This natural attraction to botany definitely preceded any actual gardening. I've only ever been distracted from it when pursuing artistic projects that weren't botanically oriented.

I first realized that I loved gardening when I had my own garden to maintain. Just doing the ordinary stuff like weeding, cutting back, pruning and deadheading brings me a lot of pleasure. As the seasons change I find I really enjoy planting

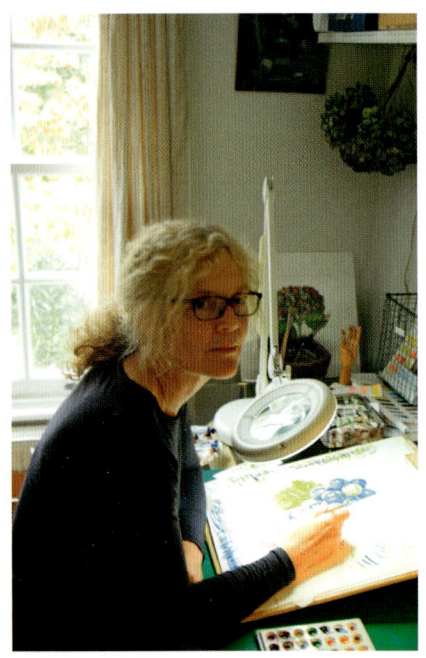

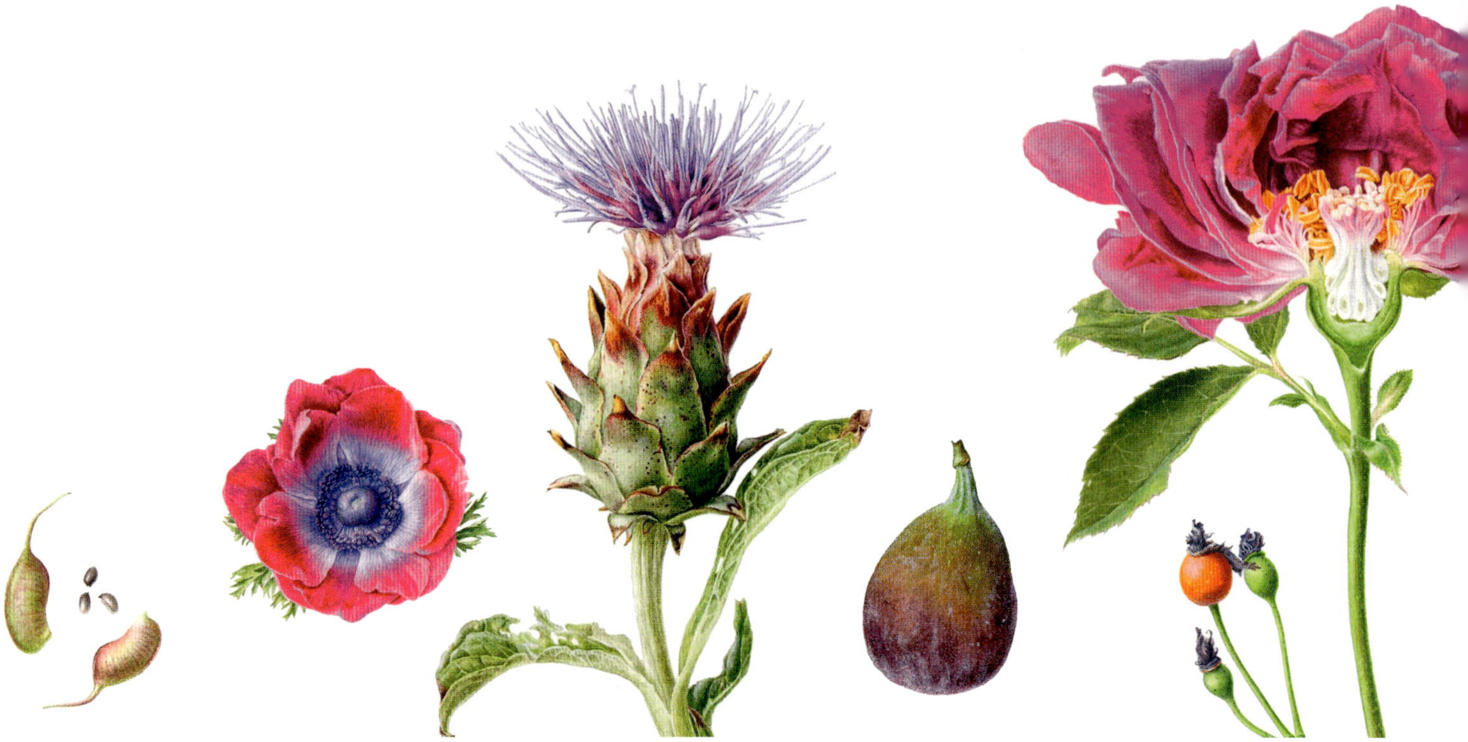

Above Carolyn working in her London studio.

Below Painted flowers, fruits and seeds from the author's garden.

up pots of beautiful spring bulbs, replacing them with dahlias for the summer and then clearing up in the autumn.

My introduction to gardening at a higher level came via the influence of my sister Nathalie – a brilliant gardener – and from working with my good friend Joanne Raven, a professional gardener who was in need of extra help in busy seasons. I learned such a lot from them both. As a result of this inspiration and experience, I decided to try to consolidate and formalize all of this new knowledge by taking a course in practical horticulture. Nathalie had previously taken the same qualifications and was now an extremely creative and knowledgeable gardener who grew many of her own plants and vegetables from seeds and cuttings in her stunning landscaped garden in France. It was this that encouraged me to want to find out a lot more.

I embarked upon a course run by the UK's Royal Horticultural Society (RHS). Some people do it out of curiosity, others do it to get work within horticulture, but I did it for both reasons. I found the course absolutely fascinating and learned a huge amount about all aspects of gardening and growing plants. I particularly liked the 'Science of Plants' modules.

It's amazing how relevant understanding the science behind plants is to becoming a good gardener. I realize now how it has improved how I paint plants too. This was affirmed recently when I received some positive feedback via my website (which is primarily to showcase my illustrations, but also mentions that I am a professional gardener). The comment I received was, 'I think the key to the authenticity of your illustrations is because you understand plants so well.' This compliment pleased me enormously.

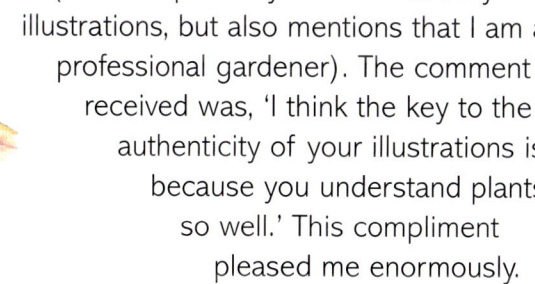
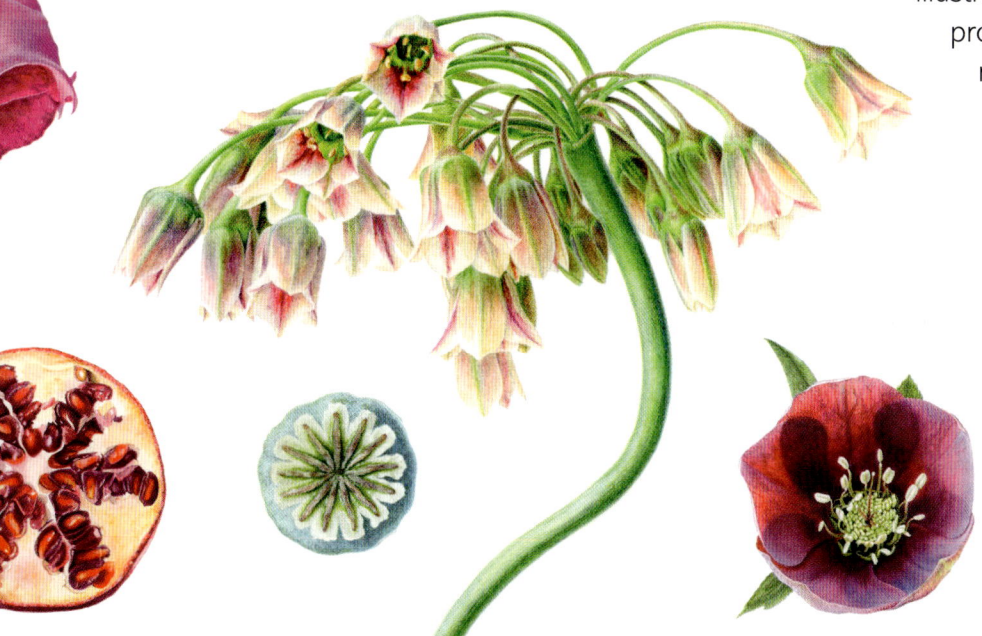
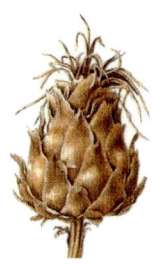

Painting vs gardening

Being a botanical illustrator with access to gardens full of beautiful plants and flowers, as well as a gardener with nature for inspiration, have absolutely become complementary roles for me. Each provides for the other. Even their differences and contrasts help level things out. For instance, my gardening work is a perfect mixture of physical and sociable whereas the illustration work I do is sedentary and solitary.

At certain times of the year it's not easy for me to be able to split my time between painting and gardening. If I get a big illustrating job in the spring or autumn it can be really tricky, but I do my best to fit everything in. I'm not so disciplined when I'm painting just for myself. The lack of a deadline means I'm easily distracted and I'll usually end up in my garden for part of the day – but that is never time wasted. Having said that, the illustrating has to take priority as there are usually strict deadlines.

The gardening provides inspiration for painting ideas; there is so much out there that catches my eye. My favourite part of painting is choosing the next subject I'm going to work on. I will see a plant in someone's garden and get genuinely excited about the prospect of illustrating it.

Below left Various botanical illustrations combined into the repeat pattern *Botanical Chinoiserie*, for a wallpaper by Mineheart.

Below right A view through dahlias, sweet peas and poppy heads in my garden.

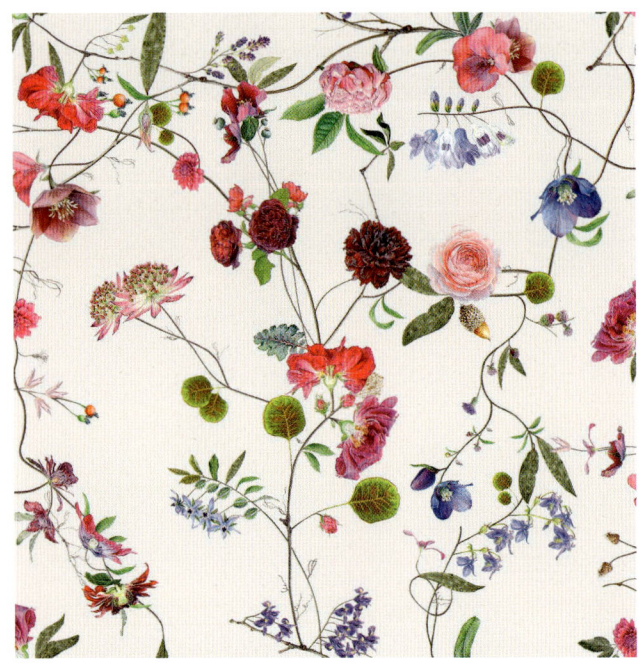

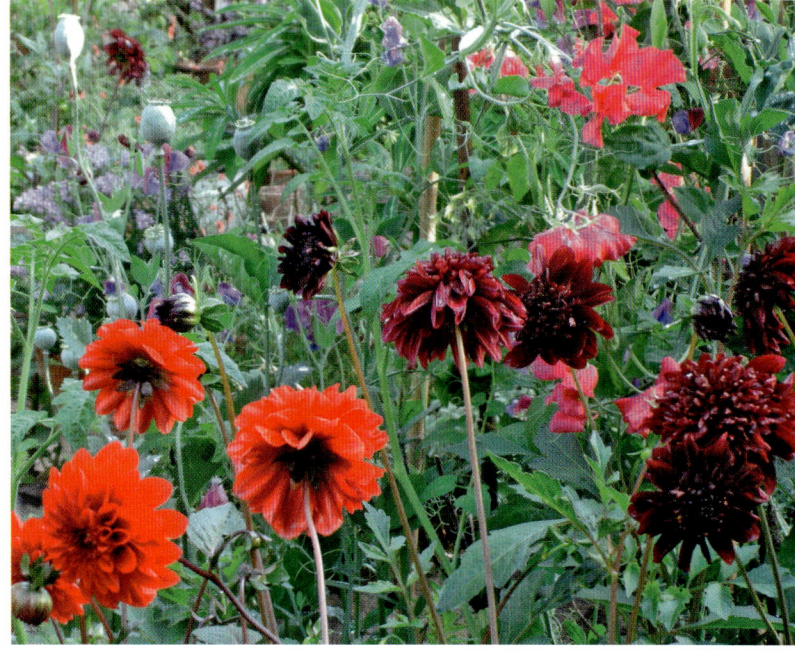

Understanding, Education and Training

After leaving school, I did an intensive one-year Art Foundation course at St Martins School of Art in London. I felt lucky to be accepted on to the course and I really enjoyed my time there. We had a lot of fun and were encouraged to quickly develop new creative skills and ideas. Back then, it was much more common to do this foundation year before committing to higher education; we learned a variety of fine art and design techniques across a broad spectrum of subjects.

At this stage, I wasn't thinking about botanical themes at all. The course, instead, equipped me with knowledge of things like composition, line quality, tone, colour mixing, photography and how to interpret design ideas after completing visual research. With the diverse portfolio I created at St Martins I decided that a design degree was the best route for me and I was accepted at Bath Academy of Art to do a Visual Communications degree in graphic design and illustration.

This sounds like I had landed where I needed to be but unfortunately I lost my focus and as a result I left after a year. I really missed my friends and the energy of London, plus I wanted to earn some money. I wanted to be nearer the centre of things so I got a job with a film production company.

I stayed in the film business for four years, working as a receptionist and then production assistant. It was a job with many challenges and lots to learn. I had to understand so much about camera equipment, lighting, getting a large crew to a shoot on time, plus everything on the shoot had to be organized perfectly or you were in big trouble! I made lots of very good friends and learned a huge amount about being organized, but realized that I didn't want to go on to be a producer – the business was too frantic for me. I was lucky as I had an extremely nice boss who would let me bring in my paints when we weren't busy. This meant that I was able to build up a portfolio of work and eventually I found myself an illustration agent. This enabled me to get work as a freelance illustrator in advertising and graphic design, often illustrating packaging for well-known brands.

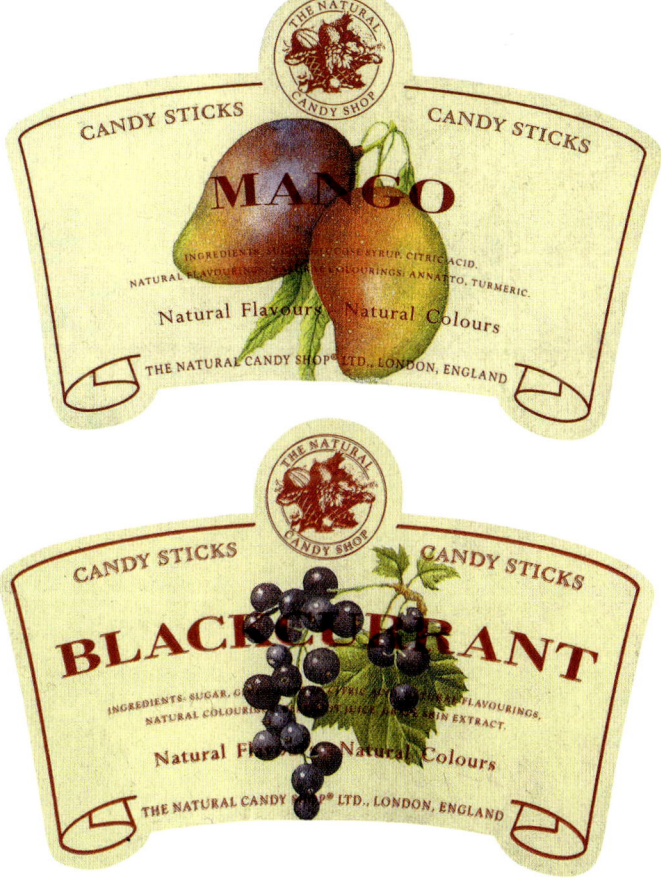

Above My early illustration work combined and overlaid with text in these labels for The Natural Candy Shop.

To begin with though, most of my work was in publishing: to illustrate and visualize projects in home and interiors books – for example, step-by-step illustrated instructions on how to make window blinds, cushion covers, upholstery and various embroidery techniques. I worked on some gardening books as well, supplementing my income by illustrating Christmas cards, with a few private commissions in between times.

In writing this book, I've tried to locate how and when the beginnings of the work I do now first arose. As soon as I started painting I worked in watercolour and have never strayed from that.

The early illustration jobs I did required real scrutiny and a lot of detail. Some of it included illustrations for gardening and woodwork and later included fruits, vegetables, and occasionally flowers. As time went on I put more and more detail into my paintings. I suppose I became very interested in painting subjects in quite a lot of detail from this time, but my botanical focus really came a bit later.

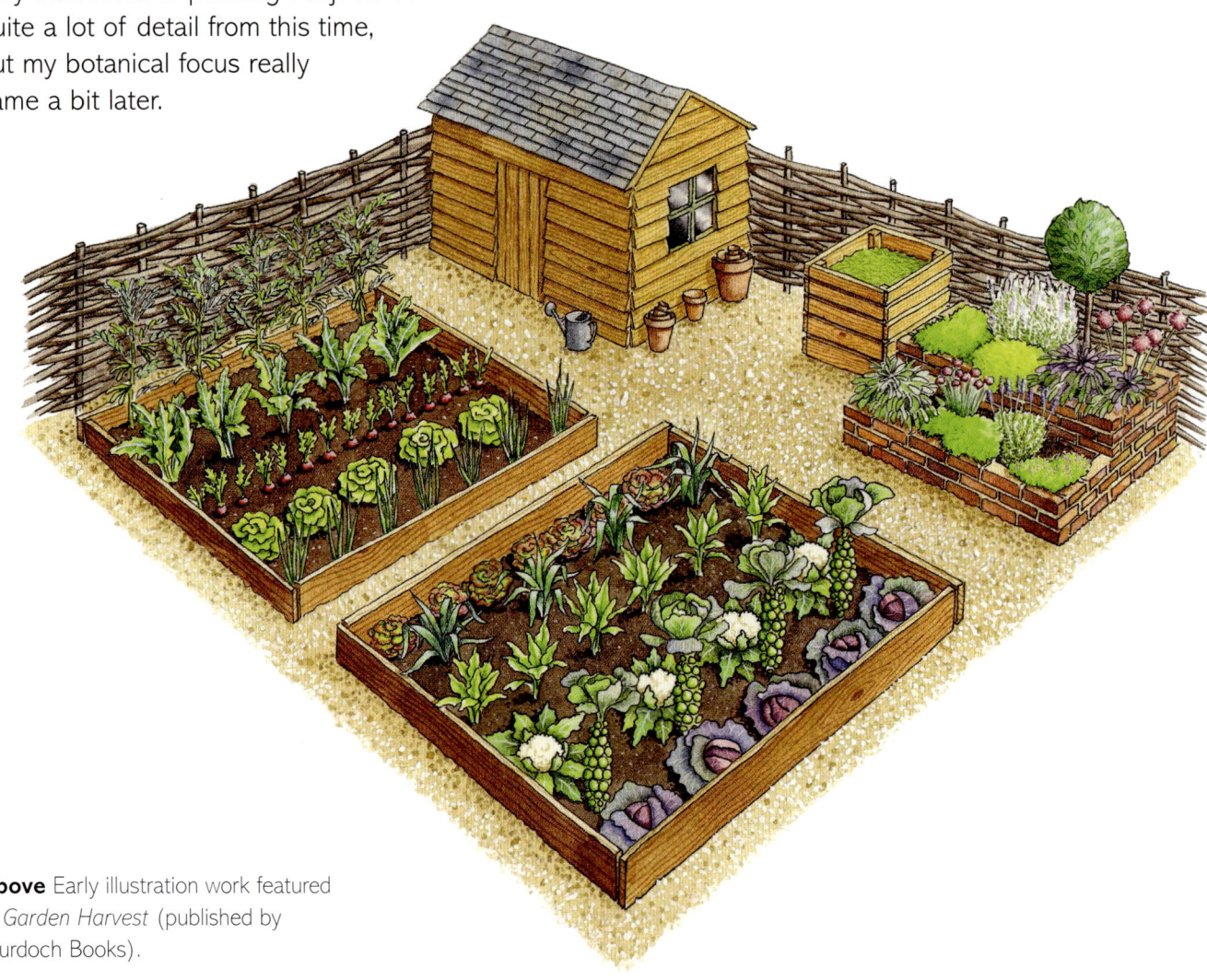

Above Early illustration work featured in *Garden Harvest* (published by Murdoch Books).

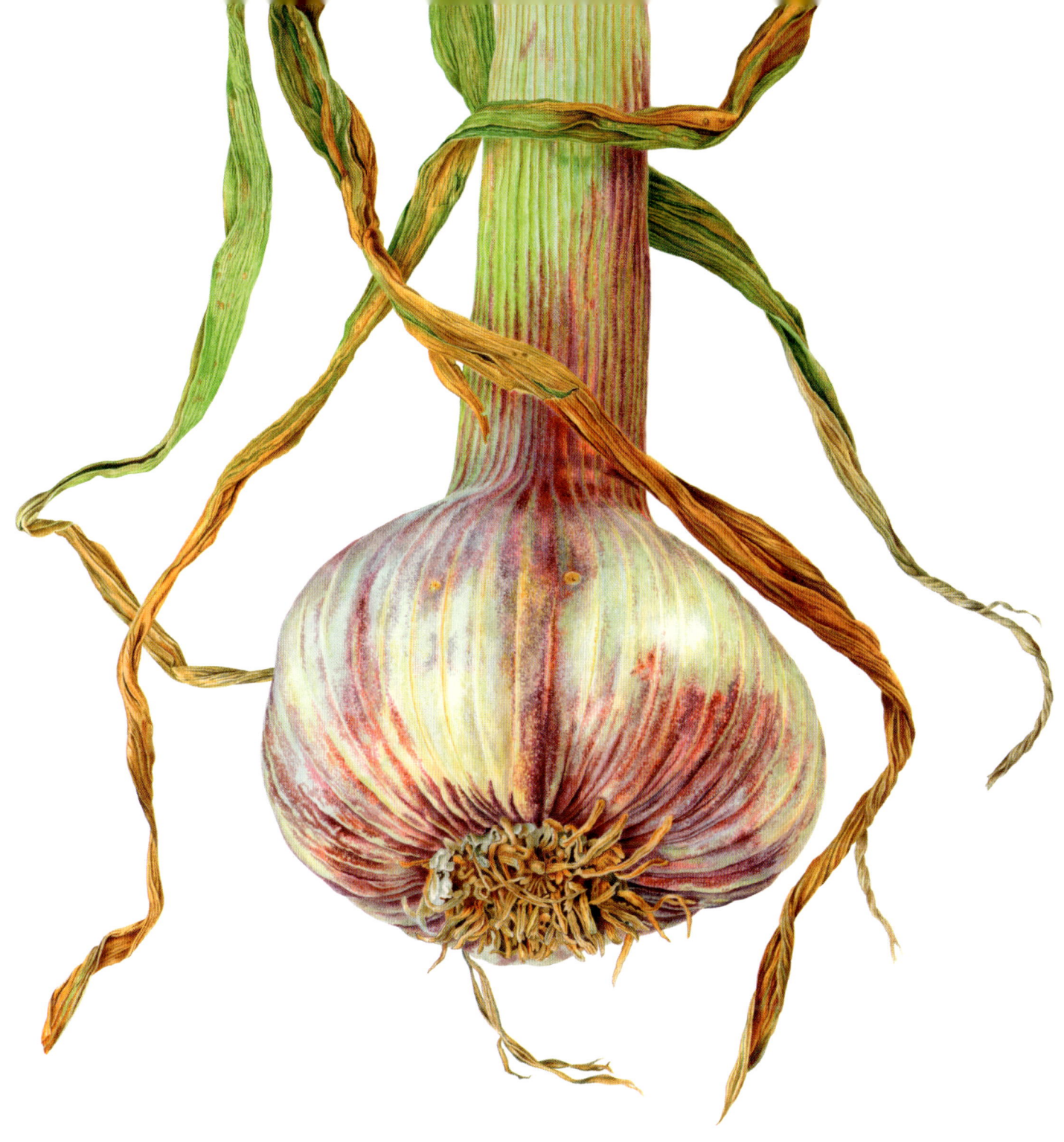

Above My interest in botanical subjects grew in part from my early experience in gardening illustation.

Botanical Diplomas – Gardening and Painting

I found myself moving naturally towards painting botanical themes after getting my first garden. Now I could grow my own subject matter. Observing it daily helped me to develop my horticultural knowledge and focus on the technical skills needed for botanical painting. This combination of gardening and painting for pleasure was also beginning to influence the kinds of commercial work I wanted to pursue.

When I received a small inheritance from my mother, I wanted to do something that would have pleased her. I chose to study for a diploma in botanical painting, which I hoped would improve my watercolour painting skills, particularly in relation to plants.

It was important to me that the course combined my horticultural interests with the plant-based painting and illustration work I increasingly wanted to do, so I applied to study at the English Gardening School based at the Chelsea Physic Garden – London's oldest botanic garden.

The Chelsea Physic Garden is tucked away behind sheltering walls beside the River Thames. Contained inside it is a unique living collection of around 5,000 different edible, useful, medicinal and historical plants. Many tender plants such as cocoa, coffee and cotton and the impressive *Echium pininana* (common names: giant viper's bugloss and tower of jewels) are able to flourish there because of the garden's warm micro-climate.

Having a painting school situated in an important botanical garden like the one at Chelsea

Physic gardens can be traced back to medieval times. They originated as apothecary gardens – plots devoted to the cultivation and display of medicinal plants. Many of these early gardens became centres for the study of plants, often instigated by the medical profession. Chelsea Physic Garden, established in 1673, is one of the most famous of these, set up so that apprentices could increase their knowledge of medical plants and herbs. Botanical drawing and painting arose in parallel because of the need to accurately record and retain that knowledge.

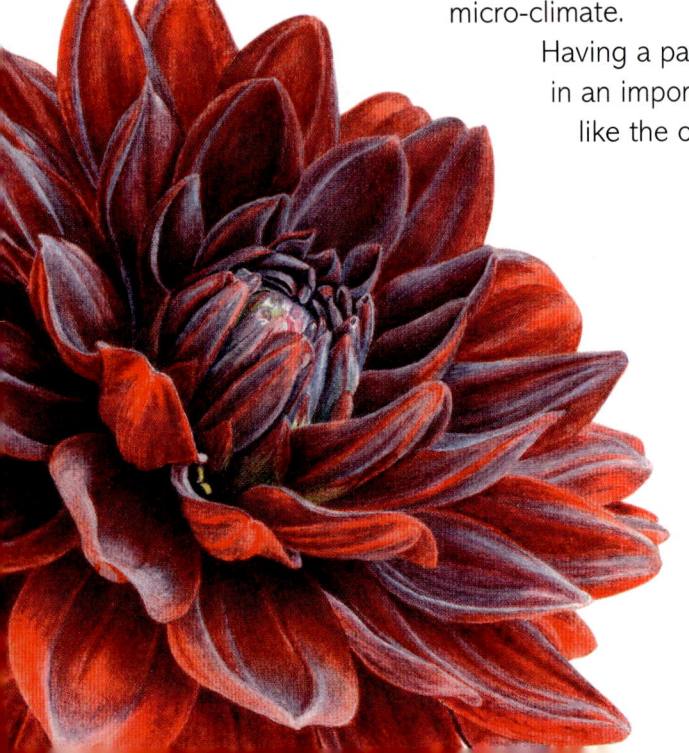

Left Detail of *Dahlia* 'Arabian Night'. A fully double decorative dahlia with dark wine-red flowers.

makes absolute sense. Botanists need high-quality illustrations for their scientific publications and botanical illustrators need a centre of excellence for training, skill sharing and a source of plant specimens.

The head gardener of the Chelsea Physic Garden at the time, Nick Bailey, was extremely helpful in letting us take occasional specimens from the order beds (plants laid out according to their families). It was amazing to have such a wealth of diverse plant material and a wonderful environment in which to study.

My course was tutored by an excellent team of internationally recognized botanical artists and illustrators including, and led by, course director Helen Allen. She taught us introductory botanical techniques, composition, aesthetics and advanced techniques in watercolour painting. Working alongside her were botanical illustrator Susanna Stuart-Smith who specializes in developing accurate scientific botanical plates for publication; Sarah Gould who shared insights into the intricacies of working with vellum; artist and author Mariella Baldwin who introduced us to various invaluable watercolour techniques and Elaine Searle who concentrated on drawing and painting fundamentals and complex forms. Anna Haigh, a botanist at the Royal Botanical Gardens in Kew, led us through the wonders of the largest and most diverse botanical collection in the world.

Here, I learned so much about the rules of botanical illustration, plant science, new painting skills and how to source inspiration from museums and archives. This inspirational botanical painting course provided me with the motivation to carry on and try to keep improving my techniques.

Botanical art and botanical illustration

Although any botanical art involves the artistic and accurate representation of plants, there are some subtle but important differences between botanical art and botanical illustration.

While both ought to be botanically and scientifically accurate, botanical art allows for a bit more artistic interpretation. An example of this might be in the composition of a painting or drawing, where a whole plant isn't represented and is also perhaps combined with other elements to enhance the work (that is, it can be more subjective for aesthetic reasons).

The purpose of a botanical illustration is to show a plant species so that it can be straightforwardly identified by botanists (in the field, for instance). These illustrations may include not only flowers and leaves but seeds, buds and roots too. They are often in monochrome.

The majority of my work is botanical art rather than botanical illustration, but I have produced some examples closer to the latter for the RHS Botanical Art Shows.

The Royal Horticultural Society (RHS)

The RHS has been important to me both as a gardener and as a botanical illustrator. My RHS Practical Horticulture course was not only amazingly relevant to a further understanding of horticulture, it began to help me more faithfully depict plants. It introduced me to details such as different leaf textures in relation to how much drought plants can tolerate, and the structure of seeds and how they best germinate. Fascinating new knowledge such as this has hopefully helped me to be a more observant and informed illustrator.

The training I received on both my courses successfully came together at the end of my painting course at the Chelsea Physic Garden's English Gardening School. At the end of a year of study we all had to produce a series of paintings to gain the diploma. I was so pleased to be awarded 'Distinction' and 'Best Student' for my collected work. I then added to the series in order to be ready for the Royal Horticultural Society's Botanical Art Show – a major annual event for botanical artists. The requirements for this are pretty strict. I found trying to create an aesthetically pleasing image while at the same time meeting the guidelines quite demanding.

To prepare for this I went to stay with my sister in the South of France, working for seven months solely on this subject. I was able to concentrate better there away from London and its distractions. I would get up at five most mornings to be ready for the sun to come up and start work. Although I find working by lamplight incredibly tiring, as winter approached there was no other option. At the end of my time there I had completed twelve paintings to hang at the RHS Botanical Art Show in London in March 2011.

I tried to make all twelve pictures work well together, so they followed a similar layout: all were square, showed some of the internal structure of the flower and were framed in exactly the same way. I wanted them to be cohesive and eye-catching from a distance; whether or not I achieved this is another matter, but the formula seemed to work well for exhibition purposes.

This was my first exhibition and I was quite shocked at how long the paintings took, having worked mostly ten-hour days, six to seven days a week, over the seven-month period. I was so pleased when the hard work paid off; I was awarded 'Best Exhibit' and a RHS Gold Medal for my series of paintings titled 'The Anatomy of Flowers'.

Right The twelve illustrations exhibited at the RHS Botanical Art Show. Many of these paintings can be seen in more detail on the following pages.

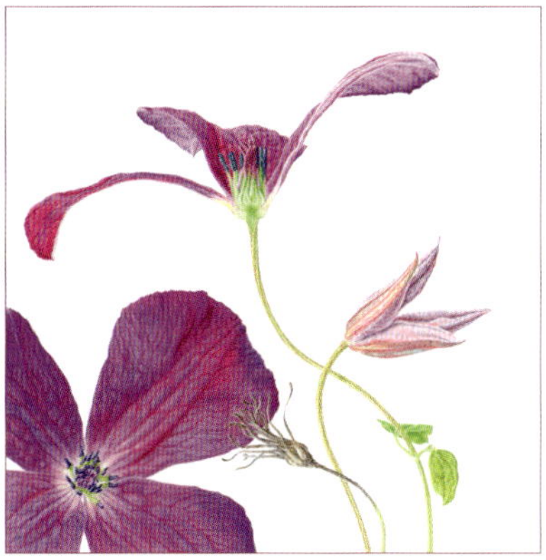

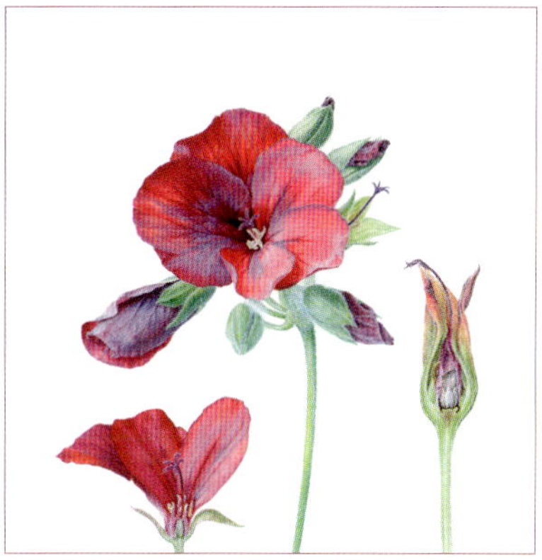

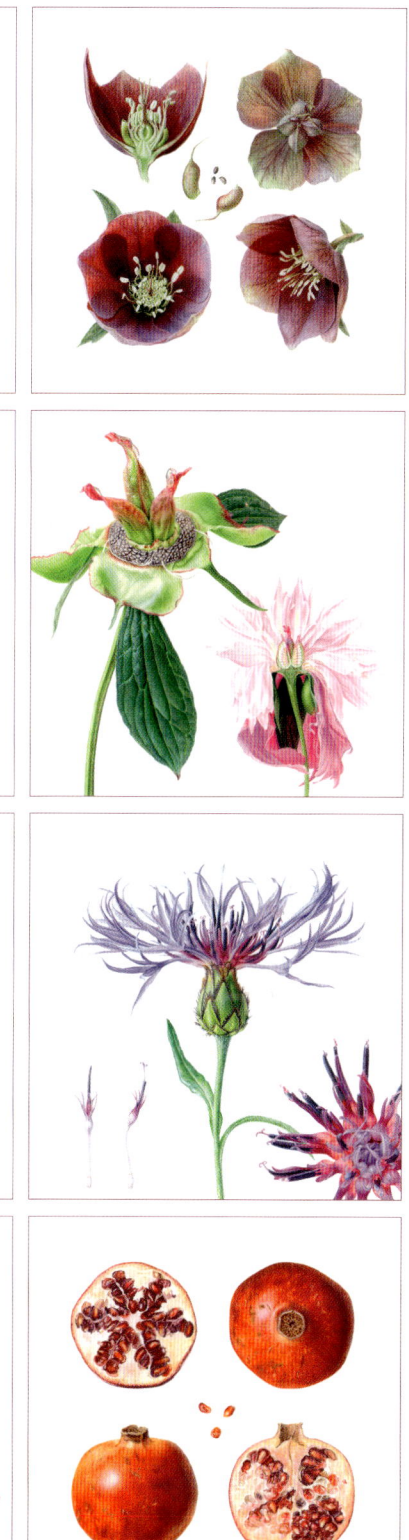

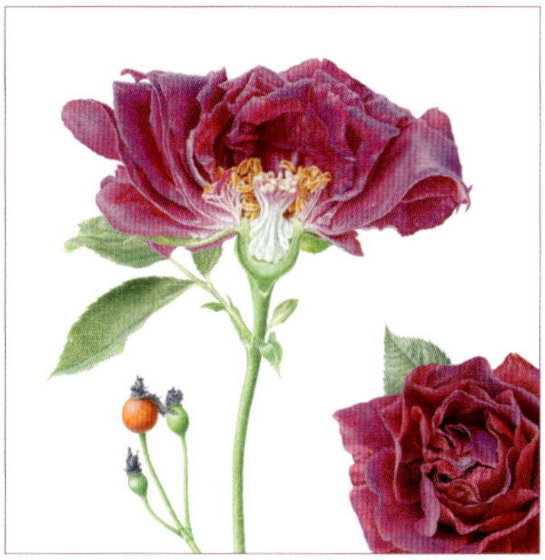

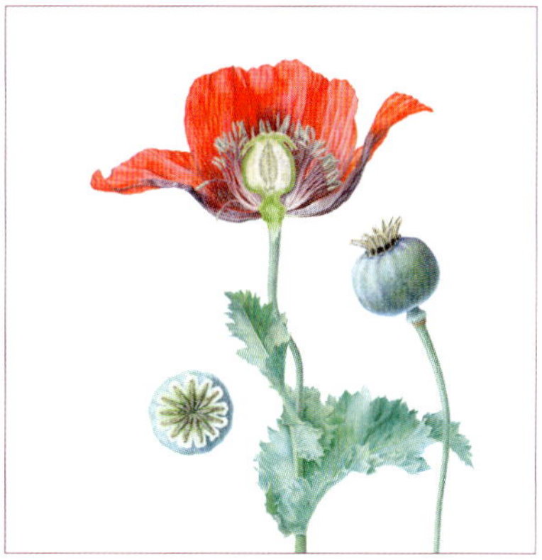

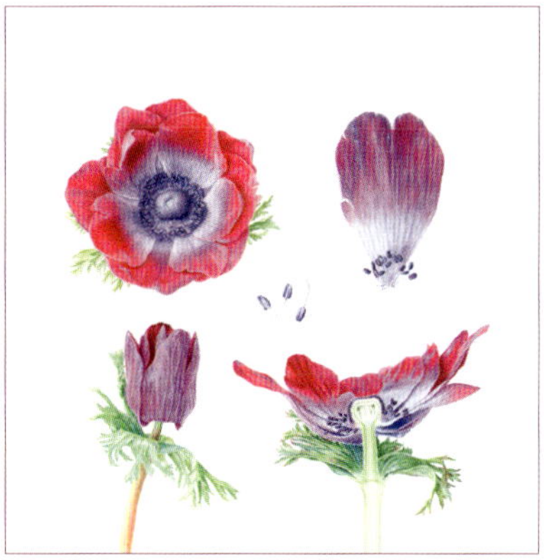

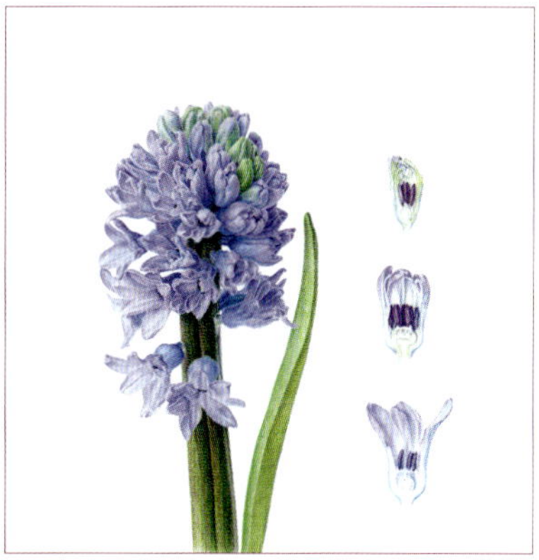

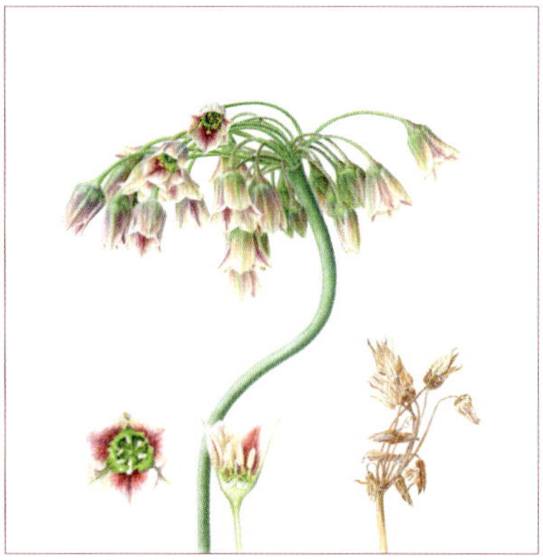

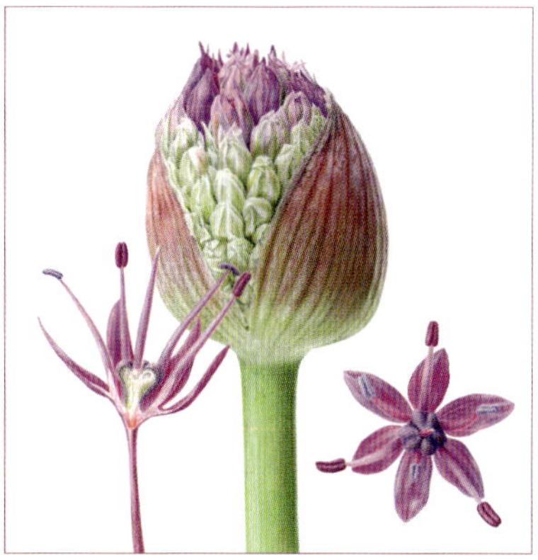

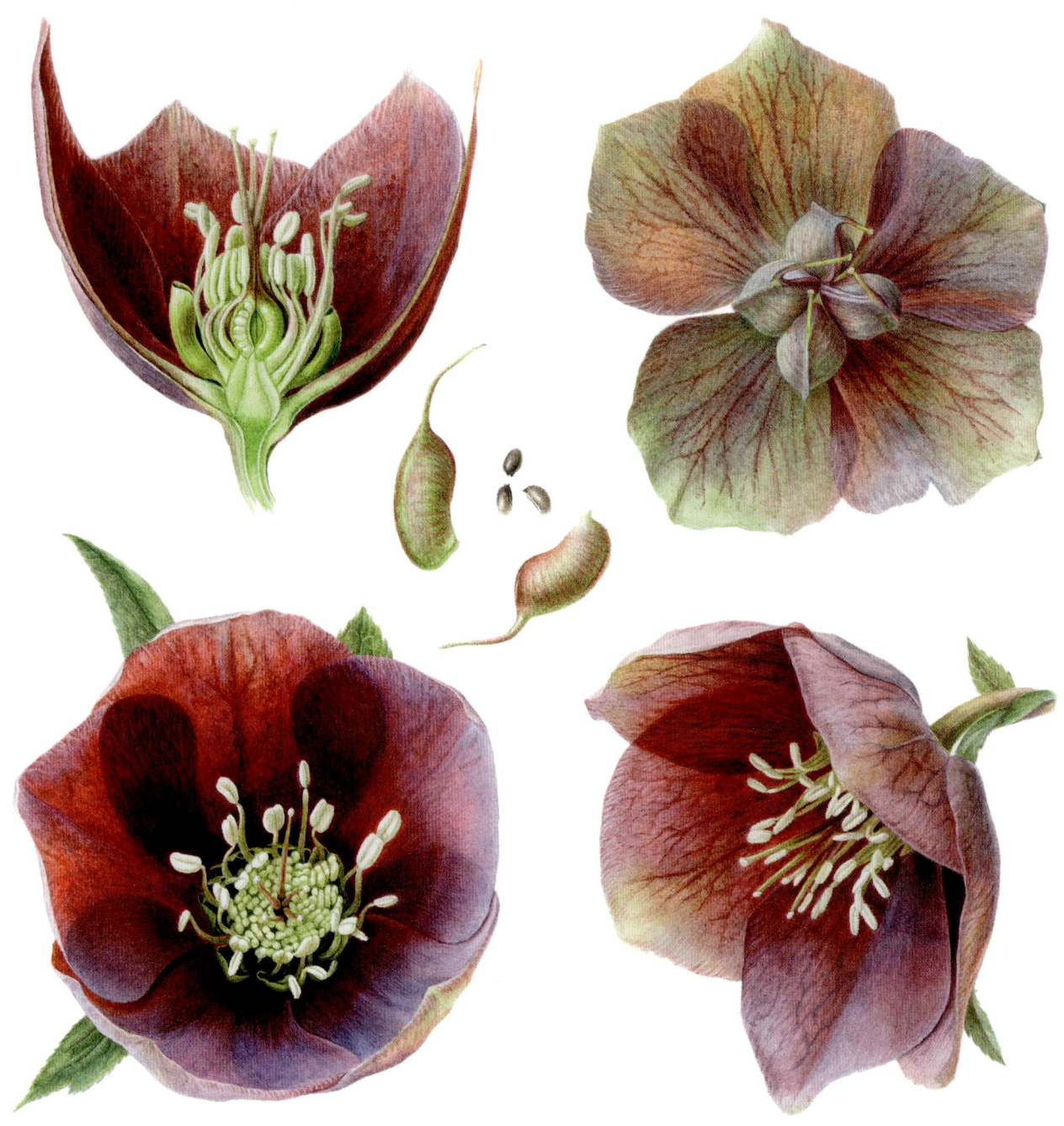

The RHS selected my painting *Helleborus* x *hybridus* from this exhibition for its Lindley Library collection. As with all of my RHS exhibition paintings, it is worked within a square format. This very much suggested that having four main elements to the composition was the right configuration for the piece.

The image shows four views of the hellebore flower. I particularly wanted to capture all the textures, colours and subtle veining of the petals that show through when backlit.

Later, my illustration *Dahlia* 'Arabian Night' was also selected by the RHS for its collection. It was inspired by this series but not exhibited at the same time.

RHS Lindley Library – Botanical Illustration Collection

The RHS was established in 1804, to 'encourage and improve the science, art and practice of horticulture' in all its branches, and almost immediately began its long tradition of commissioning artists to create beautiful artworks for their collection.

The Lindley Library housed within the headquarters of the RHS contains this art collection, which helps to tell the fascinating stories of plant histories and gardening. As well as paintings and drawings, the collection also includes photographs, books and gardening magazines.

The library currently contains 30,000 botanical art works and more than 80,000 books. They represent 400 years of botanical illustration, making this the world's most important and largest horticultural library and botanical art archive.

Its collection retains a contemporary edge because the library regularly adds new works from botanical artists and illustrators from across the world – often by those who have been awarded RHS Gold Medals. I'm really proud to know that my work is held in this collection.

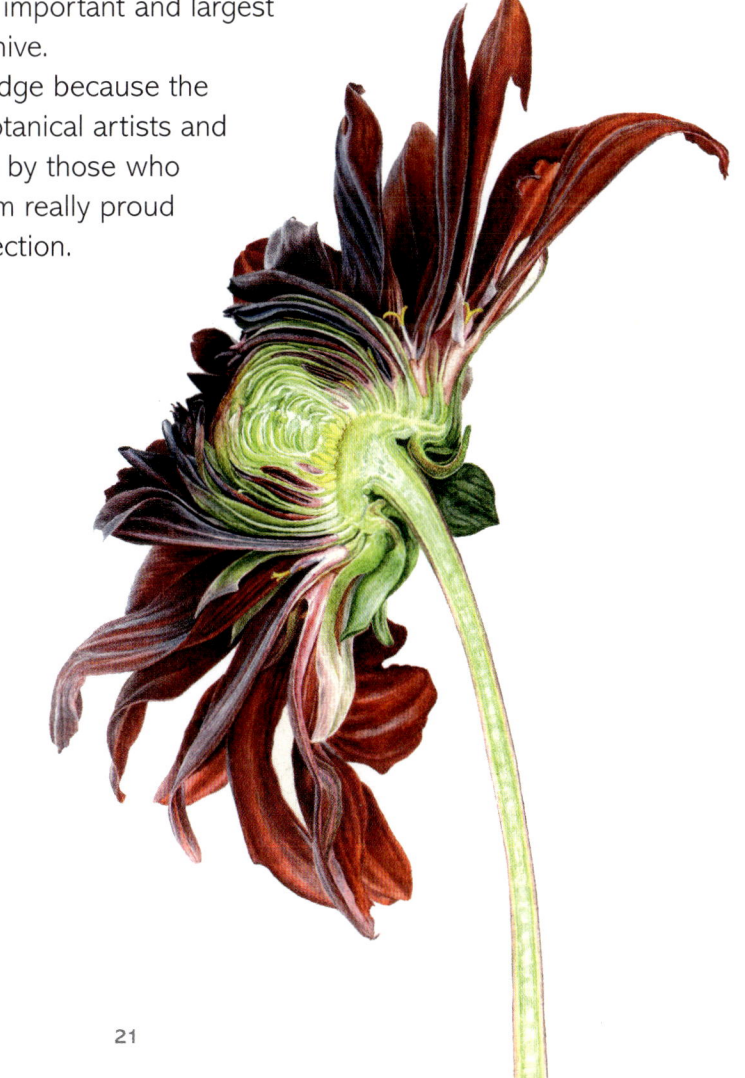

Left *Helleborus* x *hybridus*. Clockwise, from bottom left: in full flower; in cross-section; during seed production; and a side-on view showing the natural position of the flower, which is normally pointing downwards. I then added the seeds to the centre to compositionally balance out the blank space.

Right *Dahlia* 'Arabian Night' in cross section.

Next page Sunflower, St Paul's wort and Chinese skullcap.

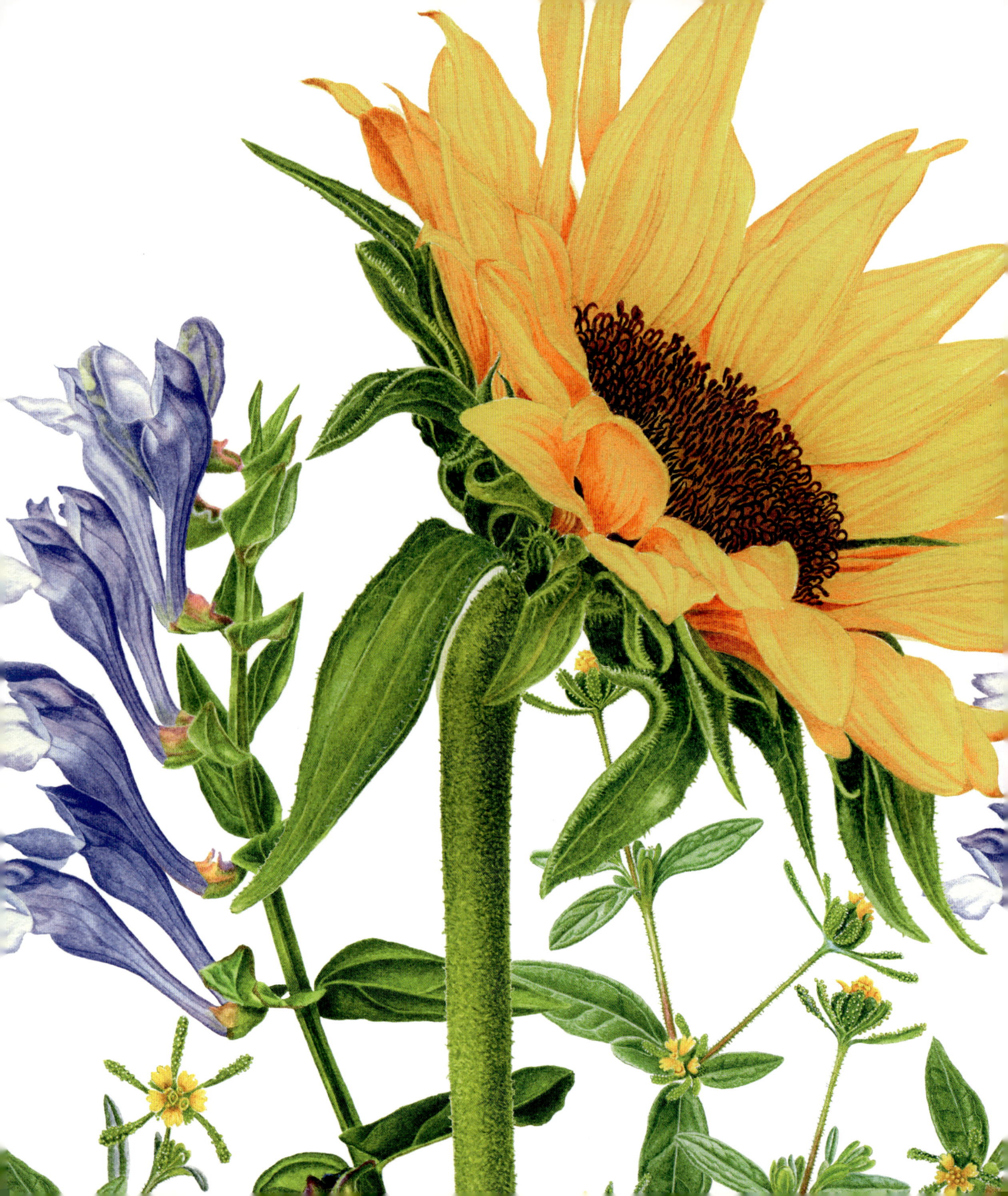

GROW

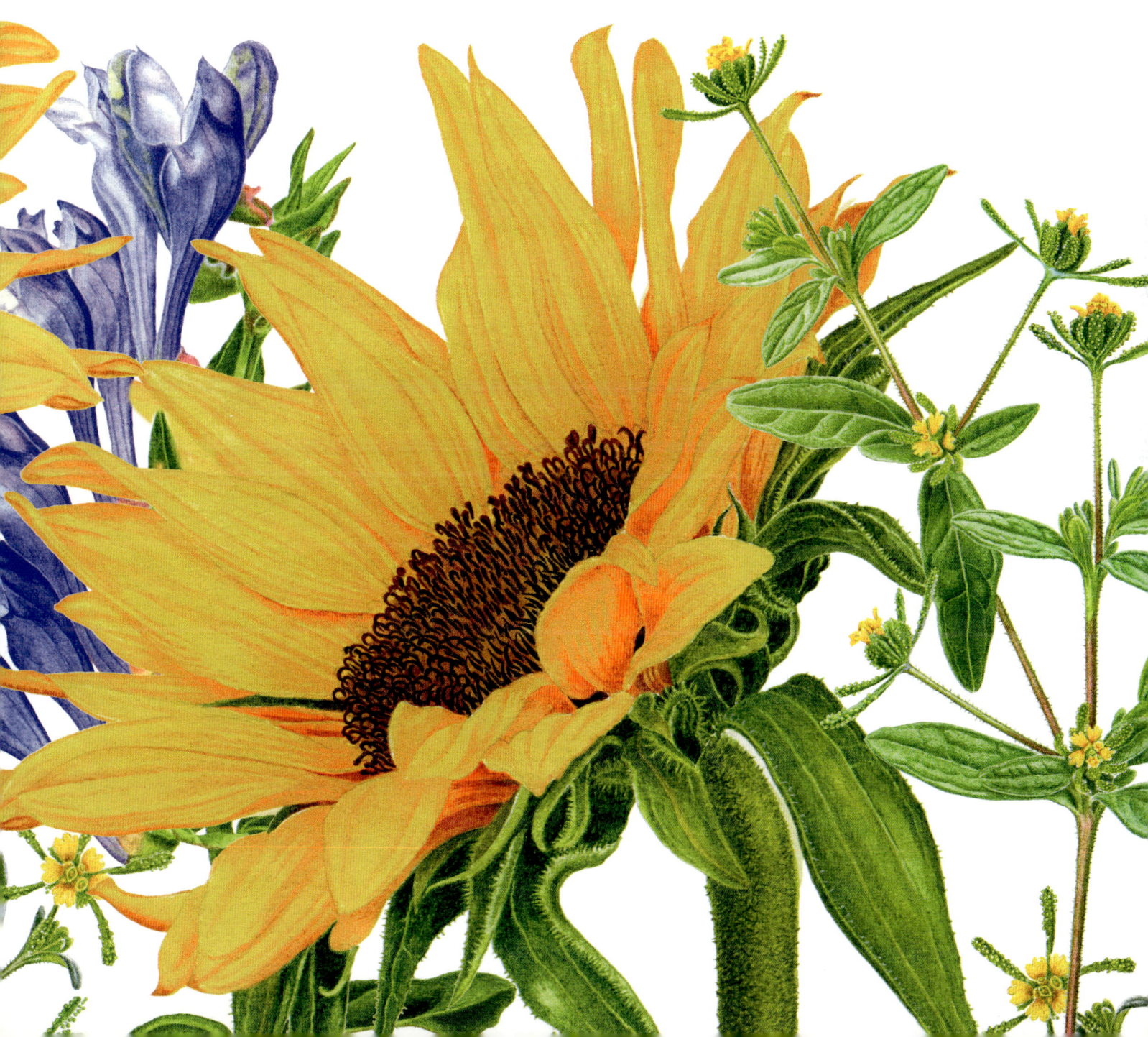

HISTORICAL INSPIRATION

All artists stand on the shoulders of those who have gone before them. Many artists have inspired me, but these three stand out.

The importance of research and the ability to *really* look is essential for any botanical artist. Observation of the plant subject is critical, but so is how it is translated on to the page. When I am going to begin a painting of a particular specimen I am mindful of others' representations of the same or similar plants. I want my research and thinking to honour some of what has preceded it. Looking at other artists' work and considering how to interpret it can provide useful insights.

The value of research visits became especially clear when I was studying for my botanical painting diploma. The course put me in the habit of visiting centres of botanical archive excellence such as the herbarium at Kew Gardens, the RHS Lindley Library and collections from the NHM's Library and Archives, where we were lucky enough to have permission to go through boxes of original paintings by great masters of botanical illustration.

Arthur Harry Church (1865–1937)

There are particular botanical works that I always return to. These include the illustrations of Victorian botanist Arthur Harry Church.

'The Anatomy of Flowers' series of illustrations I painted for the RHS exhibition (see pages 18–19) were prompted by a visit I made to the Natural History Museum in London. I already knew of Church's work but for this important project I wanted my research to include a close scrutiny of his original paintings. I was bowled over by the intricacy and incredibly modern look of his painted work and – as he was a botanist and scientist – on the clarity with which he illustrated the structure of the plants.

In the introduction (see pages 10–12) I mentioned my fascination with morphology and how the form and structure of plants meant that I would carefully take plants apart to see how

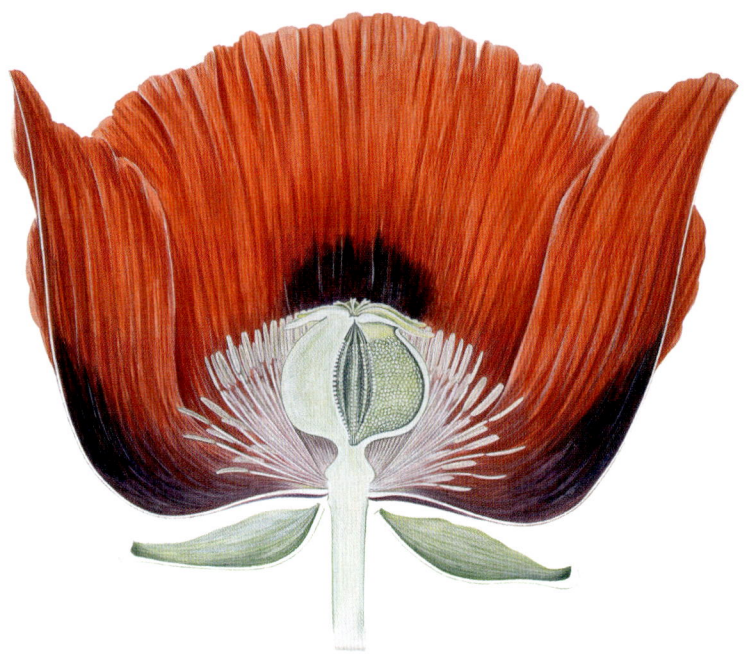

Above *Papaver somniferum* (1904), one of Arthur Harry Church's paintings from the Natural History Museum's collection that has inspired my own illustrations (shown right).

they fitted together and actually grew. Church's paintings gave me this information, and in addition the dynamic shape, colour and use of compositional space absolutely captured my imagination.

I've been illustrating for over 20 years, working for design companies, publishers and magazines, and right from the moment when I first discovered his paintings I have tried to emulate the boldness of them.

It's almost unthinkable to me that the work of Arthur Harry Church lay unpublished and unnoticed for several decades. Deserved interest was revived when Professor David Mabberley's book *Arthur Harry Church: The Anatomy of Flowers* was published in the year 2000.

Initially I was attracted to the boldness and simplicity of Church's composition. For example, in the image shown opposite he illustrated just the flowerhead of the poppy rather than doing a classic plant portrait where it would be more usual to include all parts of the plant. I found it fascinating to see the cross-section of such a common flower painted with such meticulous precision. This composition of a close-up sectioned plant immediately grabbed me, and I wanted to try it myself.

It was quite hard to cut the flower in half without ruining the petals but all was revealed after a few goes with a very sharp scalpel; it was so interesting to see what was at the centre of the poppy.

I added a few more elements to the design, making it more asymmetrical as well as some leaves. My version has views of the flower and seedpod from different angles.

Right *Papaver somniferum* showing how much the work of Arthur Harry Church has influenced my own.

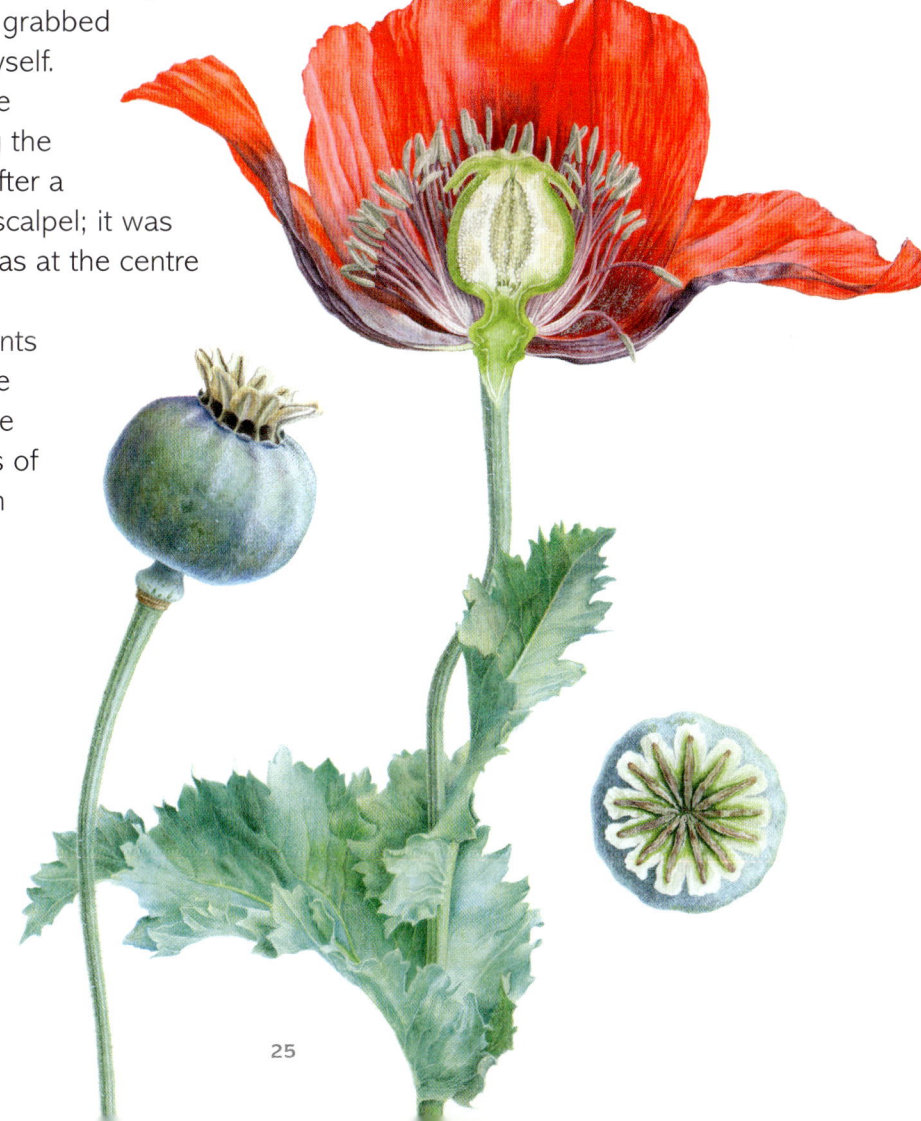

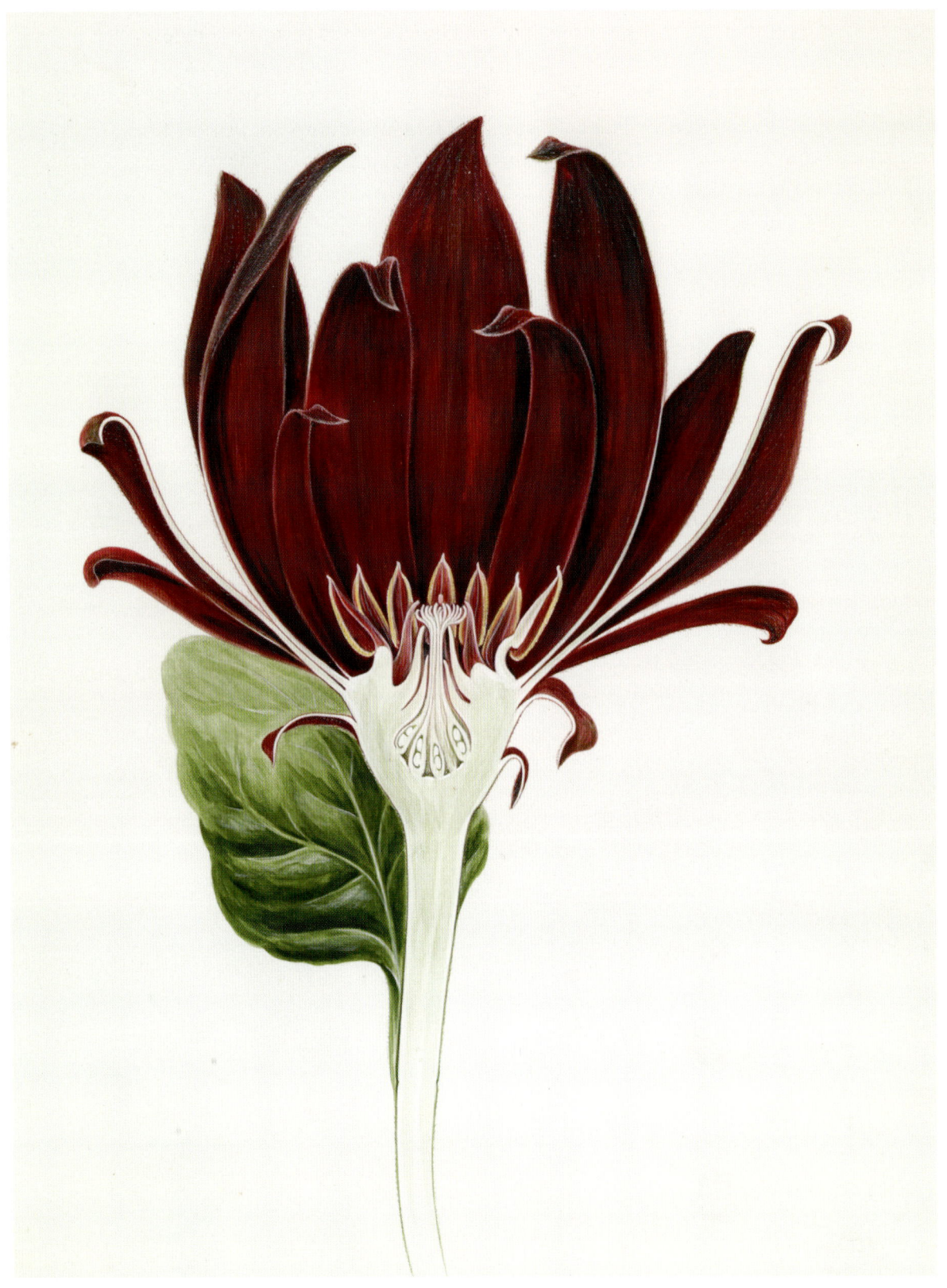

After the RHS purchased my hellebore homage to Arthur Harry Church, I was asked to bring in any other work to show them that continued this theme. One of these was my dahlia painting. This time I didn't paint the same plant but chose a flower in the same deep burgundy-red colour. After cutting my *Dahlia* 'Arabian Night' flower in half, hundreds of contrasting, closely packed petals were revealed. Colours ranged from the bright green of the young petals at the centre of the flower to the deep reds and almost black petals around the edge.

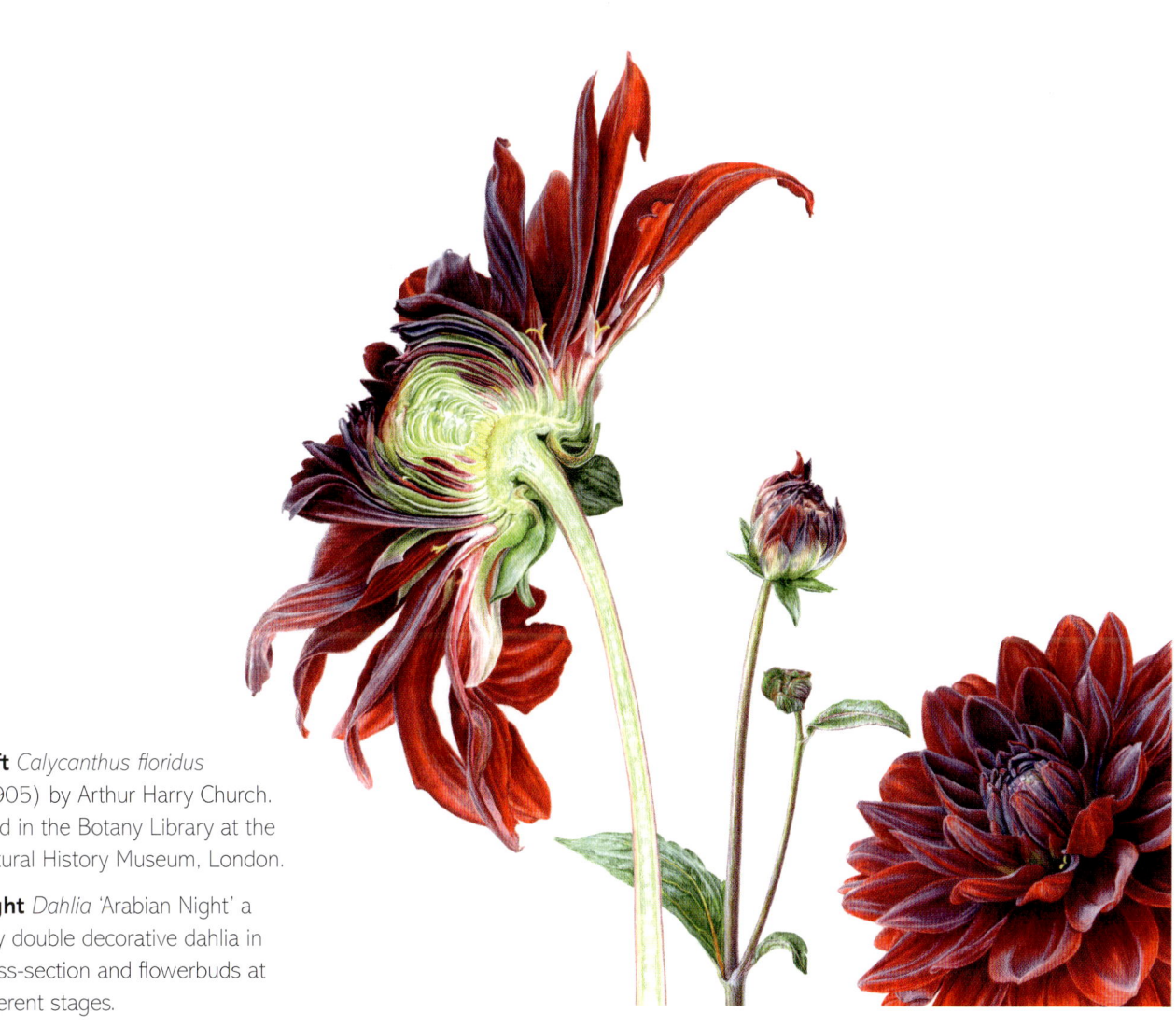

Left *Calycanthus floridus* (1905) by Arthur Harry Church. Held in the Botany Library at the Natural History Museum, London.

Right *Dahlia* 'Arabian Night' a fully double decorative dahlia in cross-section and flowerbuds at different stages.

Franz Bauer (1758–1840)

Going further back in the history of botanical illustration I so admire the work of Franz Bauer – Kew's first official Artist in Residence. Bauer's ability to make paintings of very scientific subjects, which include incredible detail and precision and yet remain aesthetically beautiful, has always intrigued and inspired me.

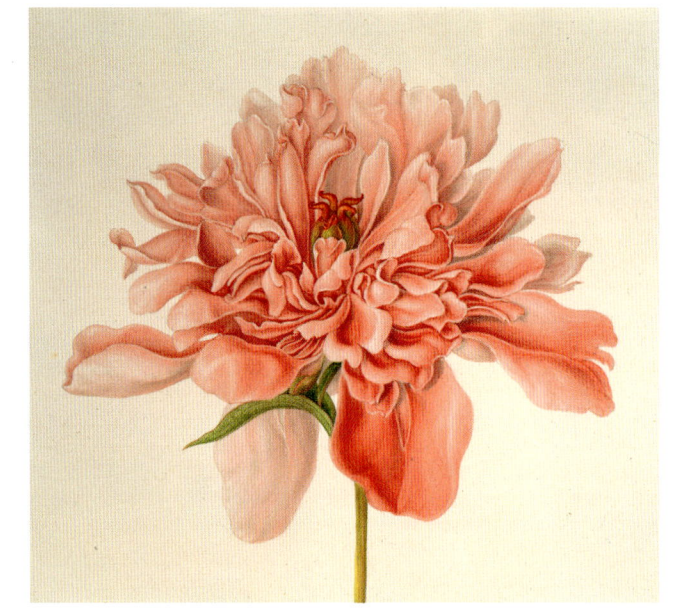

Bauer's work made use of the technology of the time. The scientific detail he was able to observe was through his use of the microscope. With it he could see the anatomy of his plant subjects clearly. He may also have had access to a camera lucida drawing aid. This would have allowed Bauer to view his specimens with a microscope and to draw them simultaneously, creating intricate and detailed studies to paint from later.

When I first saw some of Bauer's original work I immediately bought a really good magnifying lamp and some hand-held magnifying glasses so that I could try to emulate his level of precision. I have become more and more interested in the fine details within my plant subjects as time has gone on.

Above *Paeonia*, from *Drawings of Kew Plants by Franz Bauer (1758–1840)*. Held in the Botany Library at the Natural History museum, London.

Right and opposite *Paeonia lactiflora* 'The Fawn' and developing peony buds. Sometimes my paintings come together as a series over a long time span. This peony sequence is a good example.

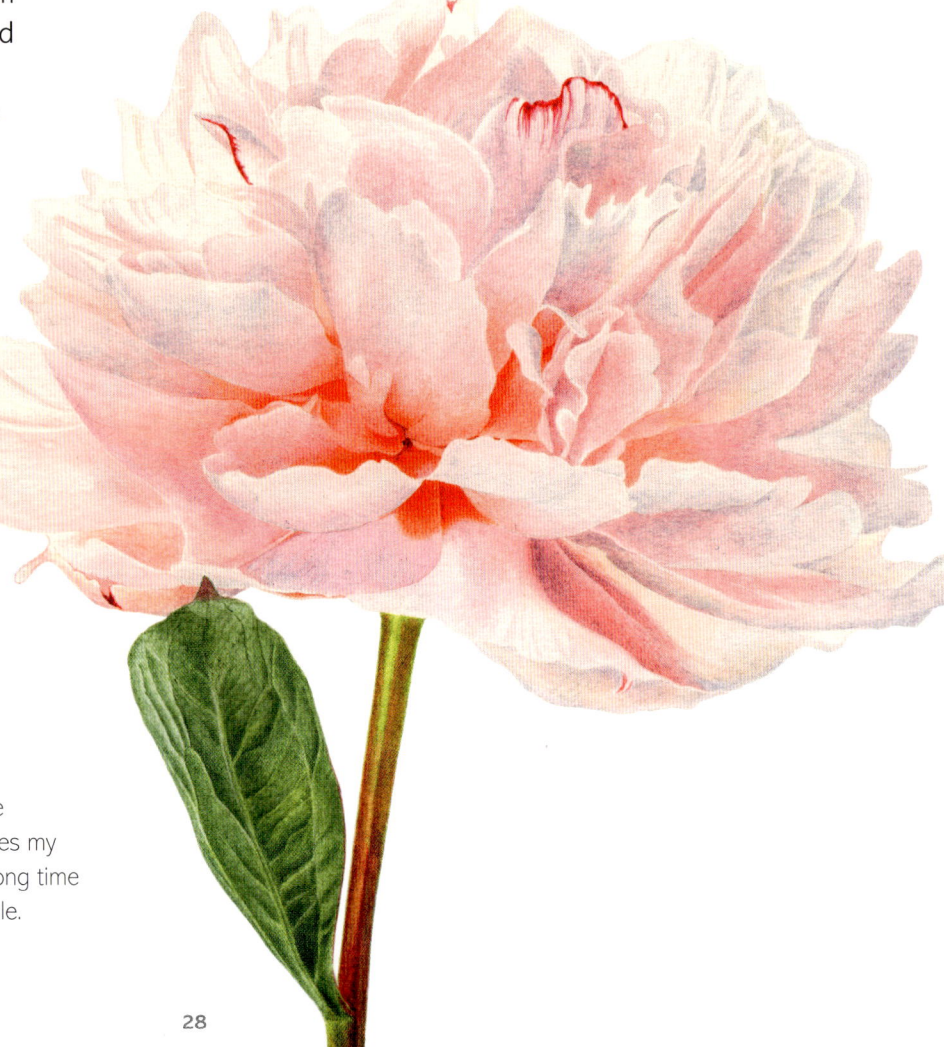

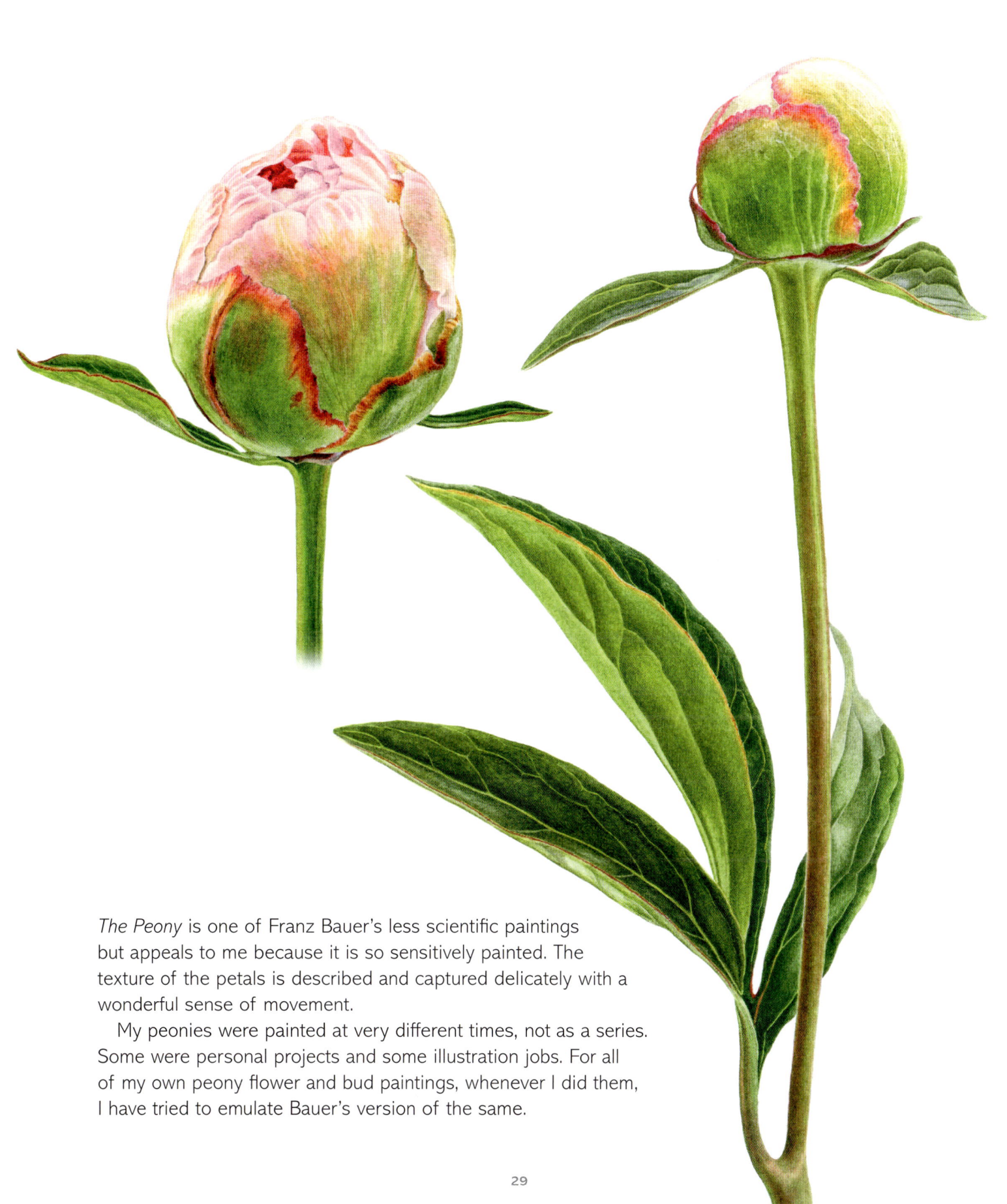

The Peony is one of Franz Bauer's less scientific paintings but appeals to me because it is so sensitively painted. The texture of the petals is described and captured delicately with a wonderful sense of movement.

My peonies were painted at very different times, not as a series. Some were personal projects and some illustration jobs. For all of my own peony flower and bud paintings, whenever I did them, I have tried to emulate Bauer's version of the same.

Indian Company of Artists

Other works that fascinate me are botanical examples found within the genre of Indian Company painting. These are mostly anonymous works that developed as a result of European (especially British) influence on Indian artists from the early 18th to the 19th century. Each region had its own distinguishable style, which grew out of, and was heavily influenced by, earlier local traditions.

The main thing I love about them is the graphic composition – they are very unfussy, extremely bold and utilize intense vibrant colour. Much botanical illustration uses a much more subtle palette, but these certainly don't. They are slightly naive perspective wise, which makes them even more interesting to look at.

Rory McEwen 1932–82

The most contemporary of my influences for this section is Rory McEwen.

I admire his use of incredible scientific accuracy but at the same time an ability to retain character and a unique style. His compositions are simple but very striking because of his brilliant positioning of the subject on the page, using lots of negative white space. He was unafraid to leave his subjects floating in the space of the page, enabling us to focus much more on specific aspects – an example might be single leaves in minute detail – even imperfect ones. Later in life he often painted larger than life but with immense detail, using the techniques of a miniaturist.

Rory McEwan's exquisite series of Heirloom Tulip paintings are to my mind perfection, I will always try to follow the example of his brilliance.

I dedicate the paintings on these pages to the botanical artists that came before me and thank them for their inspiration.

Above *Tulipa* 'Colombine' (top) and *Tulipa* 'Insulinde' (below). Rory McEwen's placement of a single flower or leaf, often within a large space, is compositionally brilliant and has hugely influenced the way I work.

Right The author working in her mostly newly planted garden in London.

ENGLAND AND FRANCE: CONTRASTING GARDENS

Gardening – and painting – in both London and Provence are very different experiences, mostly due to the weather and temperature.

I know I am so lucky to have the opportunity to live, paint and garden in Provence and London with my partner, but it does mean that I need to be very organized and make sure that I have all the essential equipment to be able to work in both places. This means having the right art materials, a botanical library for reference (which I keep on my computer), my photography kit and a good studio space, set up to work in. That includes good light and daylight lamps, a large work surface, a comfortable chair and something engaging to listen to.

I rely so much on the plants I grow for inspiration and for many of the specimens I paint. My planning has to include a sense of where I'm going to be, in what season, and for how long. I need to ensure I've timed things well so that the growing, watering, care and harvesting of my plants is to their – and my – best advantage. I don't always get it right!

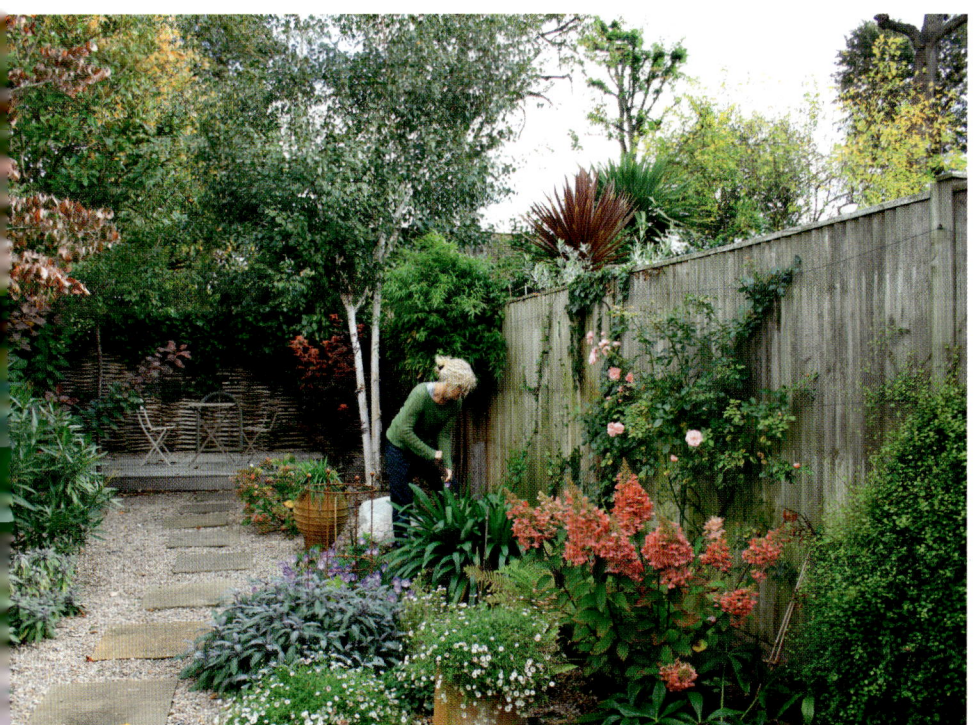

London – the garden(s)

I have several gardens to manage in London – my own, and the gardens of up to fifteen clients. Luckily, all these plots are in the same area as me, but even so I'm gradually reducing that number because of the increasingly large amount of time I spend in France.

The hardest part of gardening in London is the wet weather. I used to work in all conditions but I do that much less these days. The rest of it I find really easy, even if physically challenging, because I love it so much. It can be extremely therapeutic to be able to work out

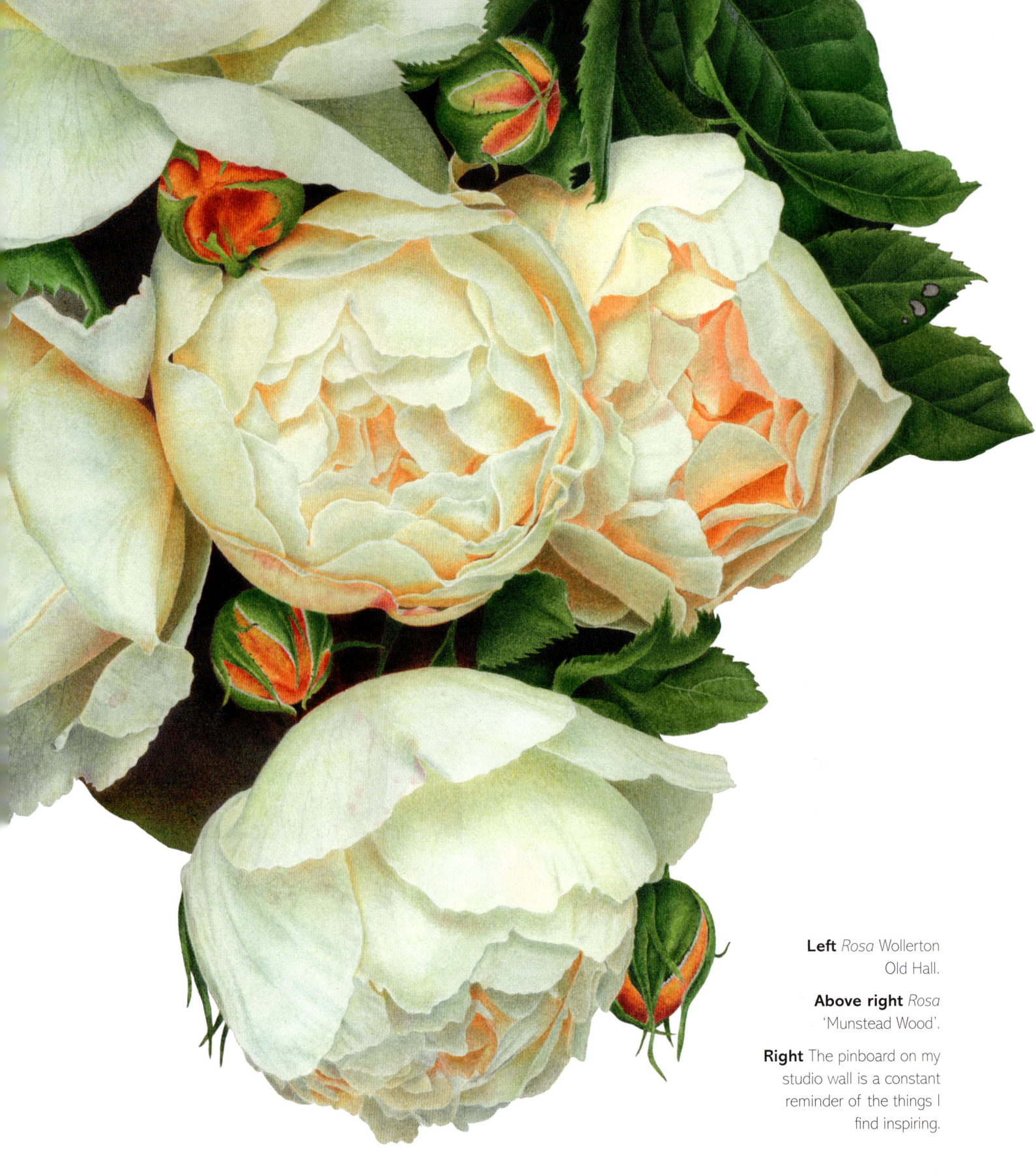

Left *Rosa* Wollerton Old Hall.

Above right *Rosa* 'Munstead Wood'.

Right The pinboard on my studio wall is a constant reminder of the things I find inspiring.

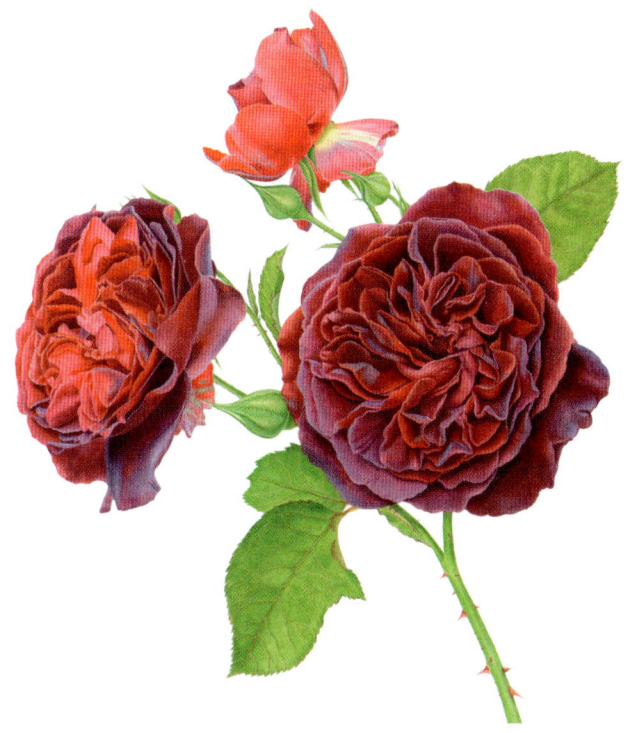

in the open air. Looking at a garden at the end of the day – my own or others' – and seeing that I've made a difference is very rewarding.

Several of these gardens belong to friends. There's something gratifying about the physical and sociable side of my gardening work and how it all links up with my painting: it's a good combination. I've also made a lot of friends working for new clients – some of whom have even commissioned me to paint flowers from their gardens.

This perfect mix of physical and sociable is so creatively sustaining, it absolutely complements the focus of my painting work.

London – the studio

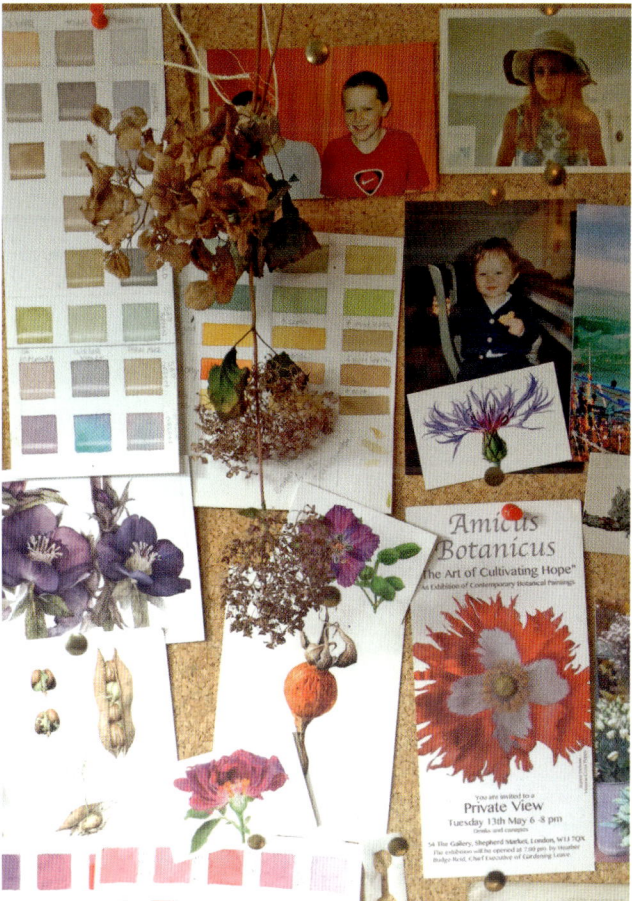

The physicality and sociability of gardening is a very different experience to when I'm working in my studio. Here I work entirely by myself and often for very long hours.

I try to turn off my phone and email while I'm painting as they can be distracting, but I really love having something interesting playing in the background: BBC Radio 4, music, or a well-read audiobook which will keep me at my work table for hours on end. This is so different to my time working outdoors, where I never garden with headphones on, preferring silence and time to think about other things.

When I have illustrating work, it more often than not has to take priority over gardening. This is because I am usually given tight deadlines to work to. The level of detail in my paintings means that they are really time-consuming and as a result I have to be incredibly disciplined.

There's not much that brings me more satisfaction than finally finishing a painting so I can move on to the next one.

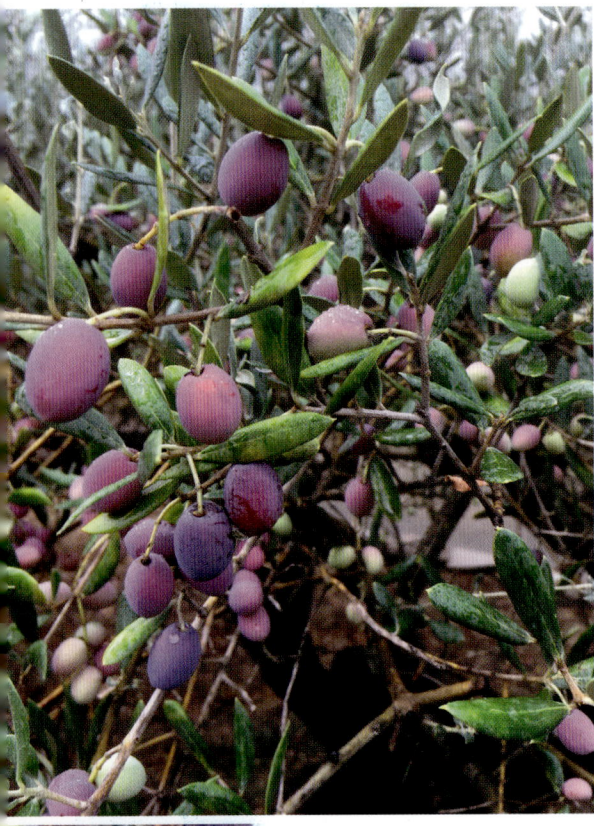

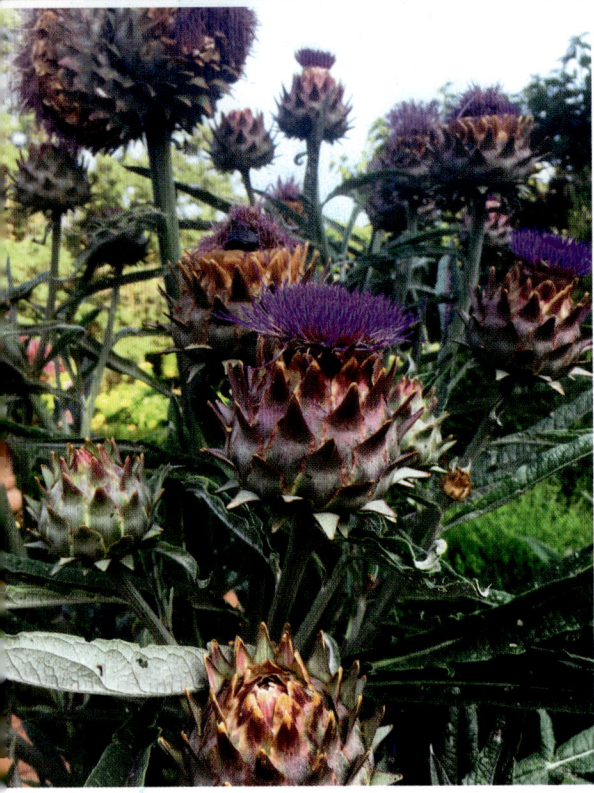

France – the garden

In contrast to our small London garden, we have a much bigger space in France. We haven't been there very long so the garden is very much a work in progress. My London gardening knowledge isn't especially relevant in France and I'm having to adapt and learn lots of new things.

This very different garden consists mostly of oak and pine trees, plus a small field of olive trees with a scattering of fig trees and grape vines. There's also a more cultivated section but it's a real challenge to grow anything because it's made up of massive rocks embedded in solid clay. The soil really is terrible! I have had lots of disasters and have had to dig up and chuck so many plants onto the compost heap.

The hot, dry weather is a challenge too. Plants that would be extremely happy in the UK in full sun absolutely cannot take the heat here. Instead I'm encouraging the growth of agaves and artichokes, which happily multiply and spread of their own accord.

These will survive in the baking summer sun and I'm cultivating any succulent plants that feel at home too – sometimes without any water for long periods of time. An indicator of the heat is the fact that by law we have to keep any low growth within 50 metres (54½ yards) of the house cut short because of the risk of forest fires.

Most of this garden has only recently been planted so only a few of the illustrations in this book are from our French garden – namely the olives, figs, grapes and cardoons – but the seeds of future potential are in place.

Over time I'm sure that some of the other things I manage to grow successfully in our hot, dry garden will find their way into my illustrating work. I'm looking forward to painting some of the succulents I'm cultivating from cuttings and offshoots, as well as the olives – at the point of just ripening – green flushed with purple and pink.

The things that I enjoy most when in France are planning a garden that will provide me with more subjects to draw and paint, trekking in the area, and Christmas harvest time – when my partner and I pick our olives and take them to the local mill to be turned into oil.

Left Cardoon thistle (*Cynara cardunculus*): a single seed, in flower and the dried seedhead.

Opposite These photographs of our garden show olives ripening on the trees and artichokes in full bloom.

France – the studio

I have a different preparation regime in my French studio. Before I start, I need to get rid of all the insects. I get lots of tiny flies and ants crawling across my paper, which is a disaster if I inadvertently squash one on the white of the paper – it's very hard to remove the stain. If you think about the potency of insect-derived cochineal colouring you'll know how strong and permanent these dots and smudges can be.

The hot weather in the summer means that painting can be challenging. Problems include getting so sweaty that my paintbrush constantly slips out of my hand, or my watercolour paints drying in the palette super-fast or on my brush before I've managed to get it as far as the paper. This isn't ideal. My solution is the purchase of a swamp cooler – a sort of fan with water in it that cools through the evaporation of the water. Not only does the paint not dry up, but neither do my eyes – as they would with a normal fan or air conditioning. Without this piece of kit it would be virtually impossible for me to work in my French studio in the hot afternoons in midsummer.

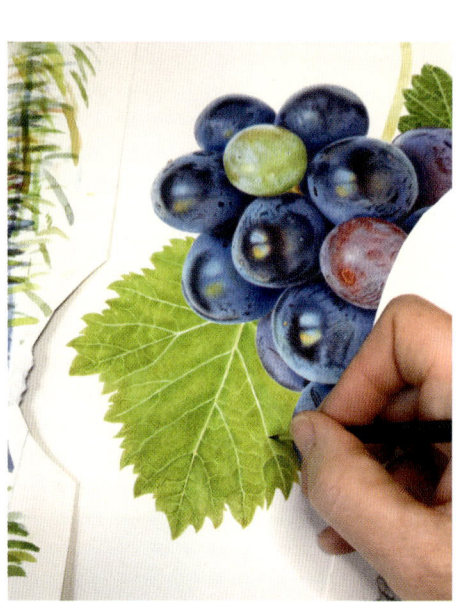

Above Grapes (*Vitis vinifera*). The grape vines in our French garden make wonderful, vibrant subjects.

Right Working in layers of green paint between the lighter network of veins on the vine leaf.

GARDEN OR FLORIST?

Just as a chef delights in growing his own fresh fruit, herbs and vegetables, the botanical artist takes pleasure in growing the best subject matter.

The Importance of Growing My Own Plants

Even though I'm so lucky to live within easy reach of some internationally renowned botanical collections in the UK, it's my own garden that supplies me with most of the subject matter I want to paint.

For obvious reasons, a lot of botanical artists are also keen gardeners. It gives us the added advantage of having easy access to botanical subjects for painting.

Being able to observe the life cycle of plants while staying with my sister in France was especially important for the paintings I needed to complete for my series 'The Anatomy of Flowers' (see pages 18–19). I needed lots of specimens I could take apart and dissect at various stages of their life span, looking closely at the reproductive stages of the flower and seeing how the seeds developed. Both mine and my sister's gardens supplied an abundance of really good reference material.

When I grow plants that I intend to paint, I collect detailed information in the form of photographs and painted colour samples. I make sure I do this as soon as I have picked a specimen: I do this at various stages of its development, and in different seasons.

As a gardener, I can choose what to plant and keep an eye out for the maturation of things: formation of new buds, the different stages of flowering and when to collect seedheads.

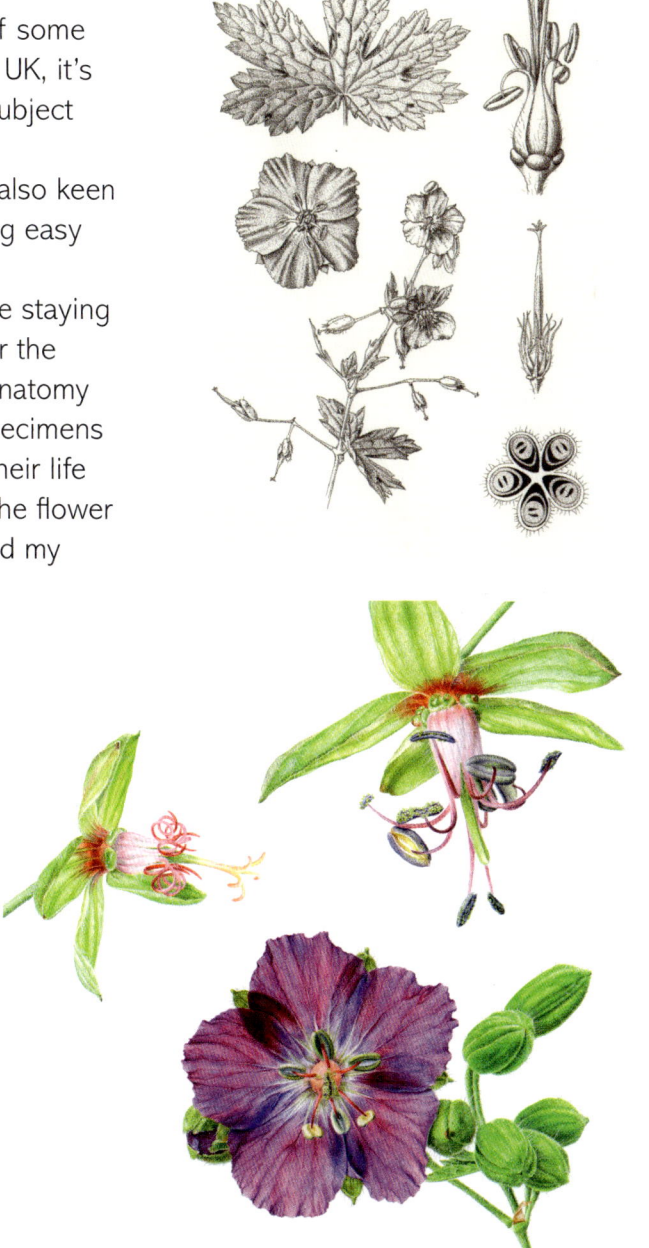

Above right A black and white ink drawing showing various parts of a perennial geranium (*Geranium phaeum*) with some of the details magnified.

Right Dusky cranesbill (*Geranium phaeum*), showing the full flower, buds and reproductive stages of this flower.

All of these observations might then be either incorporated into a work for myself (my personal portfolio) or go towards a commissioned illustration.

Decent reference of all parts of the plant really are essential for the kind of work I do. There have been instances when, halfway through a piece of work, I have found that I didn't have a good-enough record of a certain part. By then it was too late as the plant might have died, so I would be forced to abandon the painting until the following year when I was able to collect the relevant detail.

Home-grown

A lot of the flowers I grow myself are not available for sale in florists' shops because they're not commercially viable, or they just don't have a good enough shelf life. These include perennial cornflowers, clematis and many varieties of dahlias and garden roses.

It is quite difficult to source the more natural-looking varieties of garden roses in florists. Some specialist florists will stock them but they can be very expensive; if you have a garden it is obviously much better to grow your own.

Home-grown roses are so much more attractive than the cut ones that are normally available. Growing your own will give you the option of many more

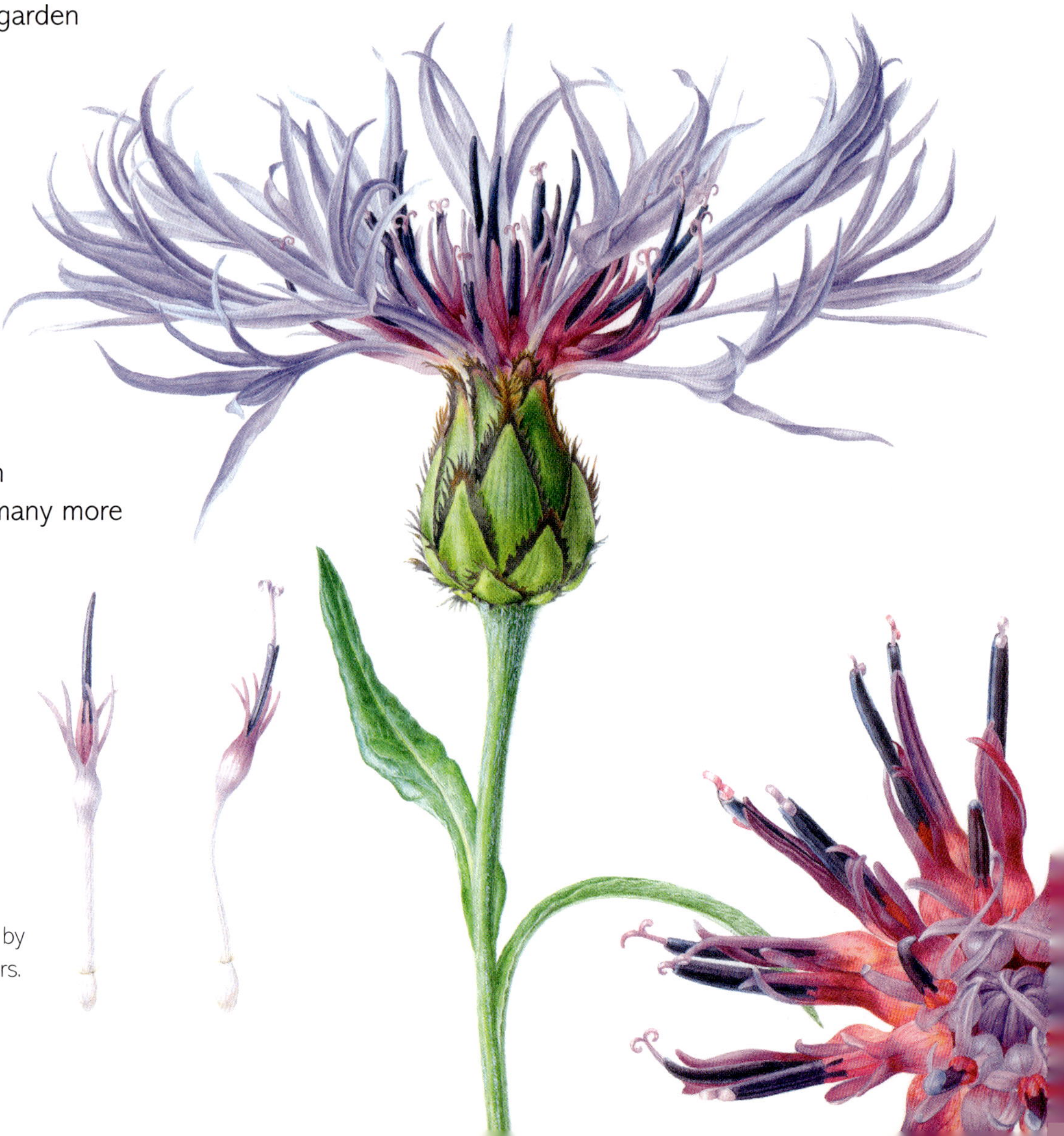

Right A perennial cornflower (*Centaurea montana*) that is loved by bees, butterflies and other pollinators.

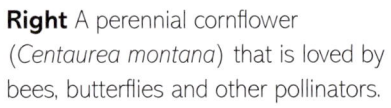

specimens to work from and the chance to see all the different stages of growth. A repeat-flowering rose is one of the most rewarding plants in my garden, producing enough beautiful fresh flowers over several months, which I cut to bring into the house.

The perennial cornflower *Centaurea montana* (shown left) is one of my favourite flowers because of its rich blue colour. They are very easy to grow, especially if you have a really sunny place in your garden.

The actual flowers are in the centre of the floret. The blue petals around the edge contain no reproductive organs but are there to attract insects, drawing them to the centre of the flower for pollination. It was essential that I could observe this plant as it grew and see these stages of pollination.

Other sources

I'm often commissioned to illustrate certain flowers or plants that I don't or can't grow myself. They might not be in season, or are exotic plants that won't grow in our London garden, nor in our much warmer and drier garden in France.

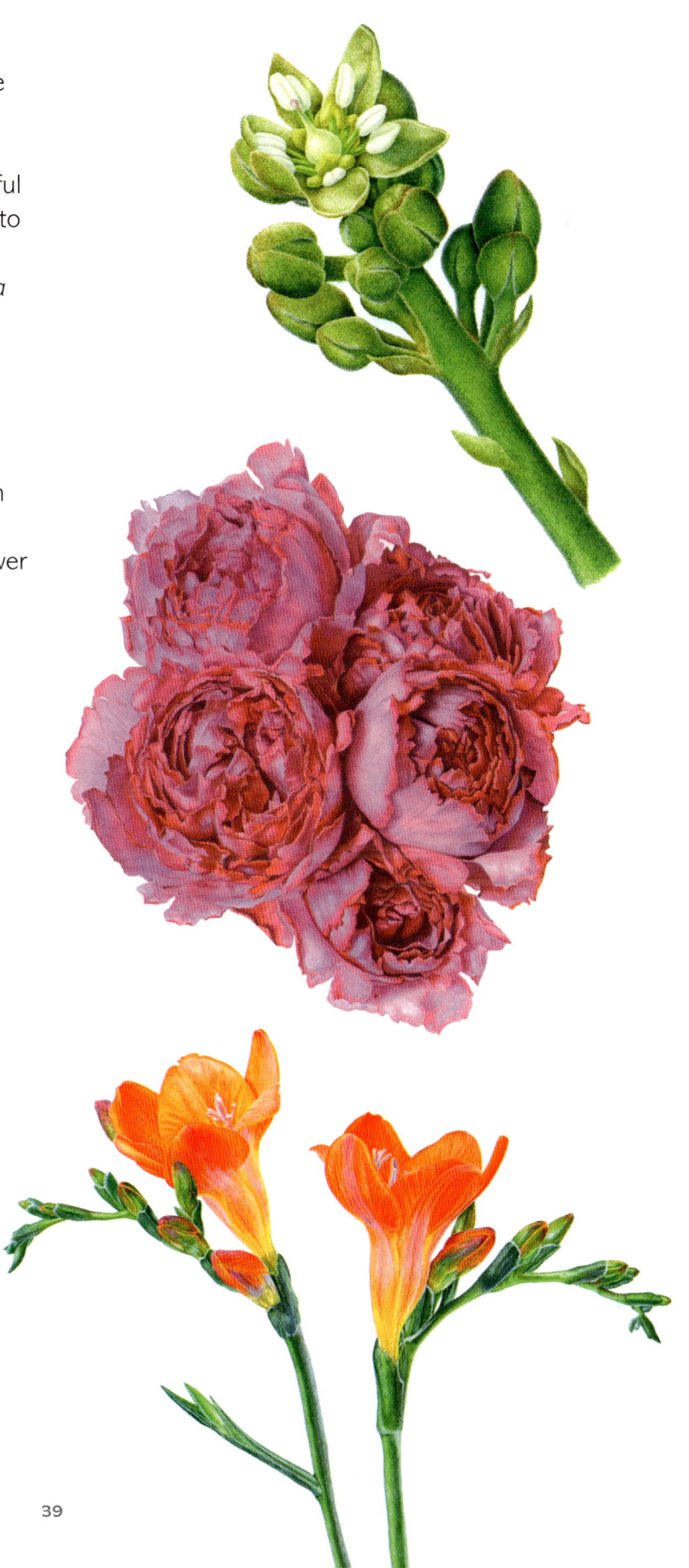

Above top Avocado flowers (*Persea americana*) are unusual in that one flower will open alternately in a male and then a female form to try to avoid self pollination. This picture shows the flower open at the functionally female stage.

Above right *Rosa* 'Yves Piaget' is a highly scented hybrid tea rose.

Right Freesias are popular cut flowers due to their bright colours and intense perfume.

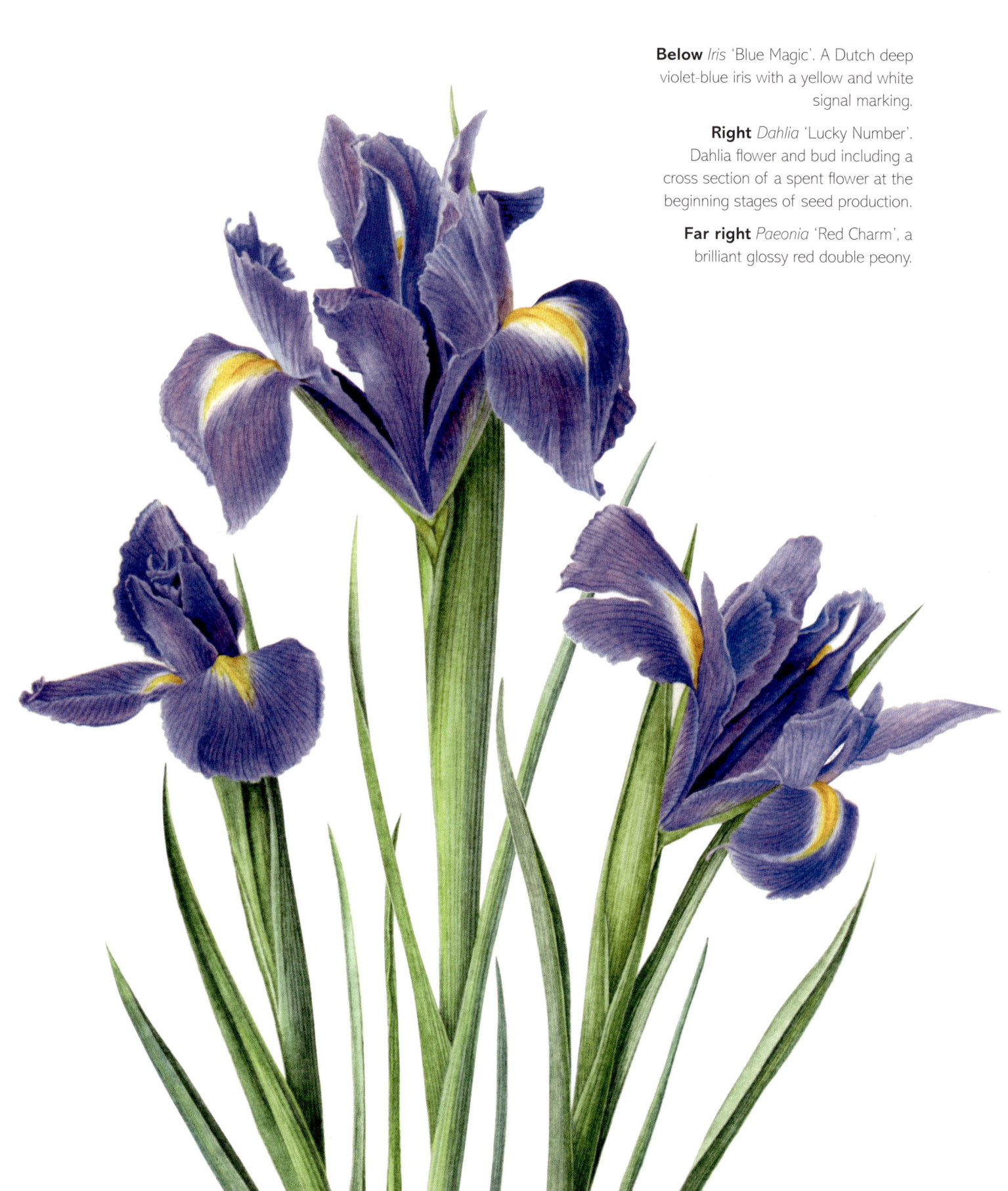

Below *Iris* 'Blue Magic'. A Dutch deep violet-blue iris with a yellow and white signal marking.

Right *Dahlia* 'Lucky Number'. Dahlia flower and bud including a cross section of a spent flower at the beginning stages of seed production.

Far right *Paeonia* 'Red Charm', a brilliant glossy red double peony.

At these times I have to either search the internet for stock photos and image references or try to source cut flowers from florists. It can be challenging to find what I'm after because standard varieties are most common and these are rarely what I need. It also depends on the season and what is available at that time. I find London's Covent Garden Market the best place for me because of its huge range of good-quality fresh flowers.

Fortunately, more and more florists are now stocking the unusual varieties I am looking for. It is now possible to buy a more diverse range of flowers, including really interesting tulips, deep purple and bright green ranunculus and wonderful peonies.

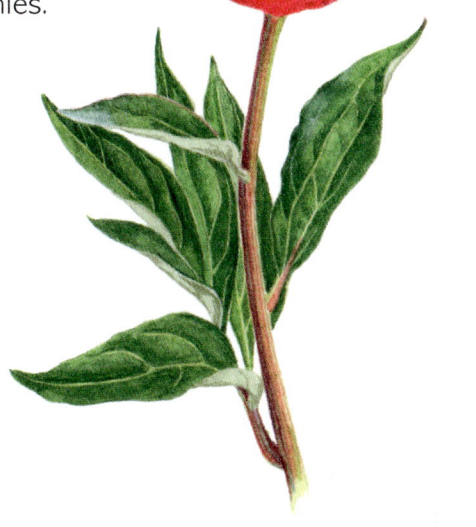

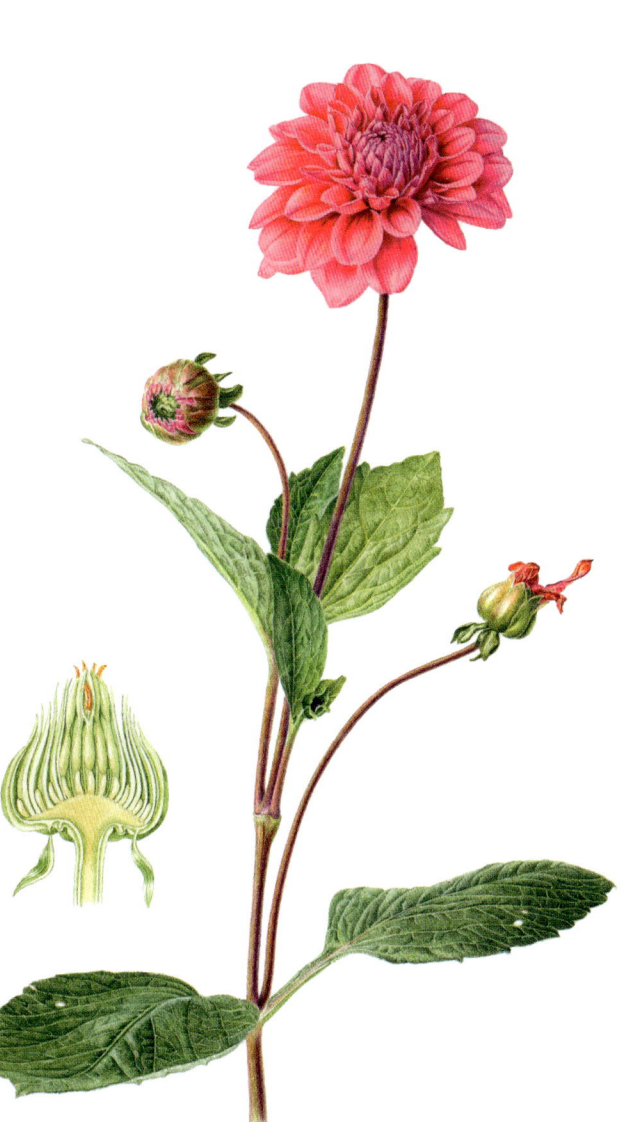

Other people's gardens

As I work in other people's gardens as well as my own, I have an extra source of interesting plants and I'm often able to take specimens home to paint – with permission, of course!

My sister-in-law, Sophie, is fanatical about dahlias. Every spring we put about twenty different varieties into large pots. In the winter these are taken out, stored in the shed and replaced with tulips for the spring. This annual ritual provides me with an amazing source of dahlias and tulips to paint that aren't normally available to buy in shops.

A Garden Favourite: Old and Garden Roses

These are varieties of roses that have been cultivated from an old rose originating from before the 18th century. *Rosa* 'Souvenir du Docteur Jamain' is probably my favourite because of its depth of colour, incredible perfume and velvety texture. I really enjoyed trying to capture the faint dusting of bloom on the petals without using white paint. Here I used a light wash of French Ultramarine and then painted over it, leaving the blue showing through in parts. This technique helped to show the wonderful texture on the surface of the petals.

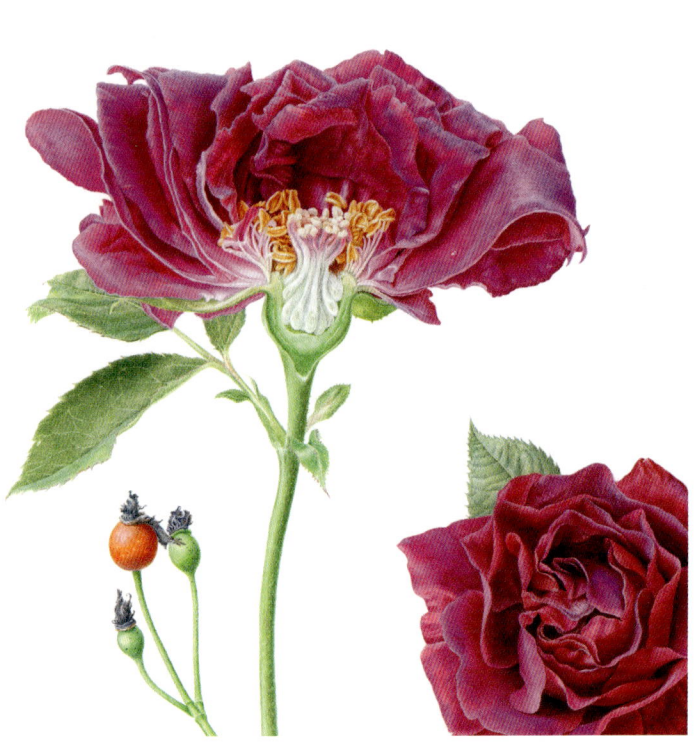

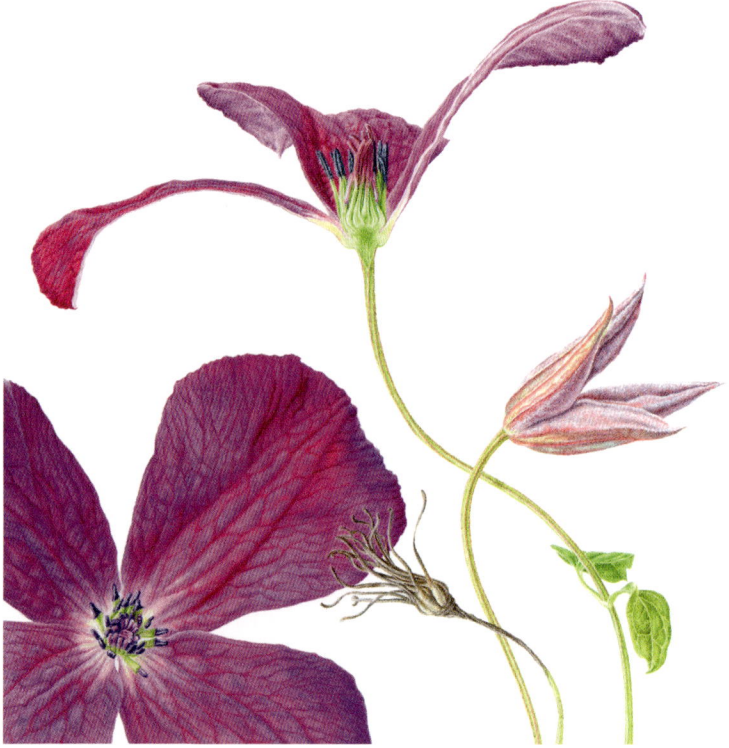

Although *Rosa* 'Souvenir du Docteur Jamain' is strictly speaking a shrub rose, I have always trained it as a climber, which makes it perfect for my small garden as it doesn't grow too massive. This repeat-flowering rose has an intense rose scent and looks fantastic with *Clematis viticella* 'Royal Velours' growing through it. The contrast of the two colours is stunning. The Evelyn Rose is another shrub rose which has an 'old rose' character, having been bred from one of the old roses in the 18th century.

Above left Showing a cross-section of *Rosa* 'Souvenir du Docteur Jamain', its rosehips and the full flower from above.

Above right Showing a cross-section of *Clematis viticella* 'Royal Velours', its bud, seed head and the full flower from above.

Opposite *Rosa* 'Evelyn'. Showing four views of this rose from bud to full bloom.

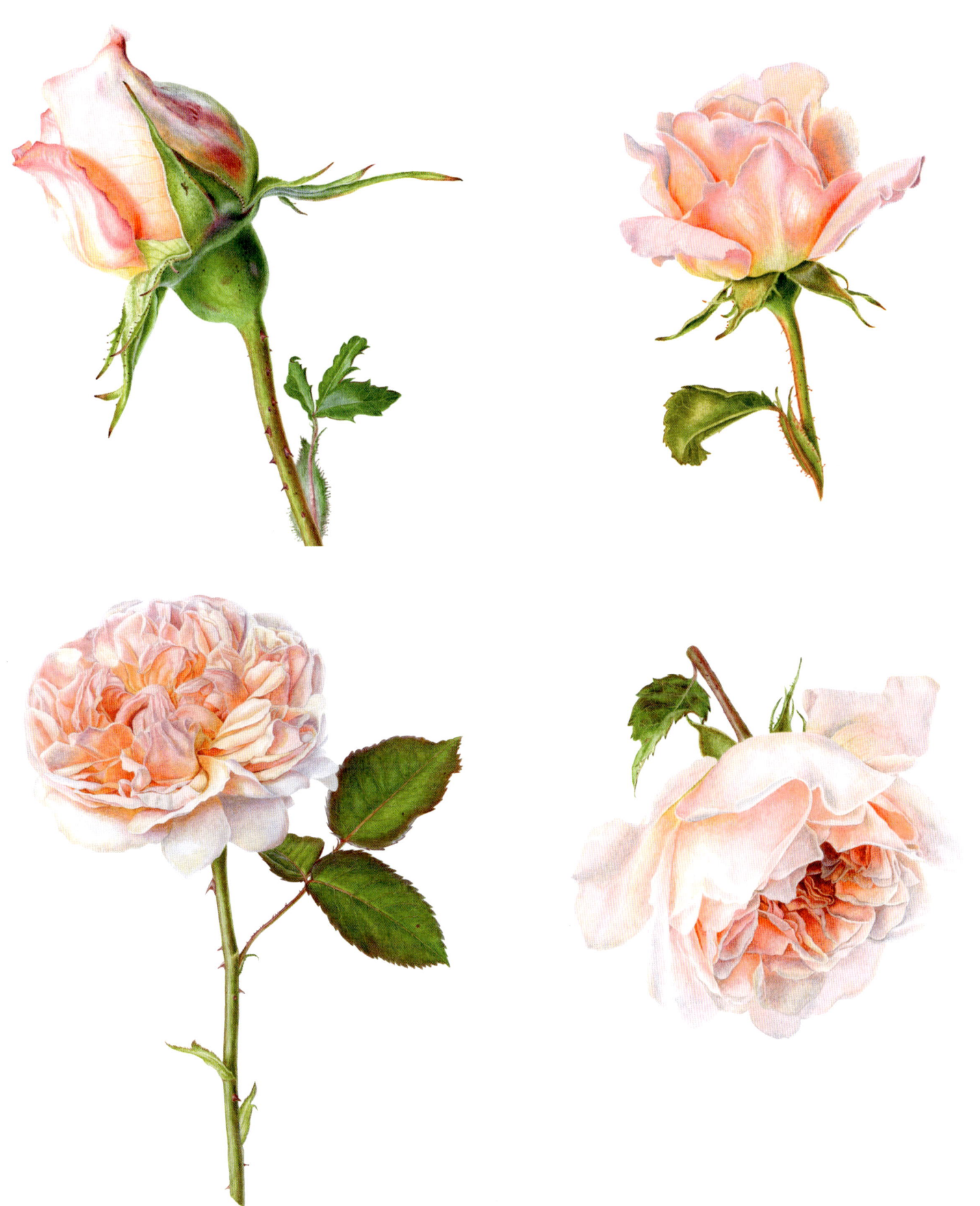

SOME FAVOURITE CONSTANTS

These are some of the plants I regularly maintain in our garden in England. The peripatetic nature of my gardening life dictates how, when and what I grow and – inevitably – what I paint.

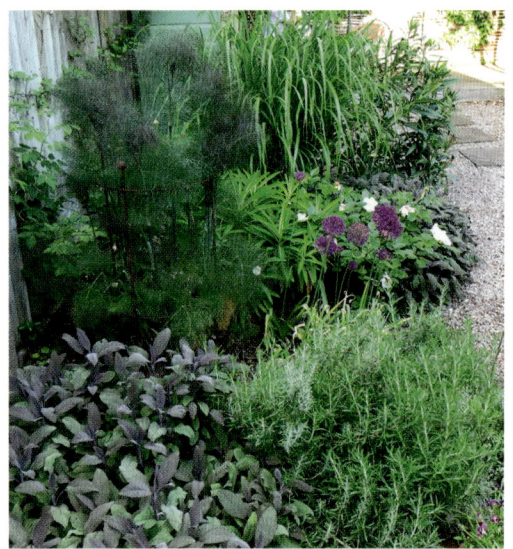
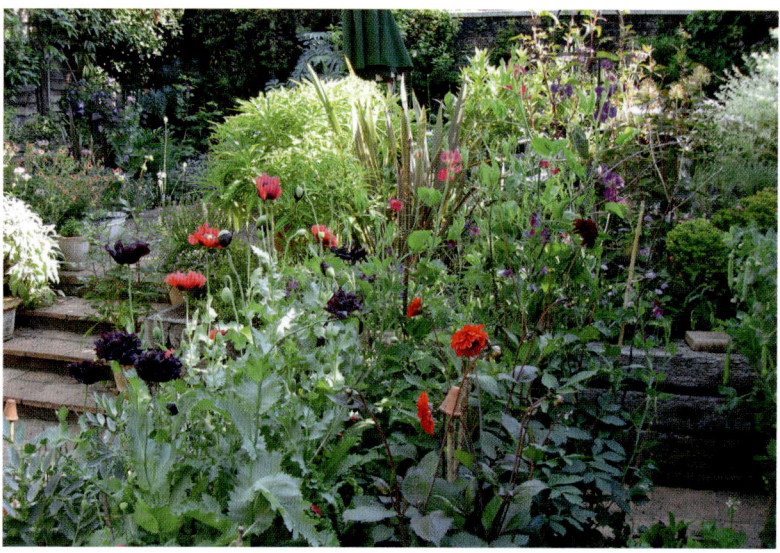

London

Our garden in London is a relatively small space and has been ours for just a couple of years. The plants are newly put in so not yet very mature and are very much in the beginning stages.

As I'm not there all of the time, the variety of plants I can have is limited and less than I've been used to. My redesign of the space meant I had to dig up nearly everything that was there before, apart from a beautiful *Cornus kousa*, an oleander and some black bamboo.

These are some of the easy, low-maintenance plants that survive well without too much bother:

Hellebores maintain themselves as they don't need lots of light or water. *Helleborus x hybridus* (right) is a close-up from one of my scientifically oriented paintings. I wanted to show the interior of the bud and seedpod, as well as the whole seedhead from the side without the petals. It was important to grow my own hellebores to be able to gather specimens at all stages of growth, from bud to seed.

Above My current 'in progress' garden in London (left) and my previous garden (right) where I had more space to grow a much larger variety of plants.

Below *Helleborus* x *hybridus*, showing the full flower in cross-section, from above and the inside of the hellebore seed.

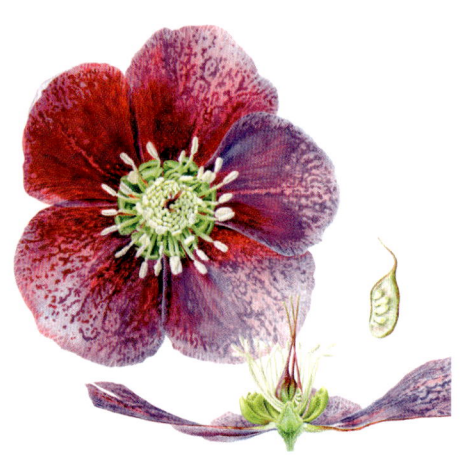

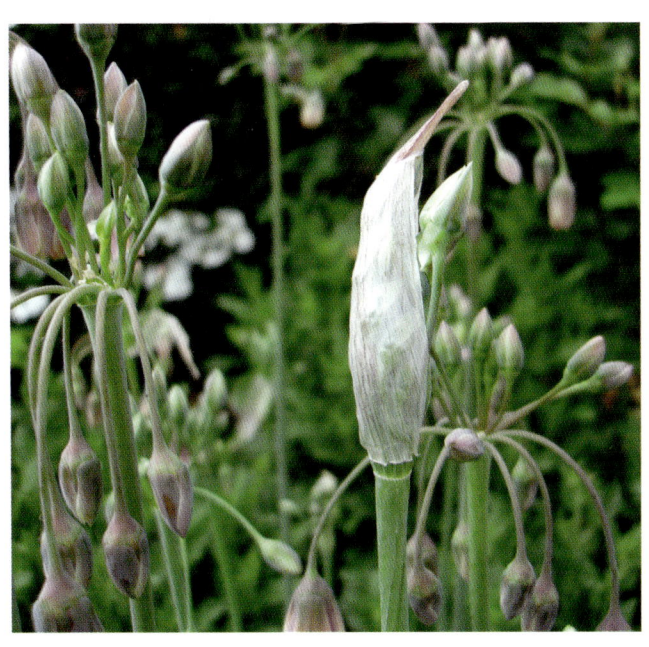

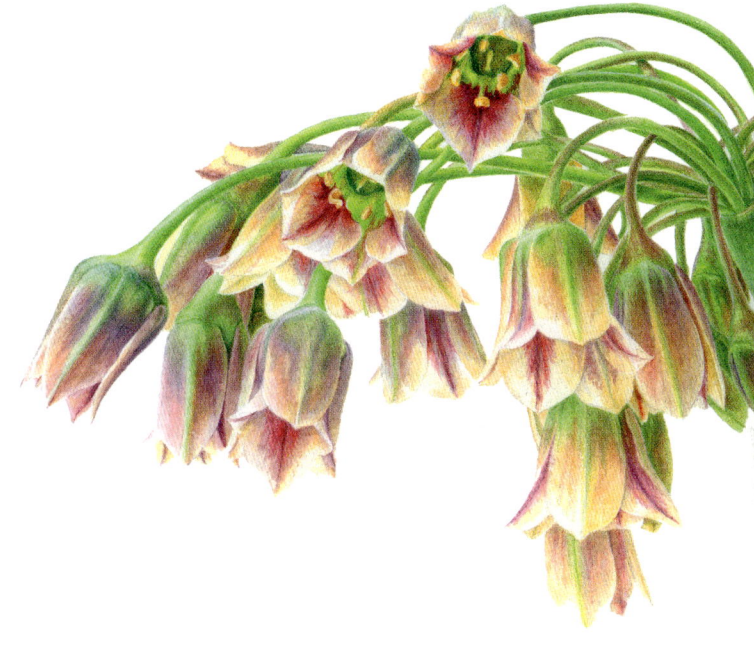

Above and above right Sicilian honey garlic (*Nectaroscordum siculum*) growing in my garden and a detail from my watercolour painting of the large, nodding flower heads.

Below Poppy (*Papaver somniferum*) to show detail of the stamens from above.

Nectaroscordum siculum (honey garlic), show above, has large, graceful umbels of white or cream flowers with subtle shades of deep pink and green within. I love the way the bell-shaped flowers droop down above their tall stem. It is very easy to grow in the sun and self-seeds all over the place. As its name suggests, the honey garlic has a very strong, slightly odd onion smell, but I'm willing to put up with it for the elegant beauty of the flowers.

Beautiful bright red poppies (*Papaver somniferum*), with black markings at the base of the petals, self-seed freely every year in our garden. Once picked they fade very quickly, so here I had to take several photographs as reference to work from. There are a variety of wonderful textures and colours within a single flower; fragile paper-like petals, powdery pollen on the stamens and the wonderful glaucous blue of the young seed head, leaves and bristly stem.

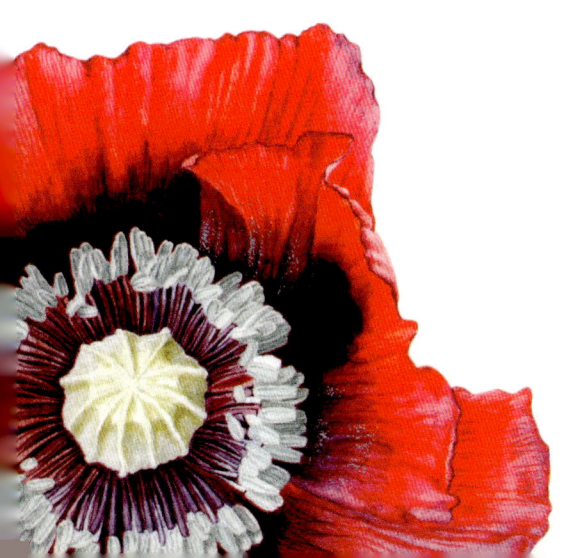

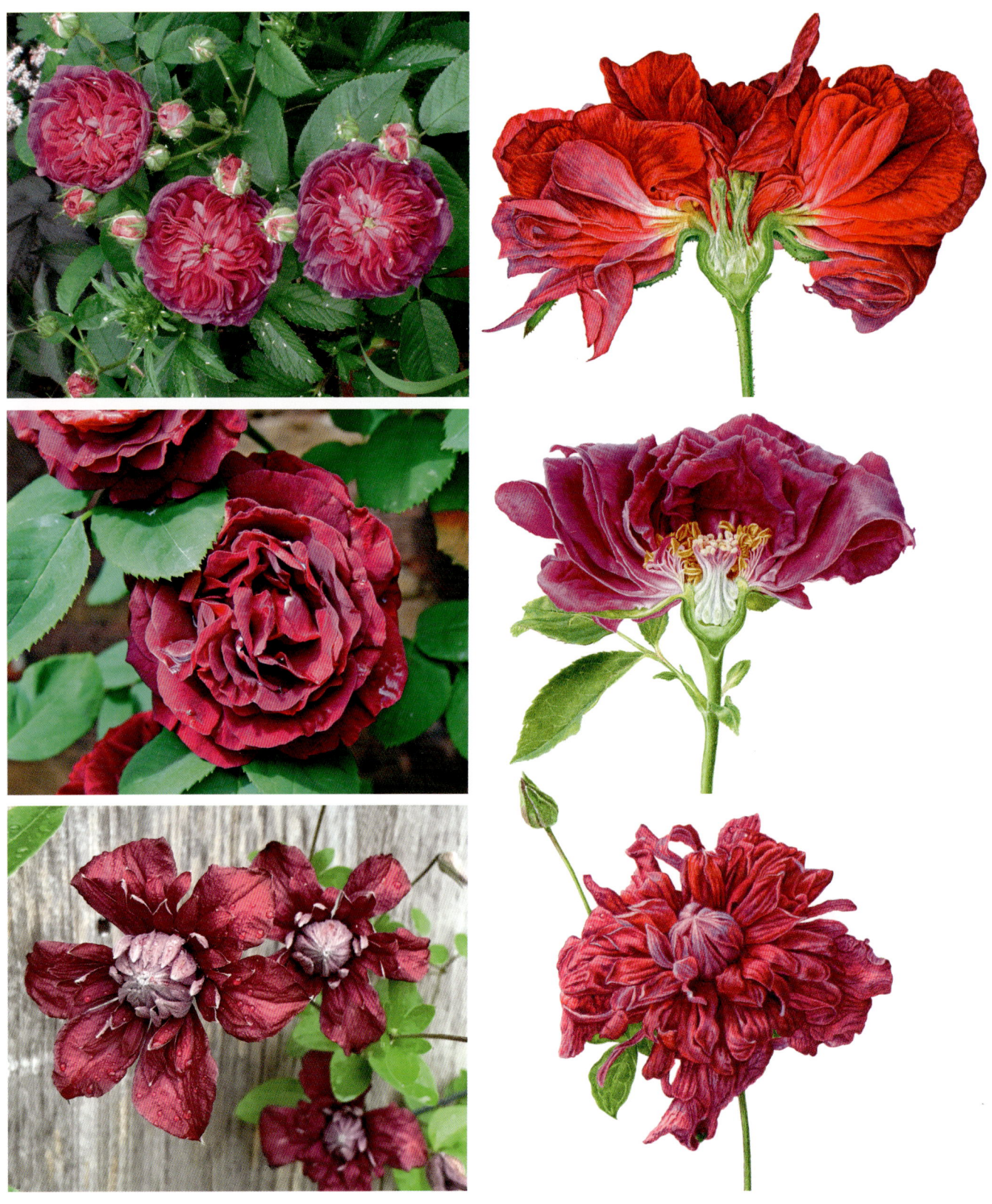

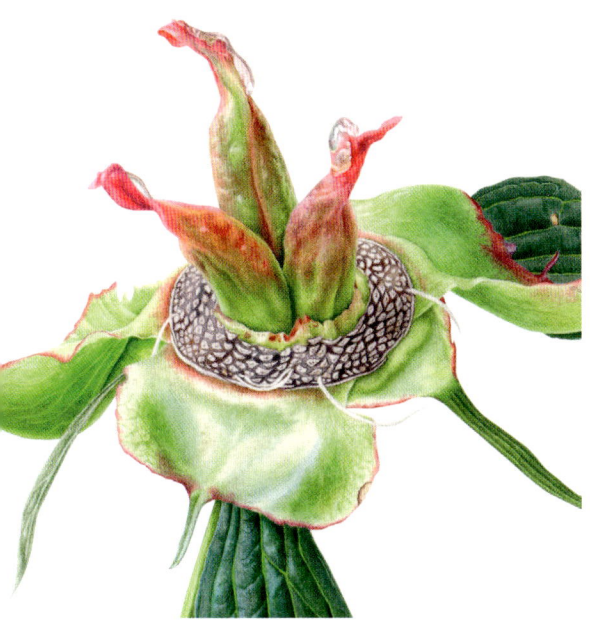

Above *Paeonia lactiflora* 'Monsieur Jules Elie'. A detail of the unusual seed head forming.

Opposite: *Rosa* 'Charles de Mills' (top) and a cross-section of a watercolour of the full flower; *Rosa* 'Souvenir du Docteur Jamain' (centre) and a watercolour of a cross-section of the full flower; and *Clematis* 'Purpurea Plena Elegans' (bottom) and a close-up of a watercolour of the flowers.

I originally grew this peony, shown left, for its beautiful pale pink flowers. When I spotted the developing seedhead I decided to focus on that instead. I found it quite incredible and had to paint it. It's very unusual and looks rather alien to me.

Geranium phaeum (dusky cranesbill) is a very easy-spreading, shade-tolerant plant. This would never grow in my garden in France as the climate there is much too hot. It has beautiful sprays of dark purple flowers.

The prominent stamens at the centre of the flower are what caught my attention, so this is how I chose to focus the composition. While painting this I found all sorts of amazing shapes and textures. I liked it just as much without its petals, as it seemed to create a very insect-like impression. Results like this happen regularly when I scrutinize plants under magnifiers.

One of my favourite (and very easy) plants to grow is *Clematis viticella* 'Purpurea Plena Elegans' (shown opposite). I absolutely love this clematis, it has a slightly antique, faded, dusky-purple colour, is multi-petalled and flowers for months.

To achieve its colour I used a relatively dark wash of French Ultramarine for the background flower colour. This is because the petals aren't smooth and shiny, but more velvety, and I didn't want any sharp highlights. I then worked in progressively deeper shades of magenta mixed with blues and a small amount of orange paint to give more warmth and to dull down the colour intensity slightly, giving a more muted effect.

I wish I could add other plants to this list of successes. However, I must admit to a few casualties, including the loss of some beautiful new roses which were dug up by foxes while I was away in France. At least I can blame this on something else, rather than a lack of gardening skills.

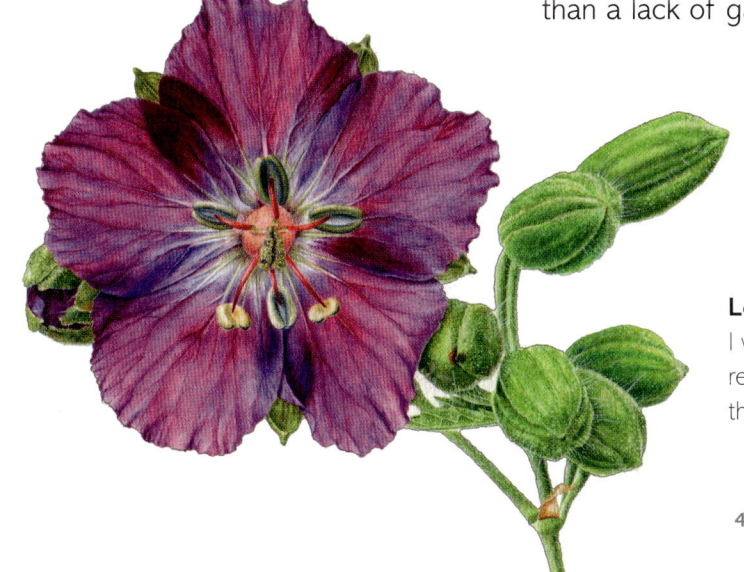

Left Dusky cranesbill (*Geranium phaeum*). I worked from a backlit specimen here to reveal the subtle shades and textures within the petals.

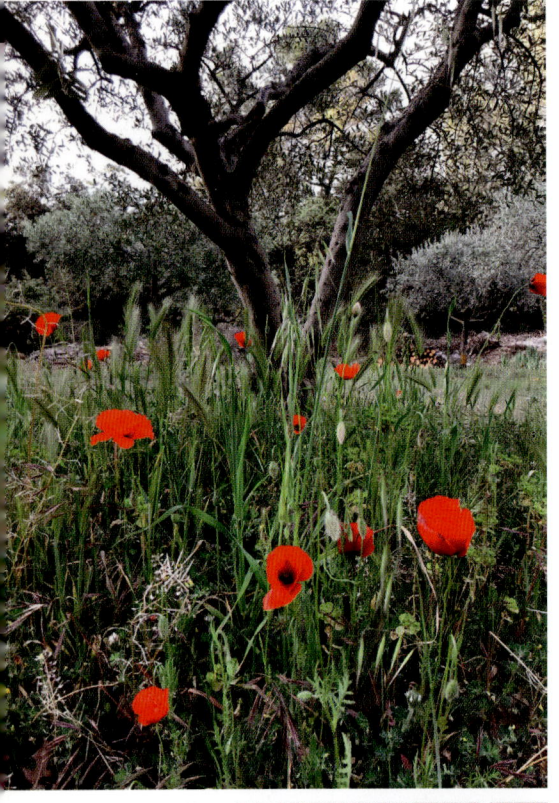

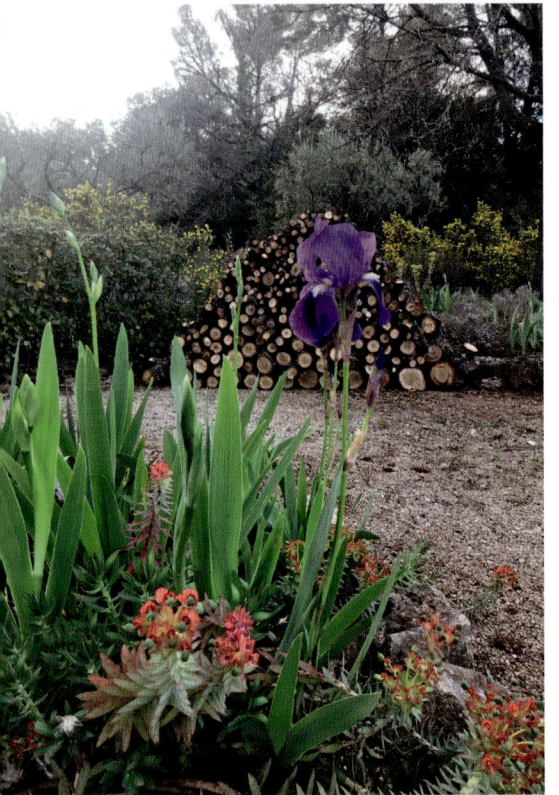

France

Our garden in France is very much a work in progress. I have had to plant easy, low-maintenance specimens, especially plants that don't need lots of water. Drought-tolerant characteristics are important, not just for ease of maintenance but because using less water eases demand on the natural environment. Agaves and succulents are particularly at home here.

Plants that grow successfully are the obvious lavenders and several herbs: various thymes, rosemary, and purple sage *Salvia officinalis* 'Purpurascens'.

The garden is challenging because of its heavy clay soil and rocky terrain, but roses seem to eventually work their roots around the rocks. I have planted several varieties of rose in France but I have yet to paint them. As they are very young plants they haven't yet produced significant flowers. I'm hoping they will eventually flourish and make great subjects.

Centaurea cyanus is an annual cornflower that is easy to grow in France. I scatter a mixture of its seeds along with poppies and nigella around the olive trees. The combination is stunning. I particularly liked the unopened bud in the painting opposite, showing the patterns of the thistle-like bracts overlapping each other.

The grapes are from a vine I planted in France. Not only are they beautiful to look at, but the taste is superb. They are nothing like shop-bought grapes, particularly if picked and eaten straight away when they are still warm from the sun.

The artichoke thistle or cardoon *Cynara cardunculus* (see page 35) is a member of the Asteraceae family. It has many cultivated forms, including the globe artichoke. All grow really well here in France.

Unfortunately, I'm unable to grow any other vegetables here at the moment as I would have to be in one place all the time to tend to them. They can't be left to fend for themselves in such a hot environment.

Left Our French garden is ideal for plants that tolerate dry conditions such as olives, poppies, iris and euphorbias.

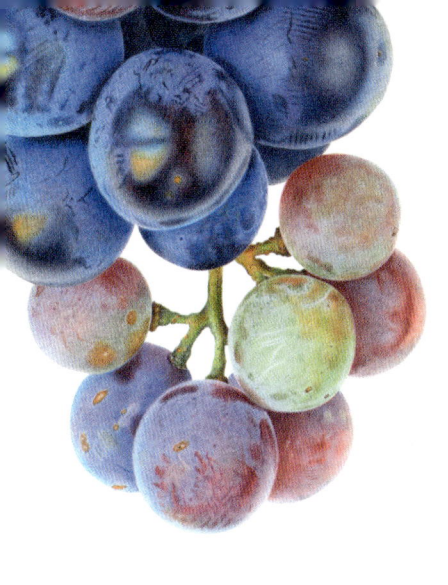

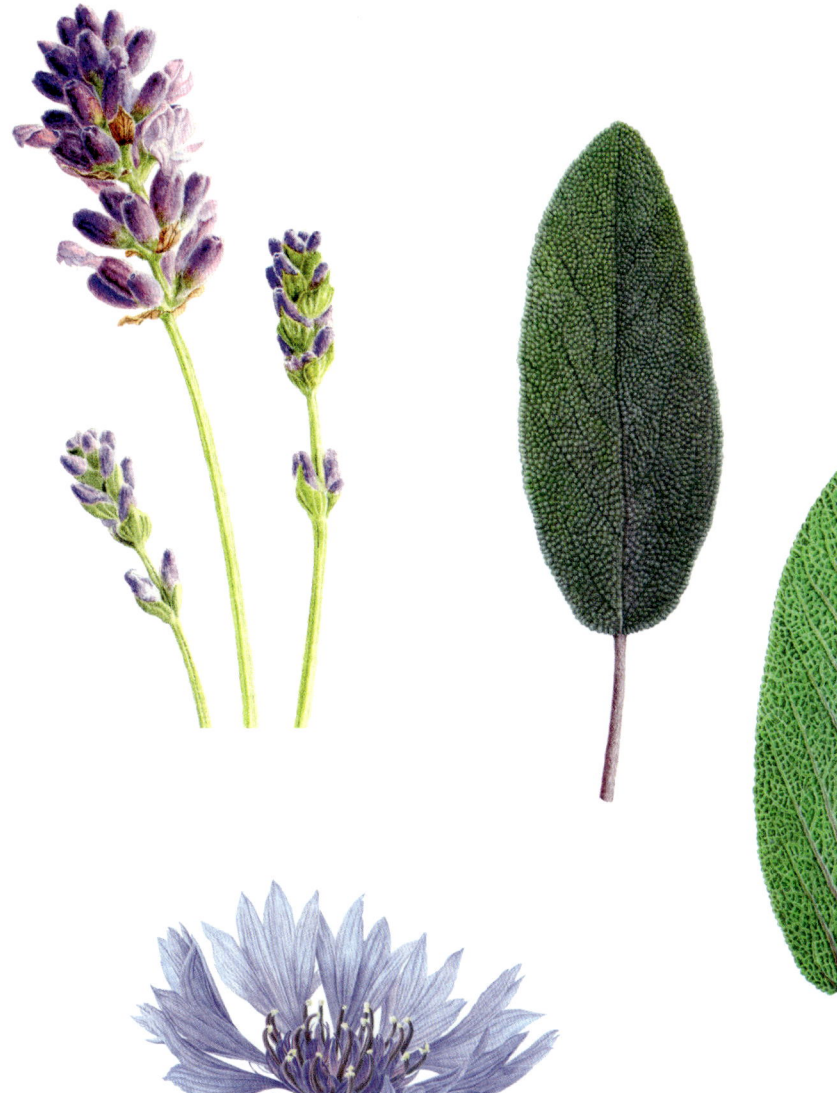

A selection of plants painted from my garden in France, including: **Clockwise from top** *Vitis vinifera*, a detail from a larger painting emphasising the light and bloom on this multicoloured bunch of grapes; *Lavandula angustifolia* 'Hidcote', my favourite lavender for its intensely deep violet-purple flowers and really neat and compact habit; Sage (*salvia*), showing the top and underside of this highly textured leaf; *Centaurea cyanus* – the thistle-like bud and open deep blue flower of this annual cornflower.

SCIENTIFIC – THE SECRETS OF FLOWERS

By the time I had my own garden I was becoming increasingly interested by the life cycles and growth patterns of plants. It made me want to pursue the idea of illustrating more of them other than just their showy flowers.

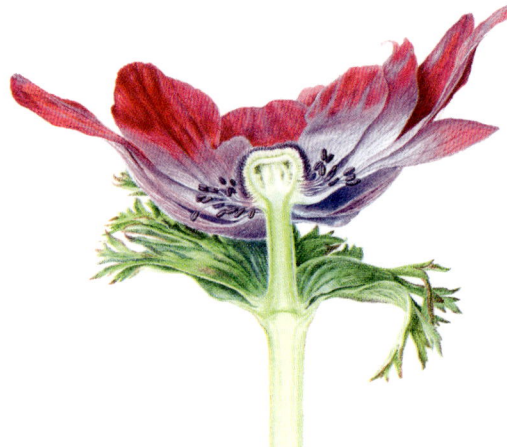

Above and below *Anemone coronaria* painted for the RHS Anatomy of Flowers exhibition and chosen specifically for the criteria of following the work of Arthur Harry Church (see page 24).

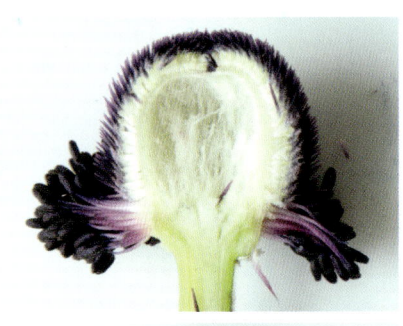

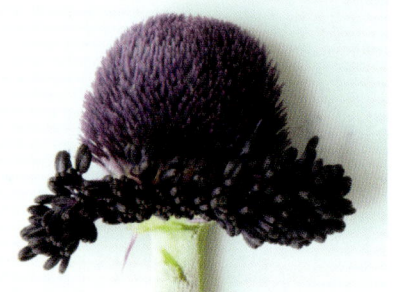

Discovering the botanical paintings of Victorian botanist and painter Arthur Harry Church was a revelation for me.

At this point I had already been studying and painting flowers for some time. By looking at his work I was seeing single flowers in a starkly different way: painted scientifically and precisely, isolated on the page and sliced lengthways through the centre of the blossom with their anatomy exposed. However, they were painted very sensitively and the colours and textures seemed so real.

In order to follow Church's methods, I chose flowers from my garden and started taking them apart. The flowers had to have an interesting interior when dissected and then some other attribute that would fit well within the square composition I had decided on. For instance, the flower from a different angle, a bud or seedpod, a stamen, or the intricate centre of the flower. Unlike Church, I wanted multiple views of a chosen plant in my paintings' compositions.

It might seem counter-intuitive to pull apart a beautiful flower, but I've found that these separate parts have their own fascinating characteristics and subtleties, with the internal arrangement of these details being specific to each plant. These are crucial elements of a scientifically oriented botanical study.

Before dissection, I looked at my plants without magnification. I was looking for the point of view that best revealed the general shape and focused on the parts that interested me. Next, I used my hand lens (10x magnification), which revealed amazing details of the enlarged parts. Taking accurate measurements as I went on and using a dissecting needle (a needle with a wooden handle) to tease apart and separate, I could see petals, stamens, sepals and ovaries in a new way. What became visible under the magnifying glass were wonderful, completely new views of the textural variations, relationships between parts and minute details in the veins, hairs, seeds and powdery pollen that I hadn't seen before.

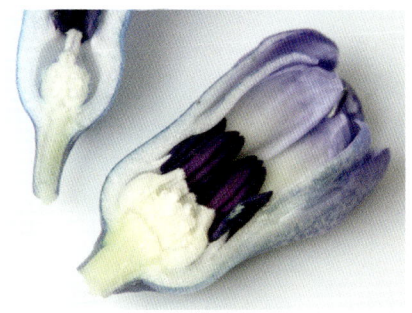
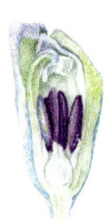
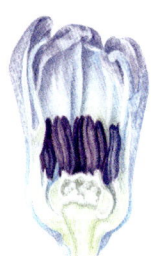
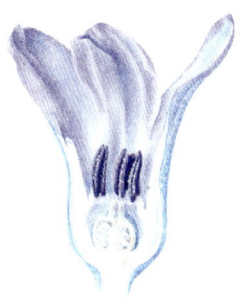

Bisection

Achieving successful symmetrical bisections through an entire flowerhead lengthways is more difficult to do – it takes a bit of practice. I had to sacrifice quite a few flowers before I was able to achieve a really good clean cut. To get a decent long section I used a very sharp surgical scalpel. The cut has to be made carefully and cleanly so as not to bruise the plant or damage the petals.

Once cut, the interior of a flower discolours very quickly. I always have a camera ready, set on a tripod, to take several photographs immediately.

The cut flower is laid on a white background. A large pair of tweezers are useful here for moving the parts around rather than using hands: it's really easy to bruise or leave your fingerprints on delicate petals, so picking them up with tweezers is a good idea. I always try to photograph using natural daylight, with the light coming from the left. This is for consistency, especially if I am going to add several elements to a composition. These photographs, taken at the moment of bisection, are crucial to the accuracy of my paintings.

I am in admiration of the botanical artists of the past who, without access to the tools and technology we now have, were still able to make such scientifically accurate works for us to use and admire.

Above and right *Hyacinthus orientalis* 'Delft Blue' showing three cross-sections of the progression of growth of a single flower and the full flowerhead of this bright blue hyacinth.

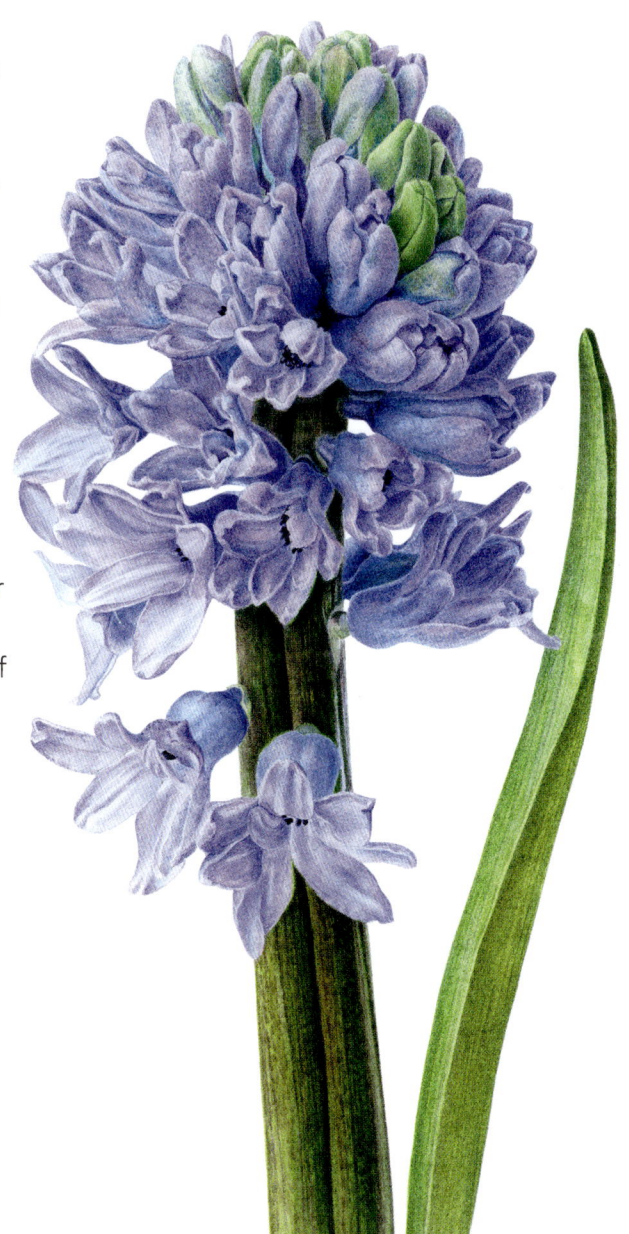

SEASONS: THE YEAR DIVIDED

All of the plants in this section are particularly significant markers of the changing seasons for me. Because of the importance of growing my own plants for my paintings, the time of year affects the choices I make.

Each season always produces something new and exciting to inspire me. Sometimes it's the returning yearly perennials, at other times it might be some annuals I've grown as part of a planting scheme; occasionally it might be something I've picked up while out on a walk. But my favourite season has to be spring because of the increased light with gradually longer and warmer days, and the beginnings of regrowth. Here are a few of the subjects I have enjoyed painting, season by season, chosen for their colour or texture or because they have a special meaning for me.

Winter

The acorn cups are from the evergreen oaks I found on Mont Sainte-Victoire near to where I live in France for part of the year. It's the mountain that Cézanne painted many times. I'm a very keen walker and went up there in autumn when the already beautiful panoramic views were made even more spectacular by the changing colours of the landscape.

I found the twig with lichen in the woods around there too, but in the middle of winter. At the base of the mountain, in the secluded forest, the colours of the mosses and lichens were really quite brilliant in the shade of

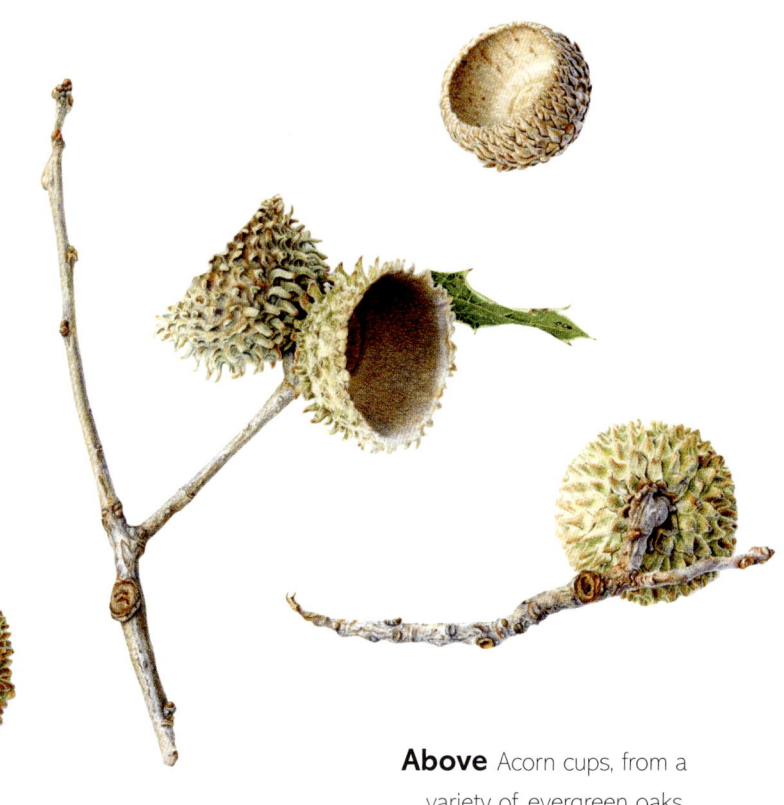

Above Acorn cups, from a variety of evergreen oaks, collected on a walk in France.

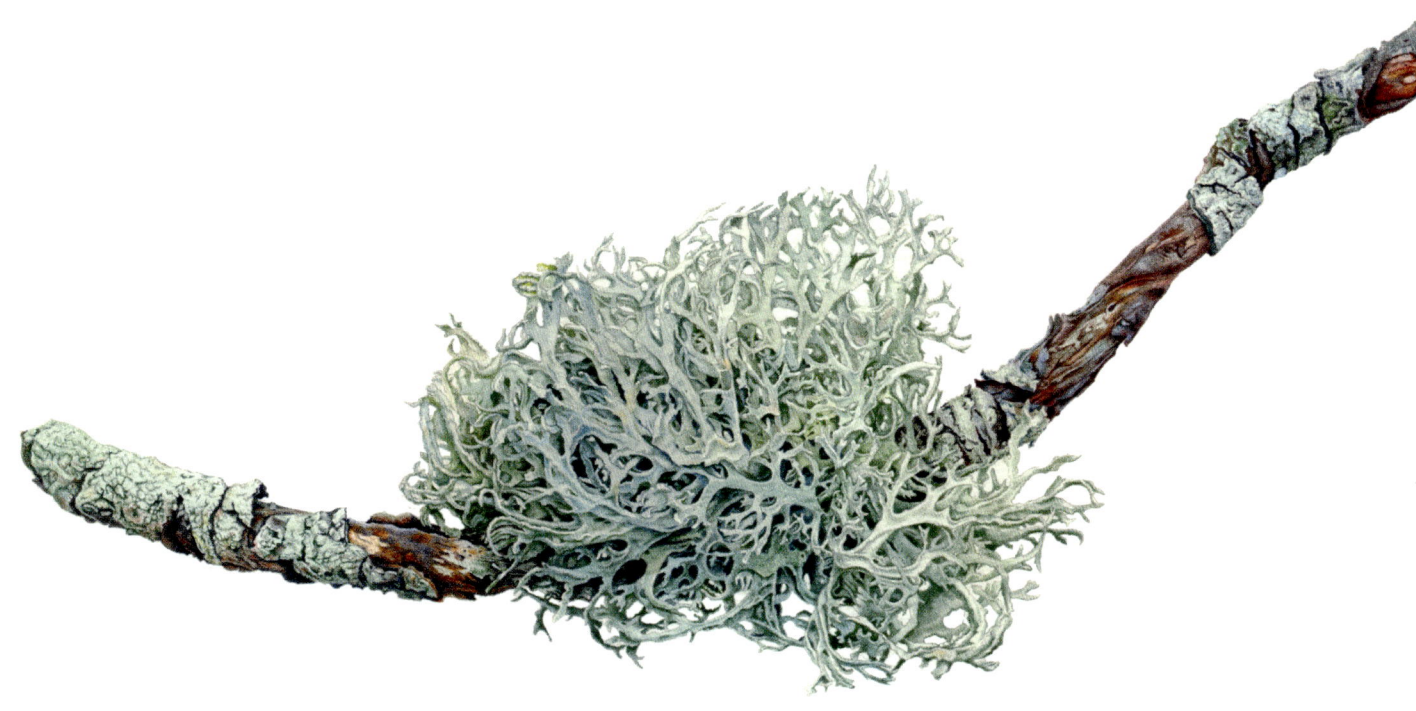

the evergreen oaks. I took home a few specimens, deciding to paint this one because I loved the seaweed-like flowing shapes of the lichen and the gnarled bark of the twig.

In the UK, pansies are really useful for providing winter colour. I completed this example to practise the technique of painting velvety texture. I started, as I often do, with fairly wet washes of French Ultramarine – making sure to avoid the white centre – gradually building up layers of magenta, Winsor Blue and Permanent Rose. As I put on the darker layers for the shadows and details of the veins, I used the same colours but as a drier mix, creating a deeper and more opaque coating.

The very dark areas are Indigo and Permanent Alizarin Crimson. When mixed with very little water they are virtually black. I prefer not to use premixed blacks as they can appear quite flat. Mixing your own gives the colour much more vibrancy.

I used a virtually dry brush for the final darker layers. This very dry brush technique can be used to give a slightly rough quality to the paint stroke. If the brush is dragged very gently over the surface, the paint will catch on to some of the fine raised texture of the paper, leaving the tiny indents of the paper below untouched. I find this helps to create a velvety look.

Above A twig with lichen collected on a walk in winter.

Below Pansy (*Viola* x *wittrockiana*).

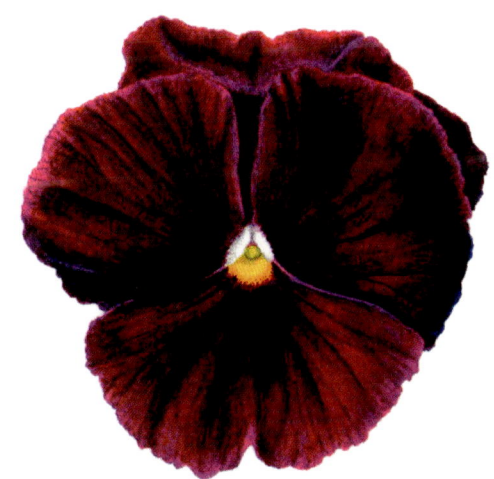

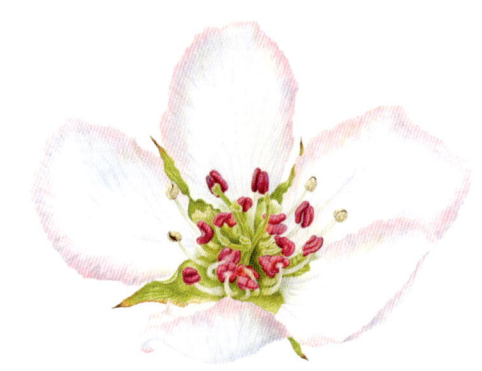

Spring

Pear blossom

Pear-tree blossom is a beautiful sight at the start of this season. Delicate white, five-petalled flowers, often with pink anthers on green stamens, they seem to float in groups on the still-leafless branches. They are a true sign of the arrival of spring. For information on the particular challenges of painting white flowers (see pages 85 and 86).

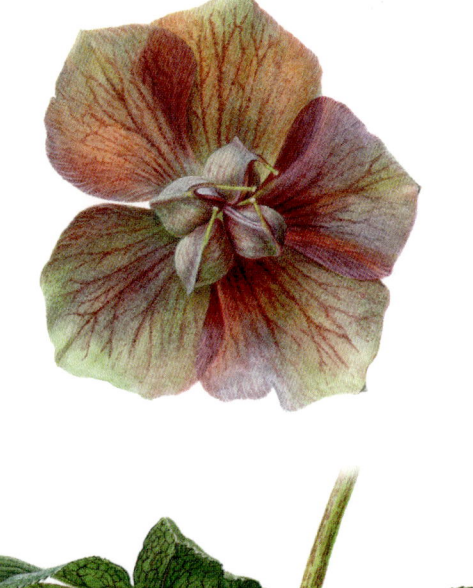

Hellebores

To me, hellebores are the first sign of very early spring. There are such a large variety of colours: white, pink, green, dark purples, and blueish blacks. These graceful bowl-shaped flowers are normally nodding downwards or outward-facing but it's always worth lifting them upright to see how beautiful they are to look at head-on. The petals – or sepals in the case of hellebores – are often translucent and look stunning with the light shining through. They can also be patterned with intricate veins and spots. The centre of the flower is equally lovely and has prominent anthers that are normally cream or pale yellow that contrast beautifully. These flowers really do glow and are so welcome as winter is coming to an end.

Above top Pear (*Pyrus*) blossom.

Right Hellebores (*Helleborus* x *hybridus*). A seedhead forming (top) and a side view of the growth habit of the downward-facing flowers (below).

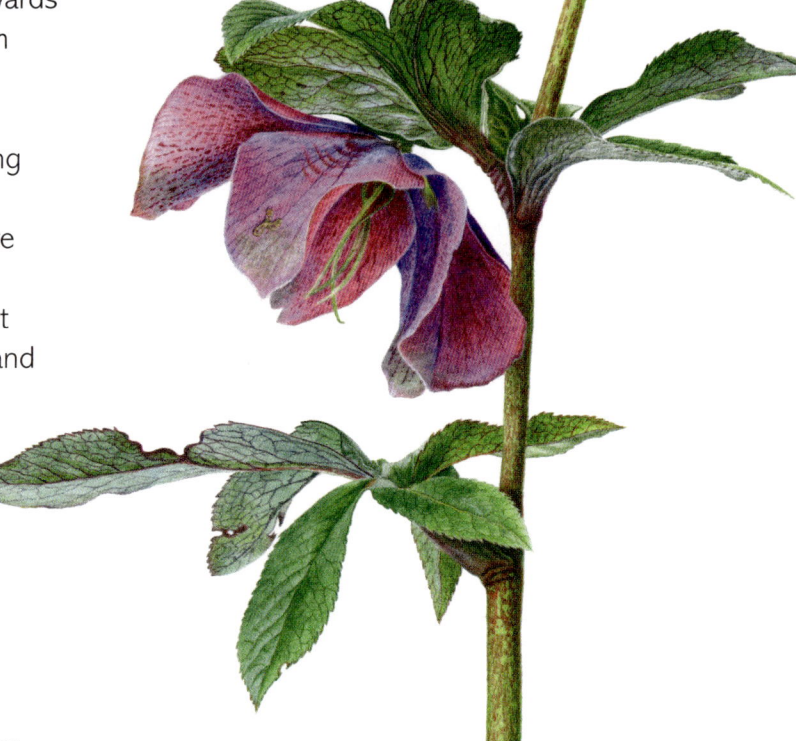

Hyacinth and tulip

These two are definitely harbingers of spring. Tulips are large, showy and brightly coloured, and come in a variety of shapes – single, double, fringed, ruffled or lily-shaped – often with interesting markings on the petals. I was drawn to Tulipa 'Black Hero' for its rich, dark colours. Hyacinths have a wonderful strong perfume that I love in the garden, but it's sometimes a bit overpowering inside the house.

Below left *Tulipa* 'Black Hero'. This is a double version of the beautiful Tulip 'Queen of the Night'.

Below right *Hyacinthus orientalis* 'Delft Blue'. A beautiful blue, the name inspired by the famous Dutch Delftware pottery.

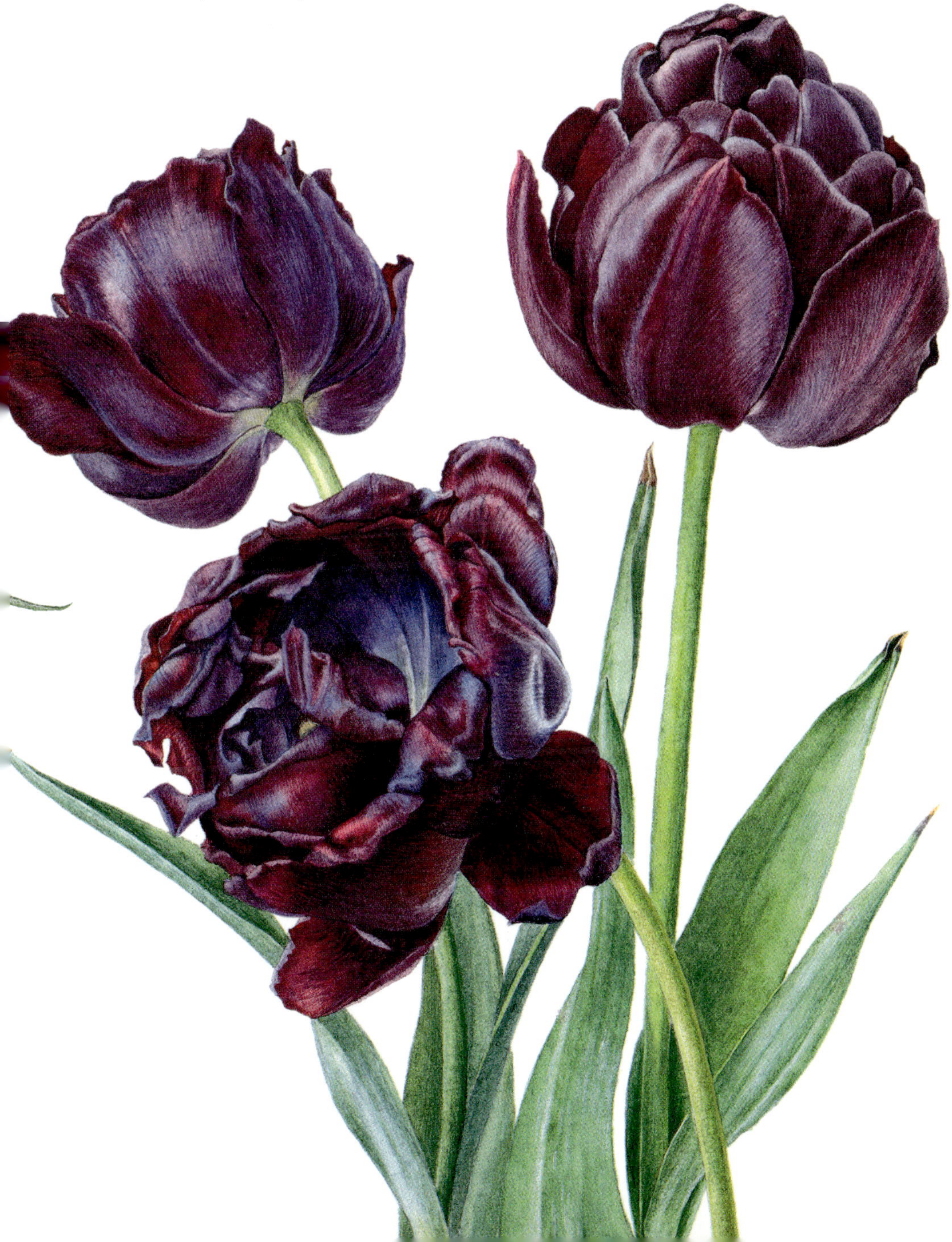

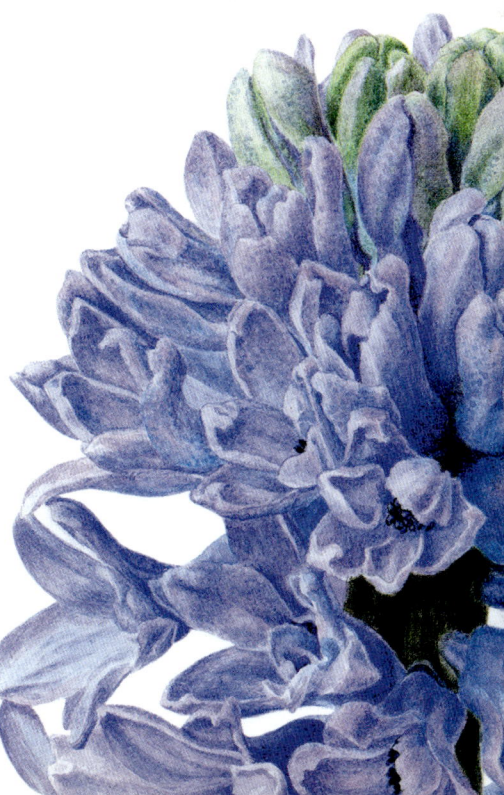

Summer

Astrantia 'Star of Fire'

A cottage-garden flower, common name masterwort, with beautiful pincushion-shaped flowers surrounded by deep pink bracts.

Allium caeruleum and Allium angulosum

I like the clusters of bright blue and pink star-shaped flowers that appear to float in midair. I painted these before they had reached maturity. *A. caeruleum* eventually forms a globe shape and *A. angulosum* a hemispherical mound, but I preferred to paint them at this stage, showing the uprights of their tiny green pedicels (flower stalks).

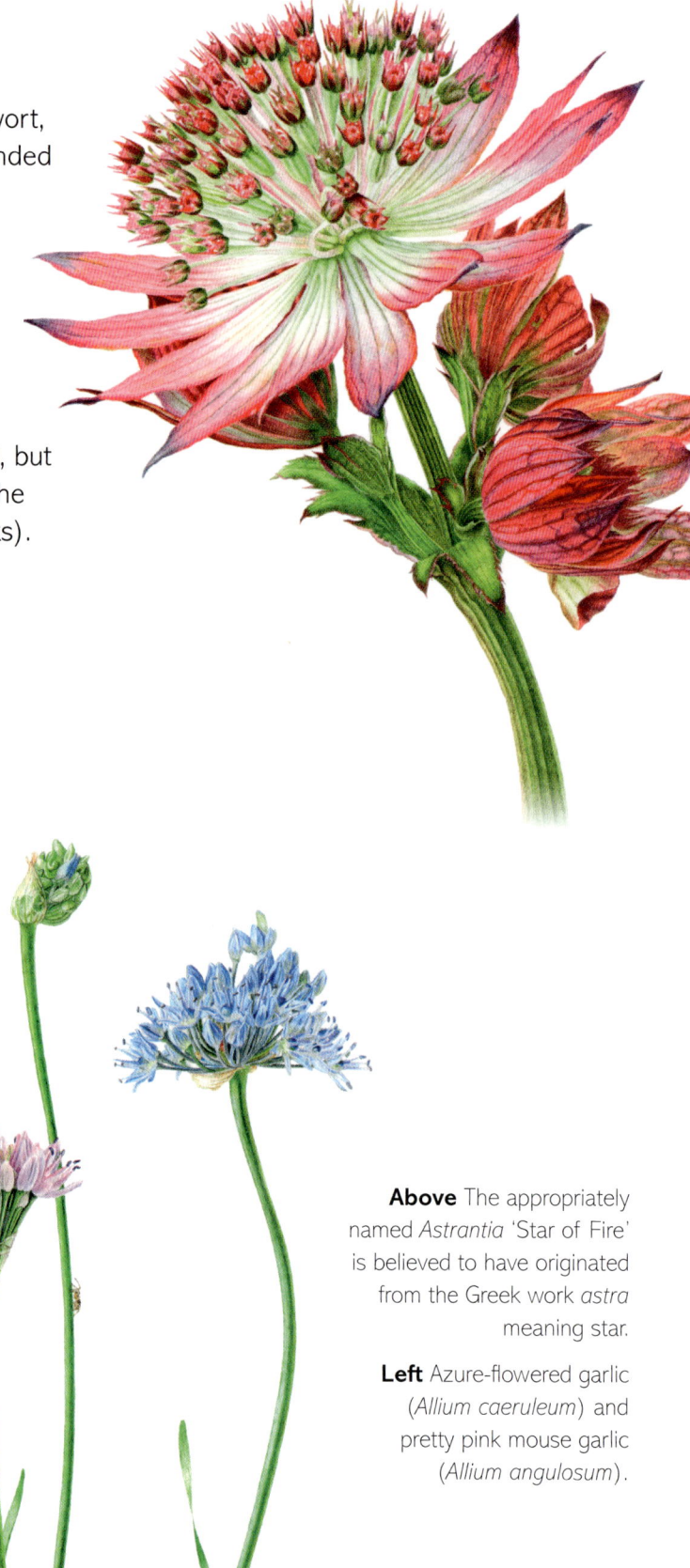

Above The appropriately named *Astrantia* 'Star of Fire' is believed to have originated from the Greek work *astra* meaning star.

Left Azure-flowered garlic (*Allium caeruleum*) and pretty pink mouse garlic (*Allium angulosum*).

Charles de Mills rose

This fantastically deep crimson/purple rose (shown right) has a mass of tightly packed petals. It doesn't flower for very long and now I'm no longer in the UK all of the time, I often miss it when it blooms. However, it remains a definite favourite of mine.

Strawberry

A true sign of the British summer, this fruit is a very complicated thing to draw. Placing the seeds or achenes in the right place to show the form and perspective of the strawberry entailed a lot of trial and error. Much rubbing out of the initial drawing occurred before I felt confident to start painting.

Pelargoniums

I source the most brilliantly coloured and interesting pelargoniums I can. I love 'Mystery' with it's deep-coloured crimson, velvety textured flowers and almost black centre. Regular deadheading means it repeat flowers throughout the summer.

Top *Rosa* 'Charles de Mills'. An old rose with deep magenta-red closely packed petals.

Centre Strawberry.

Right Detail of a *Pelargonium* 'Mystery' showing two cross-sections of the flower at different stages.

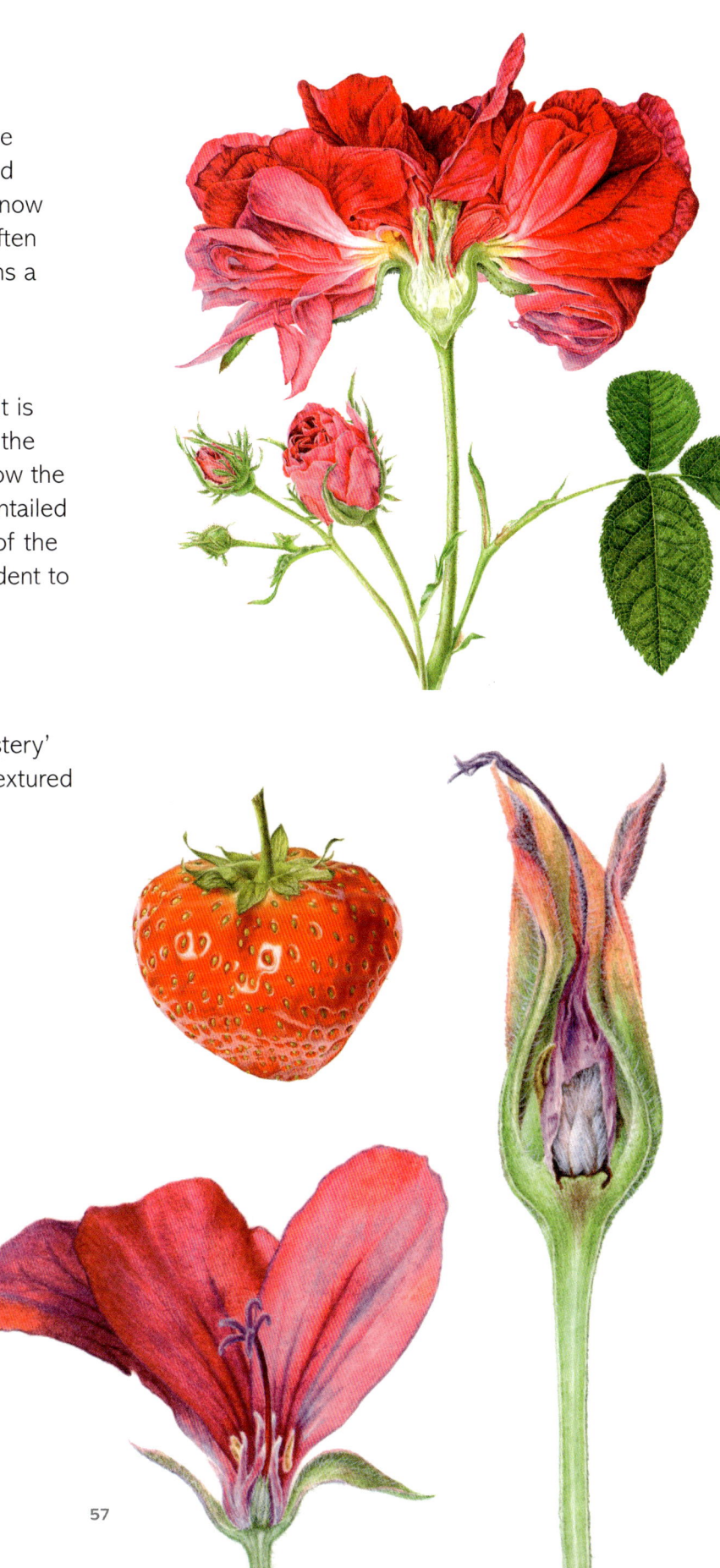

Helenium 'Moerheim Beauty'

This plant has striking, fiery flowers that are intensely deep orange and red in colour. Its rich tones and dramatic reflexed (downward) petals inspired me to paint it close-up.

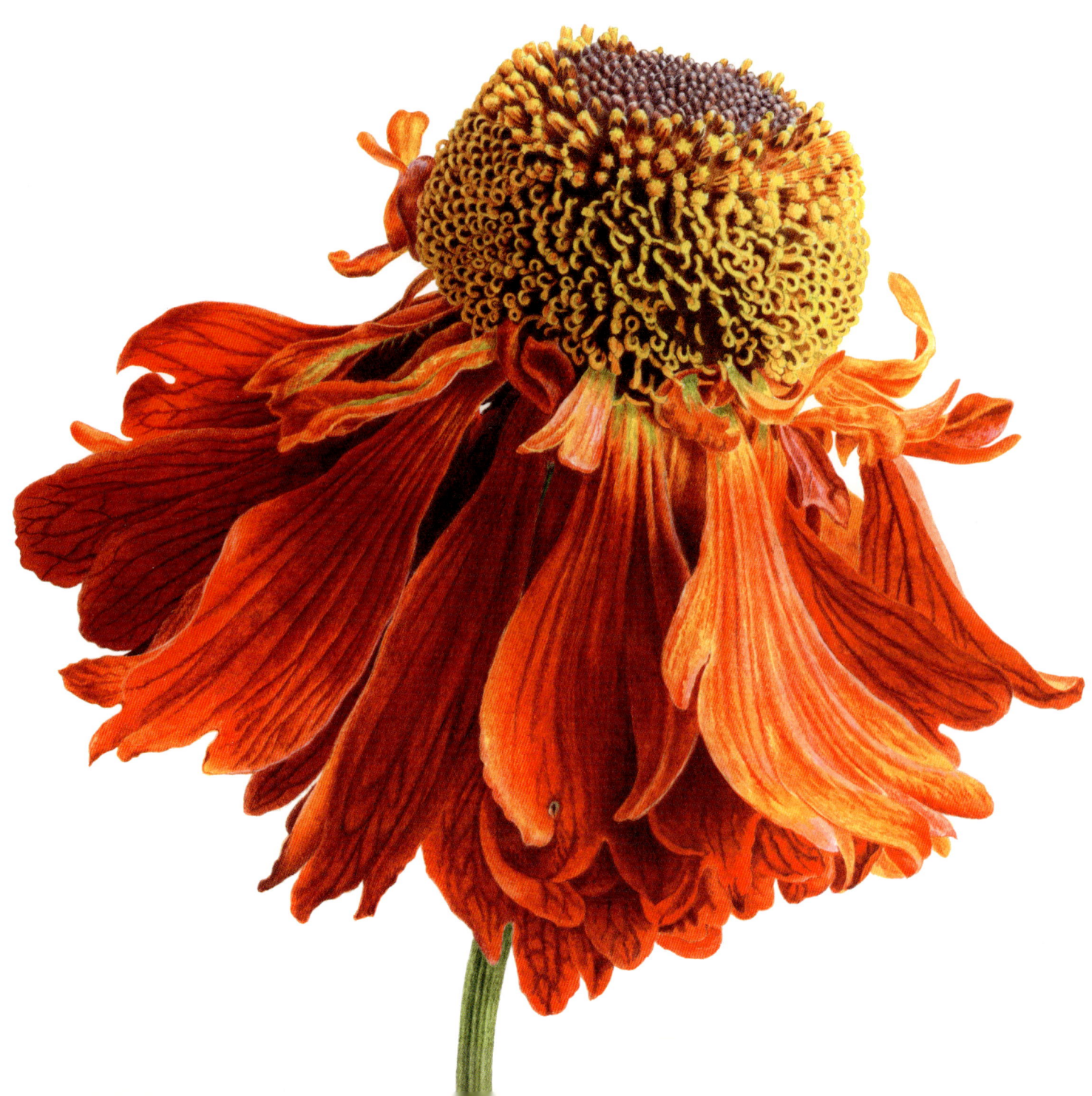

Dahlias

Dahlias in general are fantastic plants for late summer and into autumn because of their unbelievable variety of colours and shapes. If you keep picking them to bring into the house they will carry on flowering until the first frosts.

Dahlia 'Arabian Night' (see page 16) is a decorative dahlia. The fully double flowerheads and dark velvet colours of this dahlia catch the light beautifully, the surface texture of the petals creating a blue bloom. To capture this I started with washes of French Ultramarine and gradually built up layers of darker paint in increasingly dryer applications. Using a drier brush will give you a thicker paint and therefore a deeper colour, and also avoids pulling off previous layers. If the brush is too wet it's likely to lift away the background colours.

Ball dahlias like *Dahlia* 'Jowey Joshua' have a fascinating form. The patterns and arrangements of this bloom's floral parts are a perfect example of one of nature's Fibonacci sequences, a famous mathematical formula found in nature and adopted by Renaissance artists, including Leonardo da Vinci, to create 'perfect' compositions.

Left *Helenium* 'Moerheim Beauty'.

Below *Dahlia* 'Jowey Joshua'.

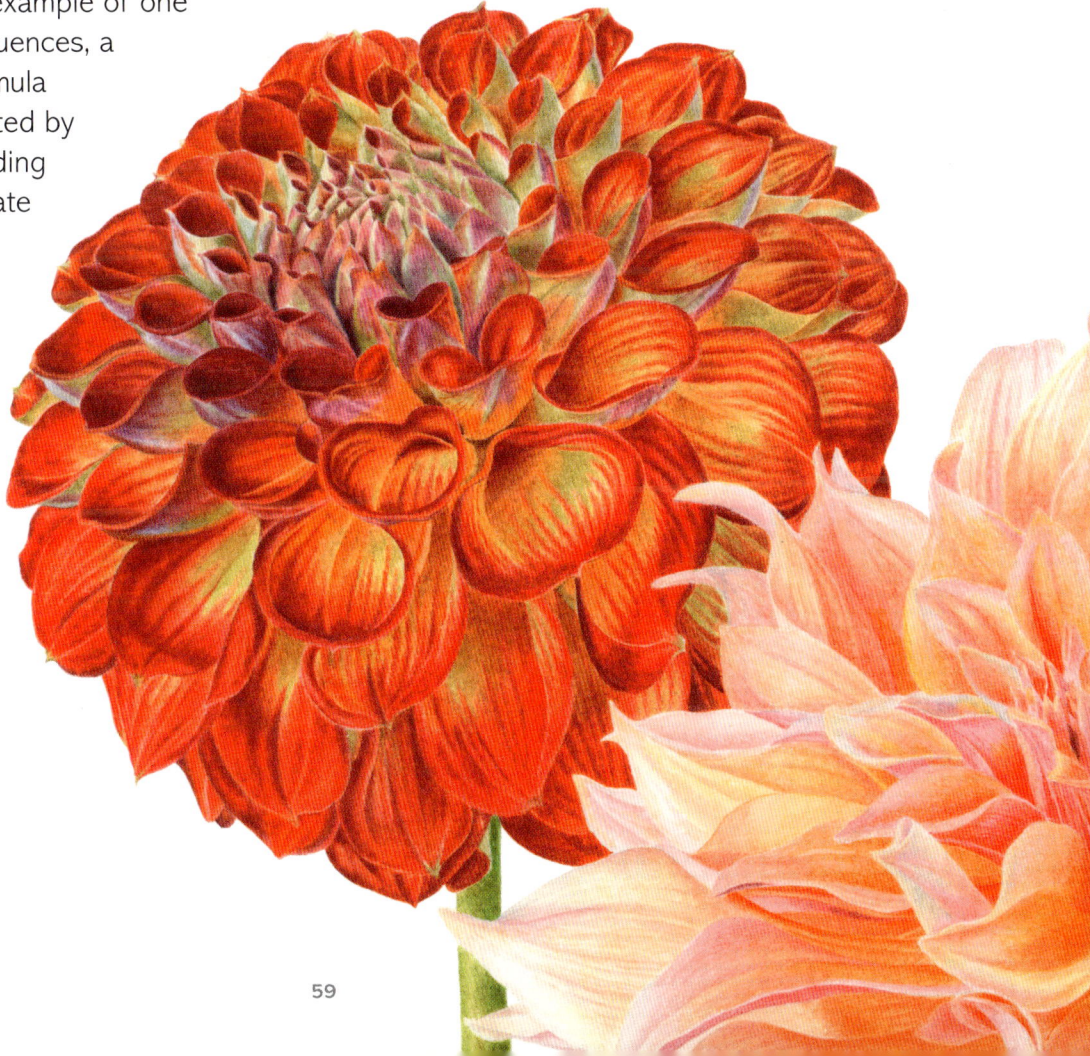

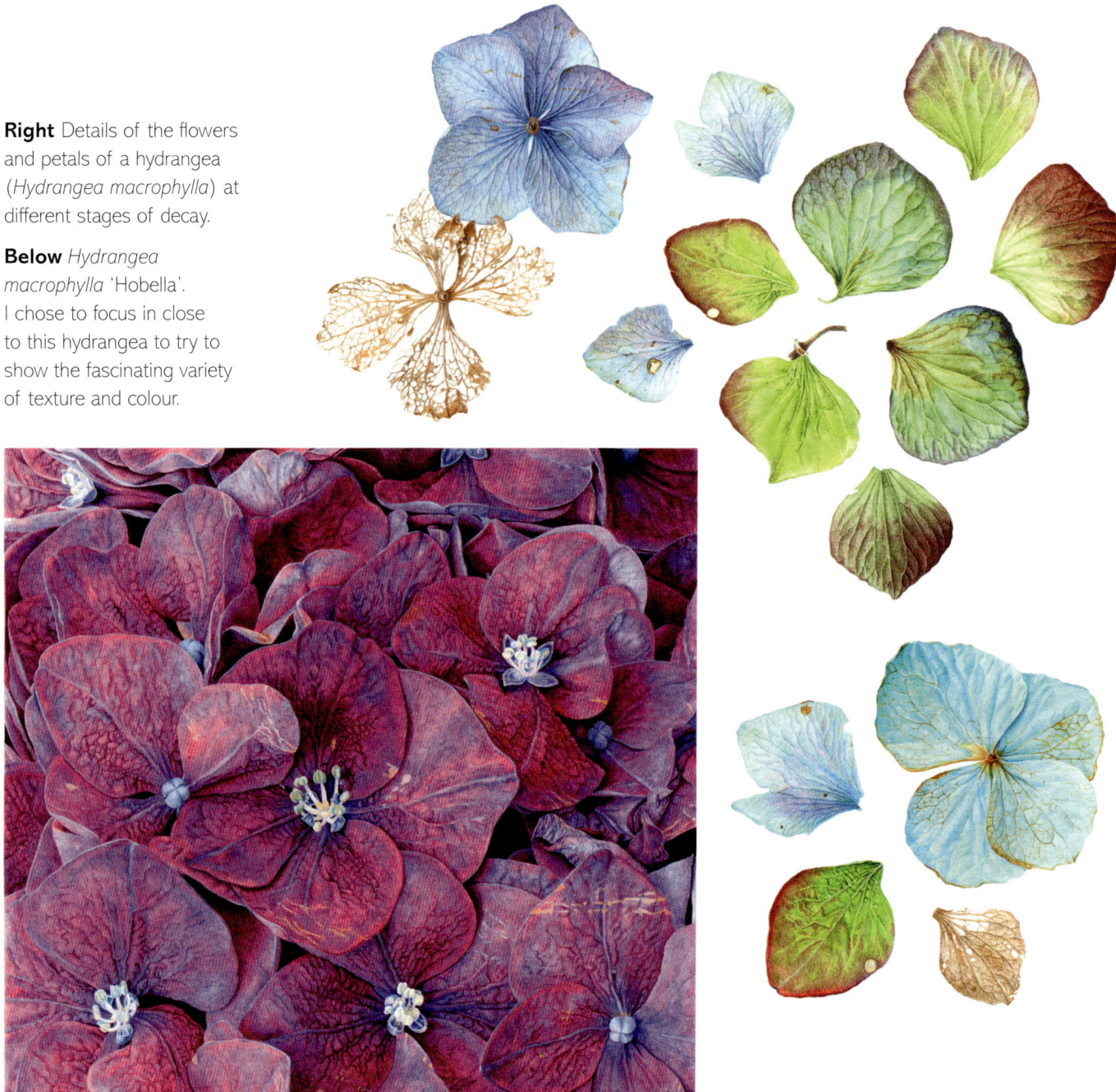

Right Details of the flowers and petals of a hydrangea (*Hydrangea macrophylla*) at different stages of decay.

Below *Hydrangea macrophylla* 'Hobella'. I chose to focus in close to this hydrangea to try to show the fascinating variety of texture and colour.

Hydrangeas

Hydrangeas are another great plant to have in the garden in late summer. A lot of perennials are at their end by this point and the hydrangea can fill a gap, lasting well into the autumn.

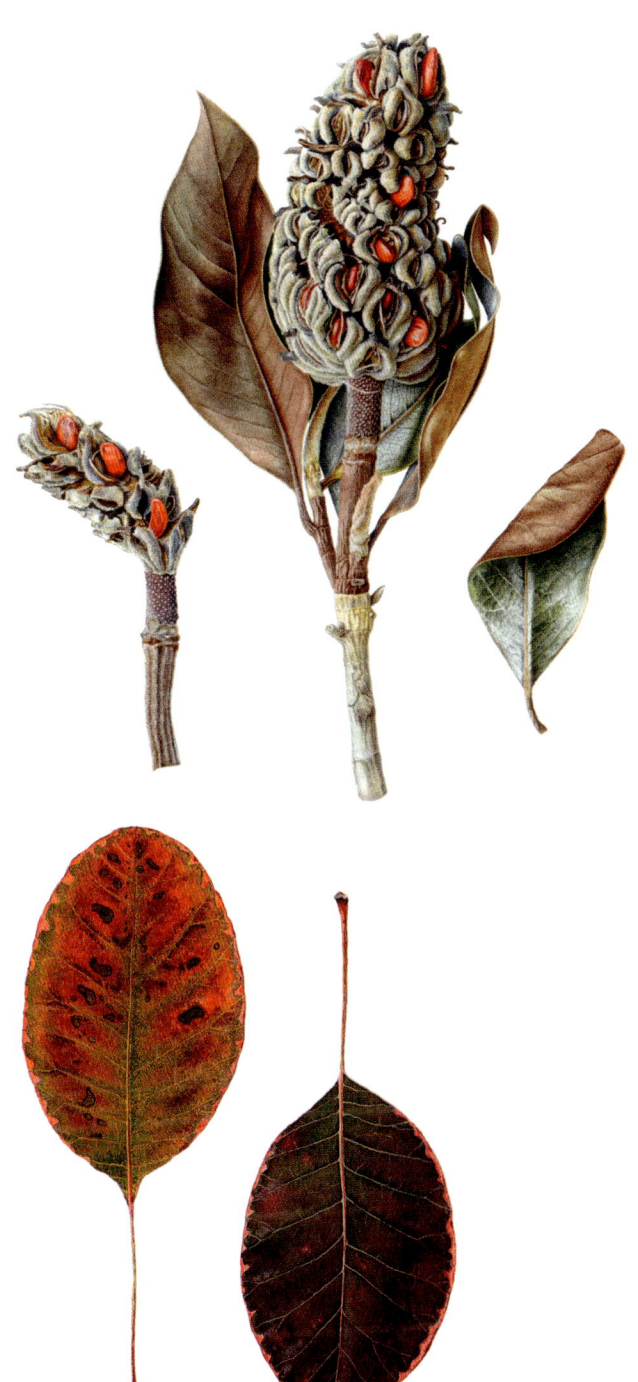

Autumn

Olive

I think this is probably my favourite tree. It has so much going for it, being evergreen, robust, needing no additional watering, and looking good all year round. I'm very keen on its silvery-grey leaves and gnarled trunk. In the early autumn, the olives are at their most beautiful (in my mind), a mixture of soft greens, pale pinks and purples, before they turn black. This one (below) was painted late in the season.

Magnolia grandiflora

The contrast of the muted browns and greens against the vivid, shiny red of the berries drew me to the subject, as did its multiple textures and patterns. There is an intriguing fluffy casing to the bright red berries, interesting patterns on the stem and a combination of a shiny upper surface and furry underside to the leaves.

Cotinus coggygria 'Royal Purple'

This is such a beautiful shrub. Its common name is smokebush because of its feathery plumes of flowers that resemble puffs of smoke. The leaves are a deep maroon in spring and turn into a fiery red in the autumn. When the sunlight catches this plant at this time of year it's almost as if it is on fire, the colour being so intense.

Top *Magnolia grandiflora* seed head with leaves. A really interesting subject to paint, focusing on the texture and subdued colours.

Above *Cotinus coggygria* 'Royal Purple'.

Right I like to paint olives while they are still full of colour, before fully ripening.

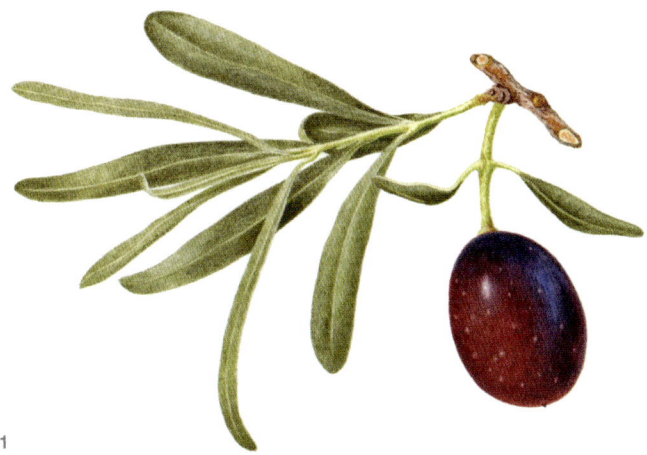

LIGHT: MORNING, MIDDAY, EVENING

A light source can dramatically change throughout the day, influencing the perception of the colour of any subject being painted.

Painting – Artificial Light

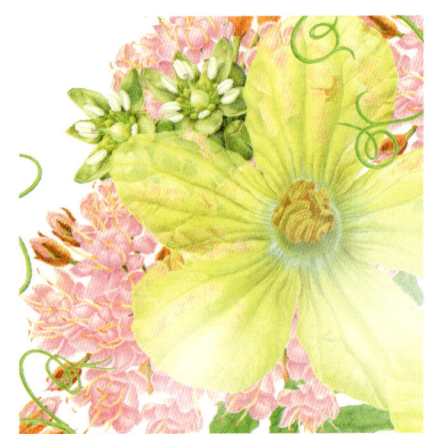

It's not only the seasons that influence how I work. The quality of light during any single day can affect what I do, too. Natural light is best, but in my studio it changes throughout the day: in the morning and evening it is a cooler blue and at midday its tones are warmer. To counter the natural cycle of things, I usually have to intervene. Without a north-facing place to work – which would give me the most consistent light – I often use daylight lamps.

To keep my overall view evenly lit, I keep a daylight lamp pointing on my subject and on my working area throughout the whole process – and consistently from the same direction – always from the left, as I am right-handed. This avoids creating a shadow on the area I'm painting.

Good lighting is essential for working in detail and allows me to paint at any time of day, all year round. Without it I would be hard pushed to fulfil my commissioned work. I'm nearly always working to a deadline so my studio set-up is important – it enables me to get things finished on time.

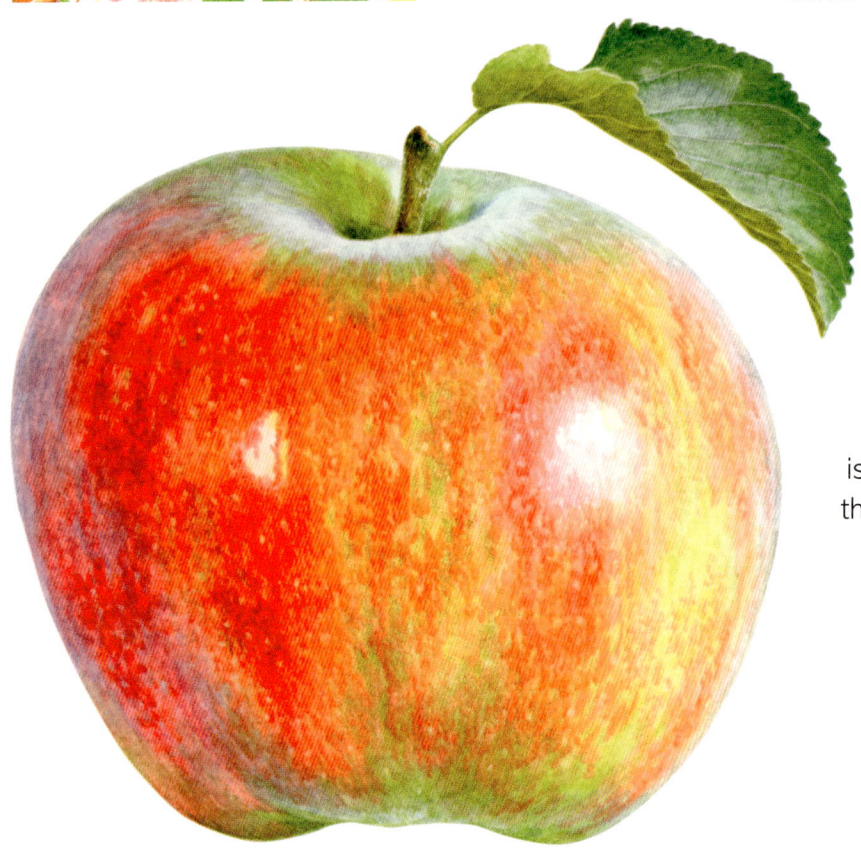

Above left Watermelon (*Citrullus lanatus*) showing the effect of light shining through the delicate translucent yellow petals.

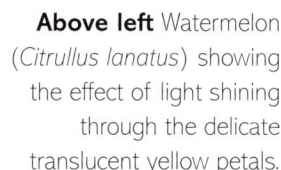

Left Showing the high shine on an apple's glossy surface.

Photography – Natural Light

Because of the nature of the work I do – very detailed paintings that take many hours to complete – it's crucial that I have supplementary photographs of my subject matter as reference back-up. Whenever I complete commissions and personal work that use a combination of painting from life and photographs, the latter are always taken by me. It's only when I'm commissioned to do illustrating jobs that I sometimes have to use stock photos. The simple reason is that more often than not the subject matter either isn't in season or available to buy.

I always photograph by daylight, not artificial light. The time of day changes colours so dramatically that I take photos in the early morning, midday and late afternoon, and then decide which colours work best for the subject.

Right White tulip showing the light coming through its petals, with blues in the shadows, but some warm tones too.

Below French algae (*Macrocystis*), neroli and prunus blossom – warm, golden light on the prunus blossom and diffused light shining through the translucent algae.

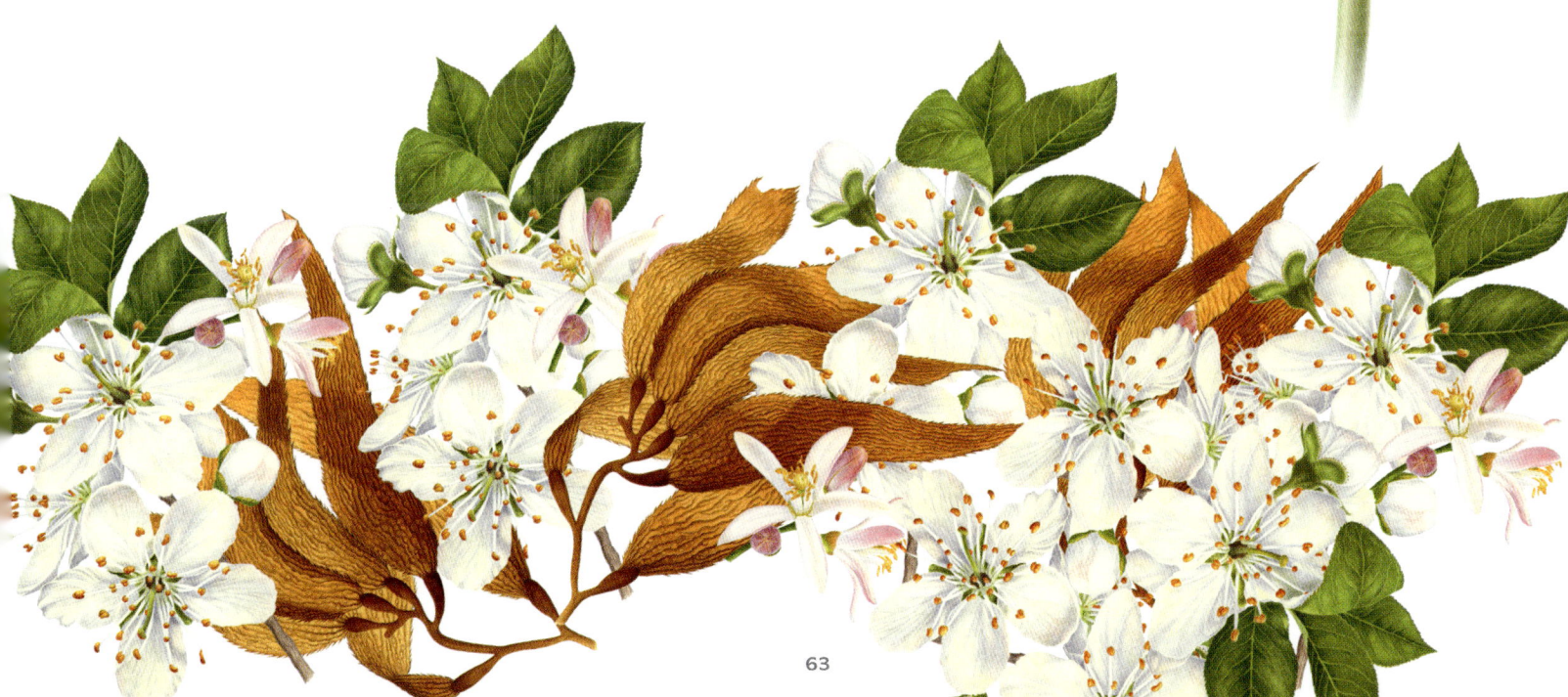

63

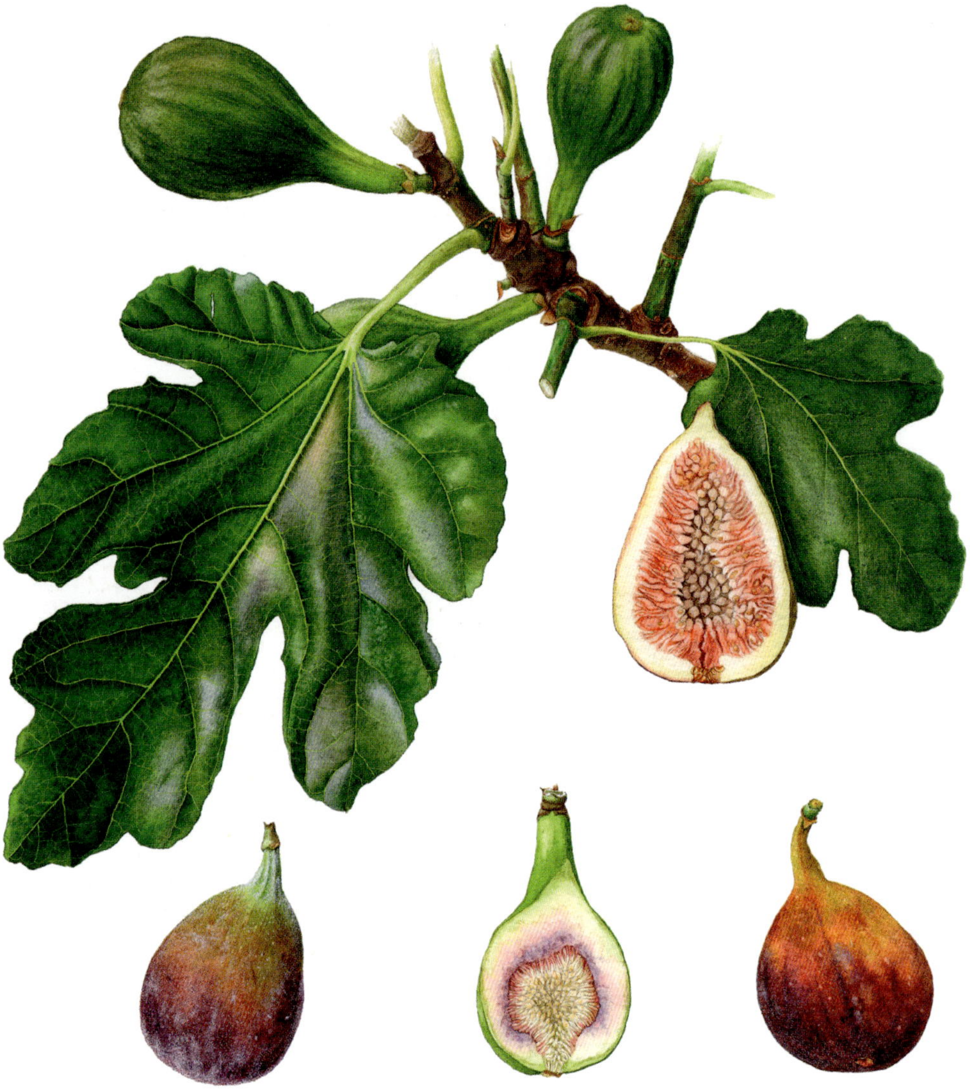

Left Figs. Contrasting light, from the brilliant gloss of the leaves to a much softer matt light on the fruits.

Right Dried lemons. A complete contrast of the effects of light on this subject. As the lemon was completely dry, it had lost all of its shine, whereas the highlights on the inside of the fruit had become even more pronounced – especially as it was reflecting on the now-black surface.

Below Iris, jasmine and neroli. I love the combination of flowers of similar colours but different sizes, the smaller blooms filling in around the larger ones.

The morning light is the best for me to take any reference photos as I like the blue tones – although very early on it's much too blue. By around 9am on a summer's day when there is a bit more warmth in the light, I find it perfect – around midday and the light becomes too yellow and rather flat.

I begin by setting my camera up on a tripod. This keeps the camera steady and enables me to get good details. I use the timer option so that as I press the button to take a picture, the shutter will open a few seconds later. This avoids any camera movement, and I get sharp images with no blurring. I normally use a macro lens to get as much detail as possible.

I always photograph everything against a white background and make sure that each element for the painting has the light coming from the same direction.

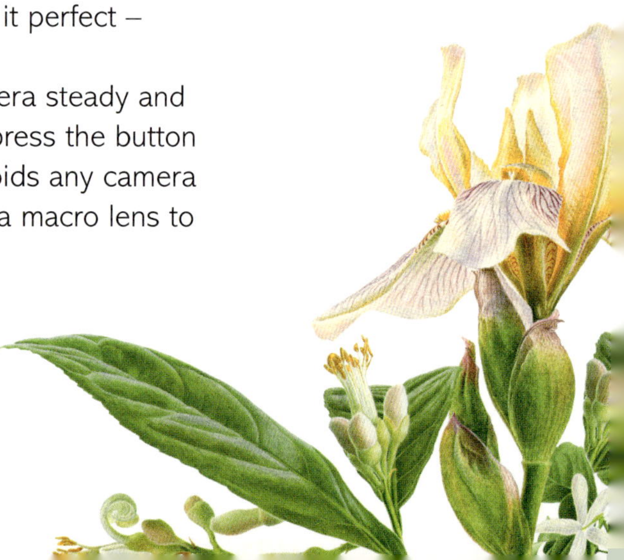

I sometimes use a large piece of white card on the opposite side to the light source in order to bounce light back on to the dark side of the subject. This makes the shadows less harsh and softens the overall effect of the final photograph.

I always take several photographs of each separate element and at different focal lengths so that I can get every part in focus as a reference to work from. I will normally end up with around a hundred photographs I can reference for any single painting. It is important that these are of all parts of the plant, facing different ways and from varying angles, so that when I come to compose my paintings I have, in effect, a complete three-dimensional record spread over many two-dimensional images.

During the process of getting good photographs to work with I will intermittently download the pictures onto my computer and check them on the screen. Often I will find that they aren't light enough, or there are elements that are out of focus, so I will go back and retake with a longer shutter speed – for more light.

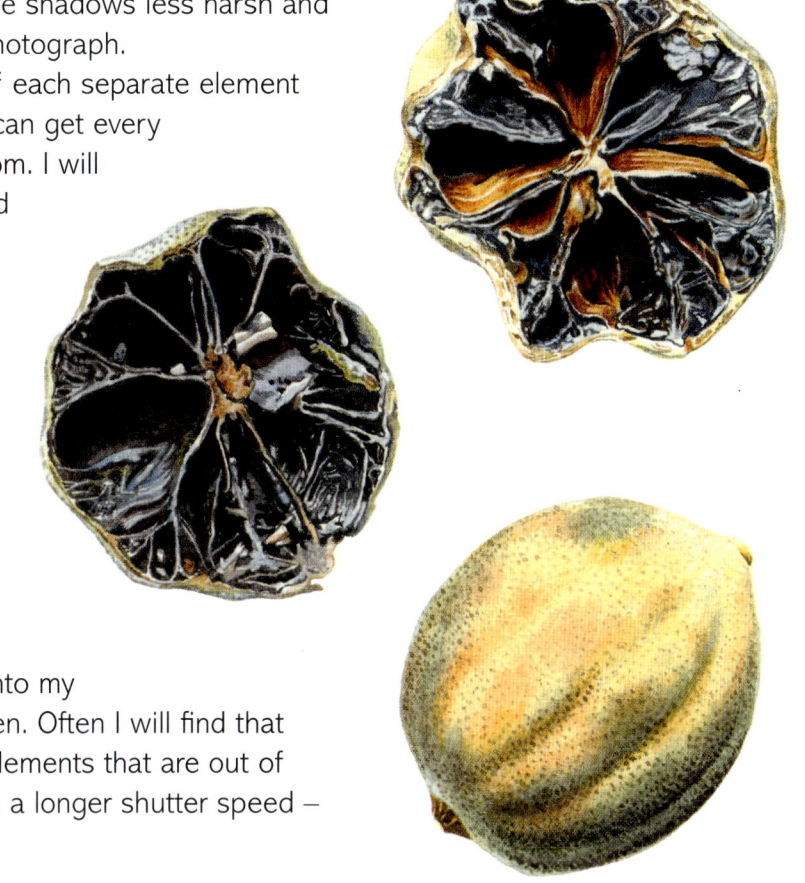

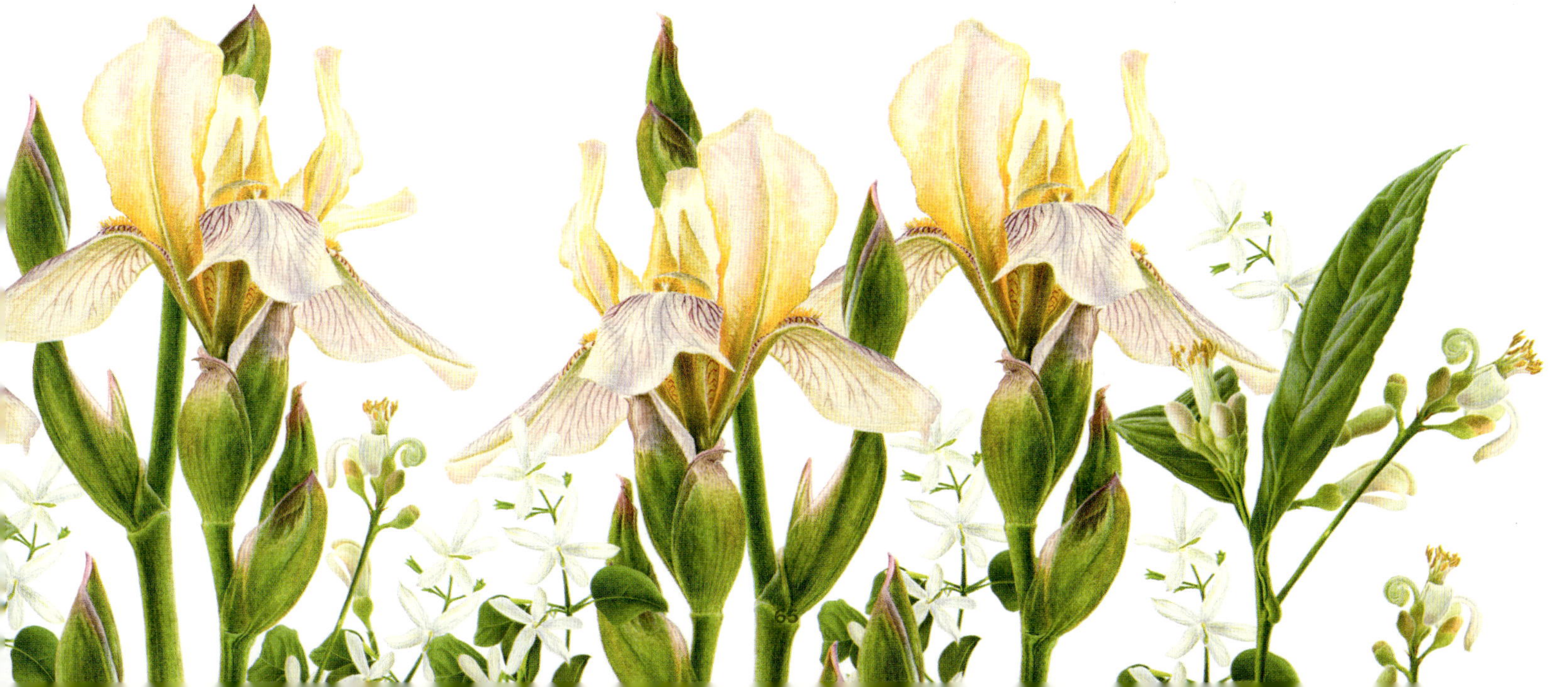

EQUIPMENT

Good tools and equipment really do make a difference, but you don't need to buy the whole art shop.

Watercolour Paper I use Arches hot-pressed paper, which has a smooth surface suitable for fine detail. I normally use blocks of paper which are glued on four sides at the edges, and use a heavy weight (300gsm) to avoid the paper buckling when wet.

Brushes I have used the same type of brush for years – most of my paintings are done with a Winsor & Newton series 7 miniature sable brush size 2, round. For larger areas of wash I use the same type but bigger, size 6. I have tried many times to use synthetic brushes but they don't seem to hold the paint so well.

Paint Personally, I prefer to use tubes rather than pans as it's a lot easier to keep the paint clean. I like to use mostly transparent colours so that I can use layers to mix colours rather than mix in the palette – this tends to give a more vibrant result. I use three different brands of watercolour paint. There are particular colours I prefer depending on the make, so my essential list of paints that I wouldn't like to be without are:

Winsor & Newton Professional Watercolour

Indanthrene Blue	Permanent Alizarin Crimson
Winsor Blue (green shade)	Permanent Rose
Winsor Blue (red shade)	Burnt Sienna
Indigo	Rose Dore
Winsor Yellow	Sepia
Yellow Ochre	Winsor Violet (Dioxazine)
Permanent Carmine	Titanium White

Daniel Smith Extra Fine Watercolours I love all Daniel Smith's Quinacridone range of paints, which have an incredible luminosity and depth of colour, but the ones I use most are Quinacridone Burnt Orange, Rose, Coral and Gold. But I also really like their Transparent Pyrrol Orange and Indian Yellow.

Schmincke From this range I use Quinacridone Magenta, Scarlet Red and French Ultramarine.

All the paints listed above have good lightfastness but I do advise anyone that has commissioned a painting from me to frame the picture with UV protective glass. There are plenty of other amazing colours but with this selection I find I don't really need any others.

Many artists use masking fluid for areas of the paper that they want to leave white but I prefer to wash the area with clean water and and apply layers, leaving the area I want white blank and using kitchen towel to dab any colour off before it dries. I keep a few old paintbrushes for the odd occasion that I do use masking fluid.

Paint Palettes I always use ceramic palettes with paint wells to separate the colours or plates for mixing paints, as the paint doesn't then separate or bead on the smooth surface. I find that plastic ones are hard to clean and leave stains. My ceramic palette has a lid so that when I've finished for the day I can protect the paint from dust for use the next day.

Painting Sundries

- Drawing boards to support and tape the paper to; I have three different sizes
- Putty rubber
- Pencils; I use mechanical pencils 0.5mm HB
- Masking tape
- Tracing paper pad
- Kitchen towel for dabbing areas of excess water and drying my brush between washes
- Stanley knife, metal ruler, cutting mat and set square for trimming paintings when they are finished.

Daylight Lamps I have a lamp with an integrated magnifier that I can use over my painting, and another lamp without one, which lights my subject from the left. Any adjustable lamp (such as an Anglepoise) with a daylight bulb is suitable.

I have my magnifying lamp mounted on a heavy base so it doesn't topple, as I'm constantly moving the lens around to focus on different parts of the painting. These are also available with a clamp rather than a heavy base but I find it means I would have to work too close to the edge of the table, which wouldn't give enough surrounding space for my materials. It's good to have a large table or desk to work at; my studio room is very small but the work surface is quite large. I like to have enough space to have all my paints, brushes, palettes and lamps within reach on my table.

Magnifiers I have a magnifying lens with a flexible arm on a clamp and another on a heavy base. Both are very useful for keeping both hands free while I look at the subject I am working from.

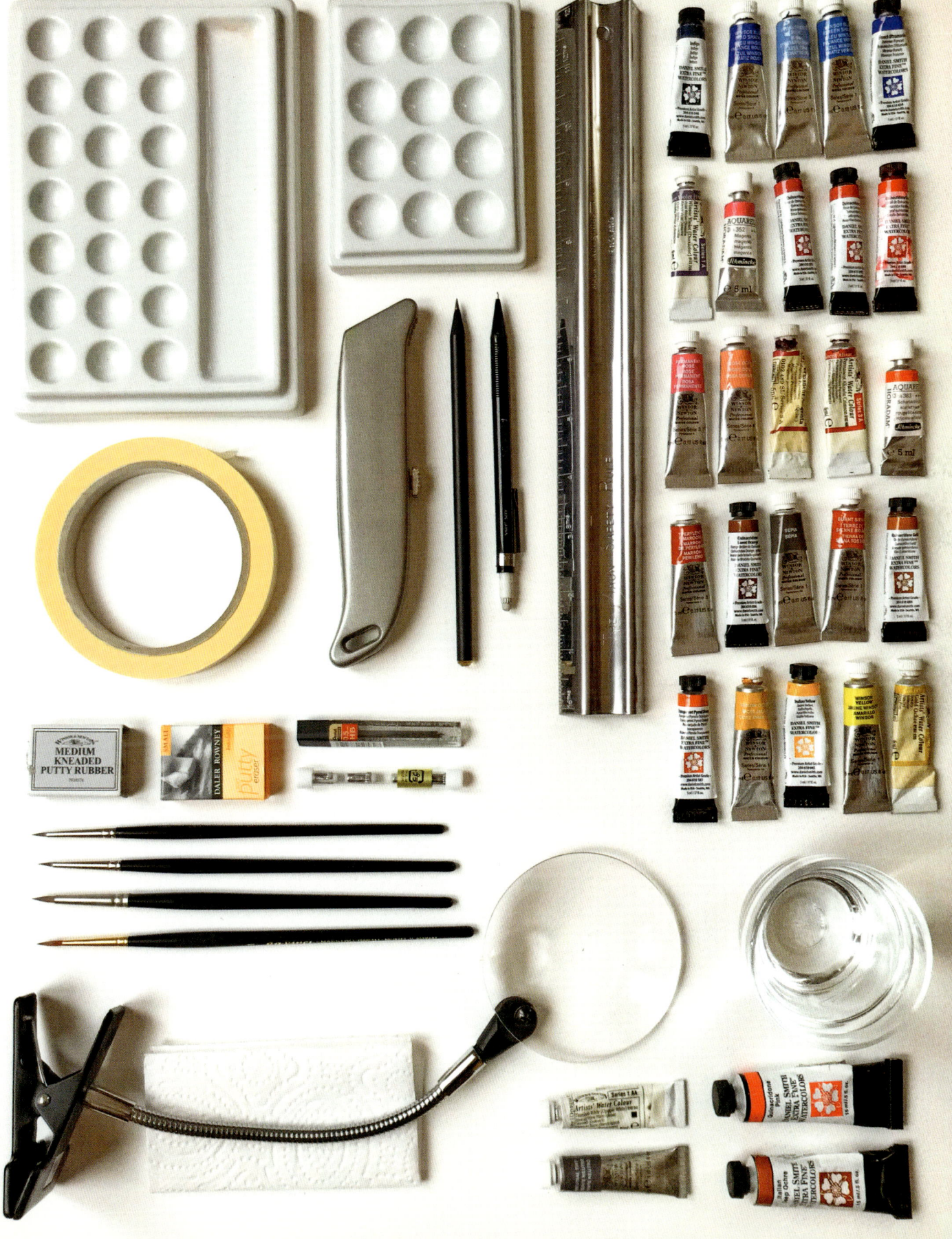

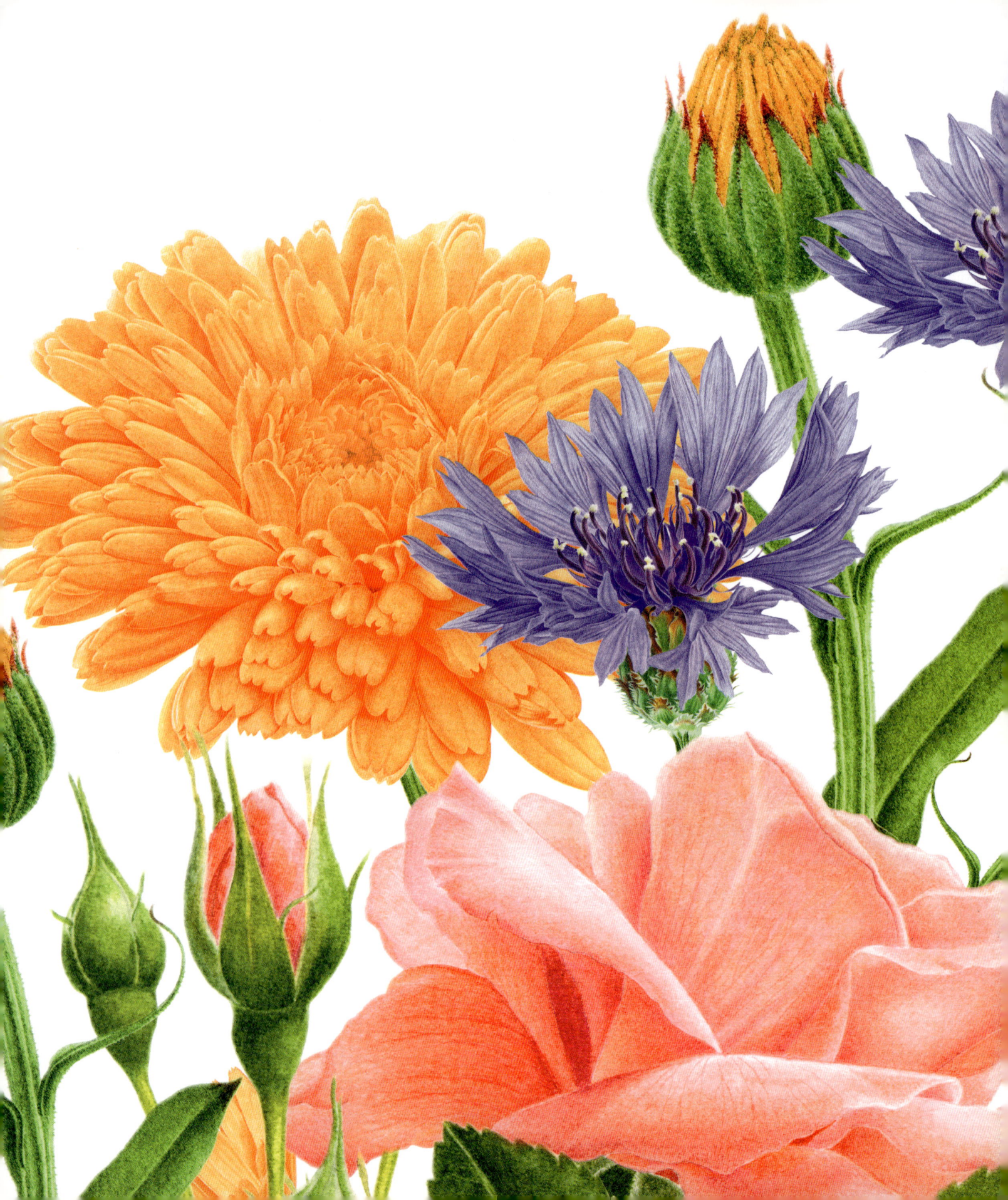

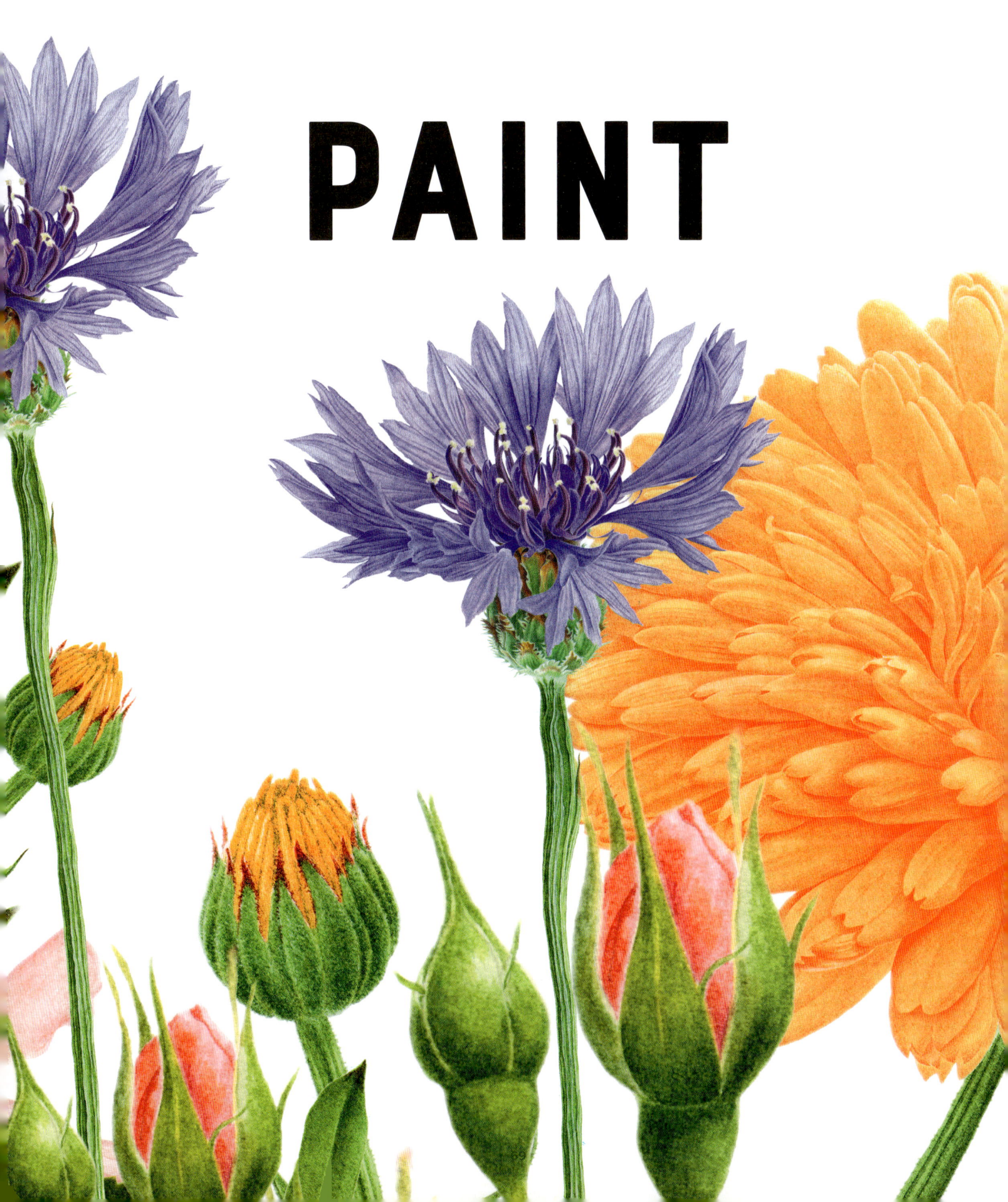

PAINT

CHOOSING A SUBJECT

Many factors help me decide what to paint: colour, texture, seasonal changes, size, growth patterns, wow factor. What ever the reason I always treat my subject matter with equal standing.

Working from Life

I always think of the term 'working from life' as referring to a painting or drawing done in a life room, or of a still-life work of something as simple as a cup and bowl, in other words entirely from the subject in front of the artist. My early work *'Violetto' Artichokes on a Plate* is in this still-life vein.

I use the phrase to refer to working from a plant specimen that will last for the duration of the time it takes me to paint it – with the precaution that I have back-up photographs just in case. This breaks the 'rules' of what working from life generally means (i.e. not working from a photograph), but it's really important to my painting process that I have a 'preserved' view of my subject for reference. I will work entirely 'from life' on one of my illustrations only if the subject matter is something that won't move or change too much, or if it's a quick study with less detail for reference.

It might sound obvious, but making a detailed observational painting from a botanical subject has to account for how long it is going to last in its current form. Petals drop, brightness fades and leaves wither as things dry out. Any painting decisions made will depend on what the expectations of the work are going to be: the approximate time it might take you to complete the task, and how long you think your subject will maintain its shape and colour – or whatever else attracted you to it in the first place.

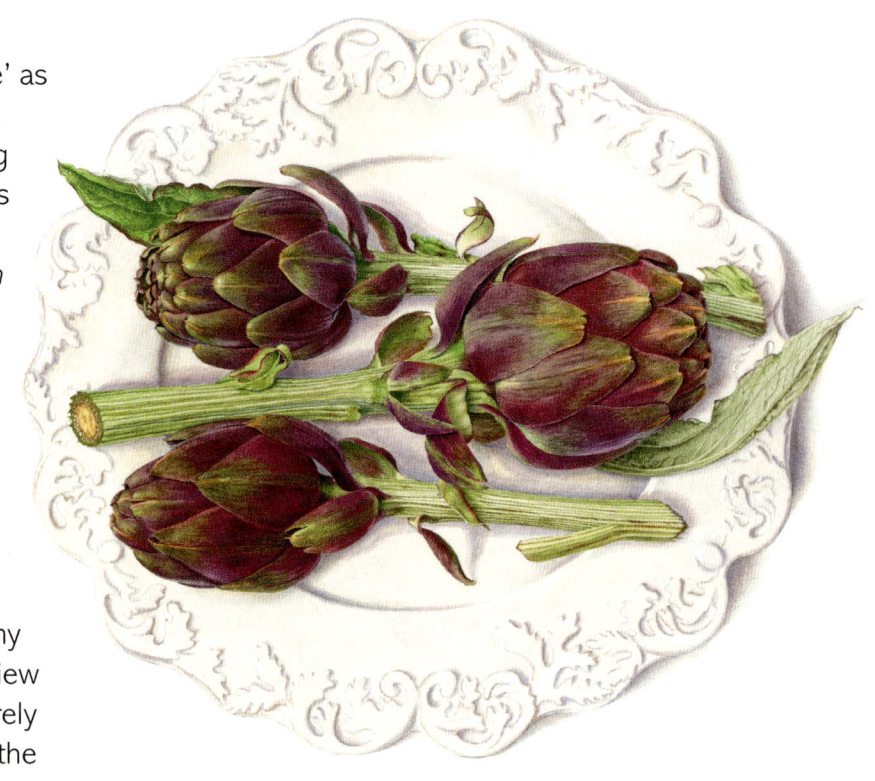

Above Purple artichokes (*Cynara cardundculus* 'Violetto') on a plate. An early work – my painting style is similar now but the set-up of the elements make for a different kind of composition.

Of course, sometimes natural changes in your subject might not matter to you; your study might be a speedier sketchbook or notebook rendition done outdoors, its mission to capture the moment; it could be a practice piece for a more-considered, lengthier work; or you might even have decided to factor in some of the changing characteristics of a plant as it ages to suggest time elapsed.

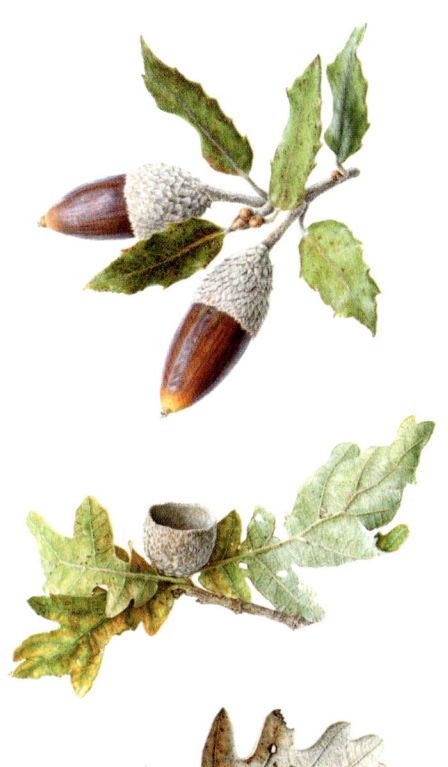

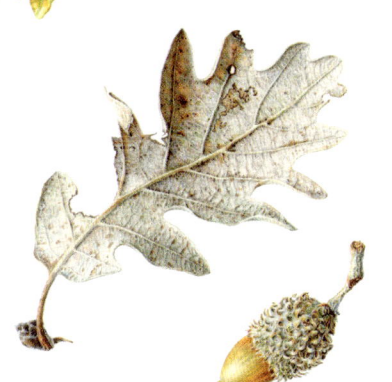

Dry Specimens

Acorns, seedpods and dried plants fall in to my 'won't move' category. I know they'll remain stable enough and relatively unchanged for the length of time it will take me to paint them. Many fruit and vegetables fall into this camp too.

Dry specimens become my subject matter especially in the autumn/fall and winter months when there are fewer flowering plants around. To be clear – this is not because they are in any way second-best or inferior as a subject of study – it's because the season I'm in influences how and what I want to paint. The cooler seasons lead me to seek out acorns, various seedpods and rosehips.

There were so many colours hidden within these seemingly monochromatic, neutrally hued subjects. I discovered blues, greens, yellows and orange browns when I studied them really closely.

Previous spread Marigold (*Calendula officinalis*), an unknown variety of rose and cornflower (*Centaurea montana*).

Above Holly oak (*Quercus ilex*), Pyrenean oak (*Quercus pyrenaica*) and Kermes oak with leaf (*Quercus coccifera*).

Right Detail of a faded rose.

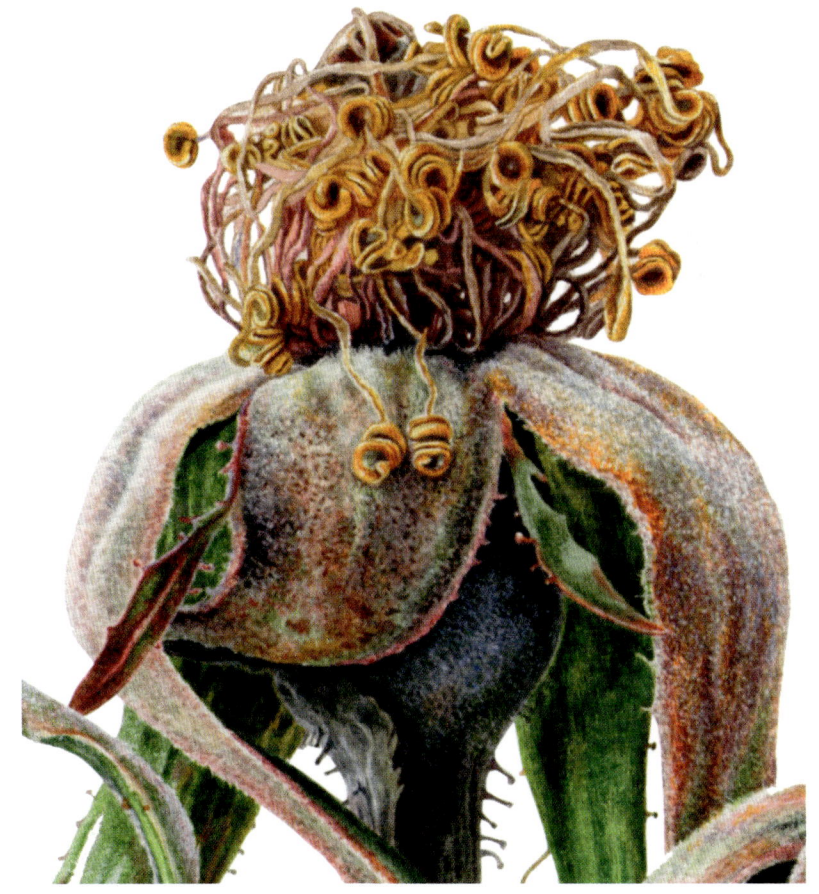

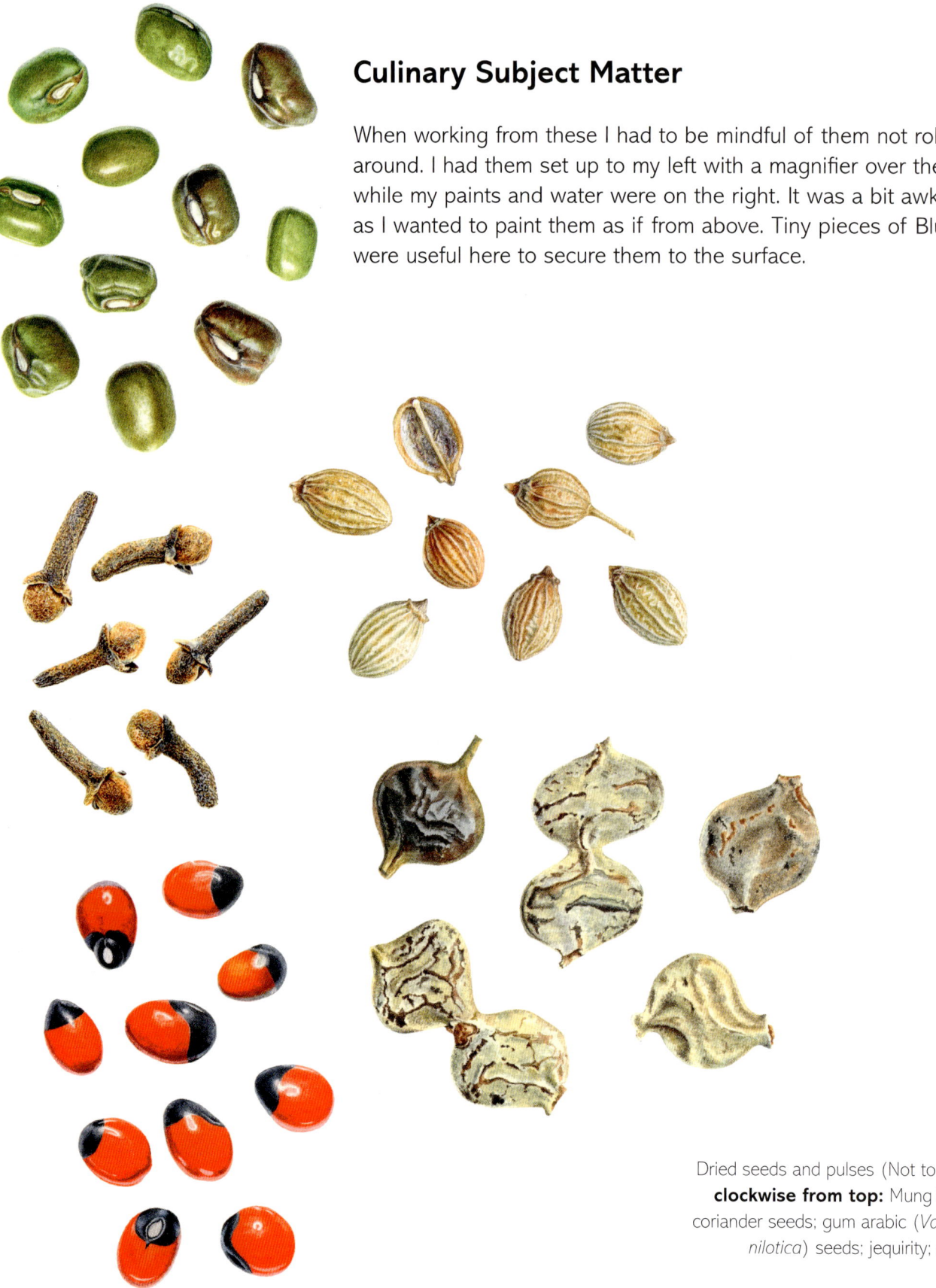

Culinary Subject Matter

When working from these I had to be mindful of them not rolling around. I had them set up to my left with a magnifier over them, while my paints and water were on the right. It was a bit awkward as I wanted to paint them as if from above. Tiny pieces of Blu-tack were useful here to secure them to the surface.

Dried seeds and pulses (Not to scale)
clockwise from top: Mung beans; coriander seeds; gum arabic (*Vachellia nilotica*) seeds; jequirity; cloves.

Flowers

Some flowers, such as roses and heleniums (see page 91) last long enough for me to paint them from life, while others, such as poppies and perennial cornflowers, will require photographic backup.

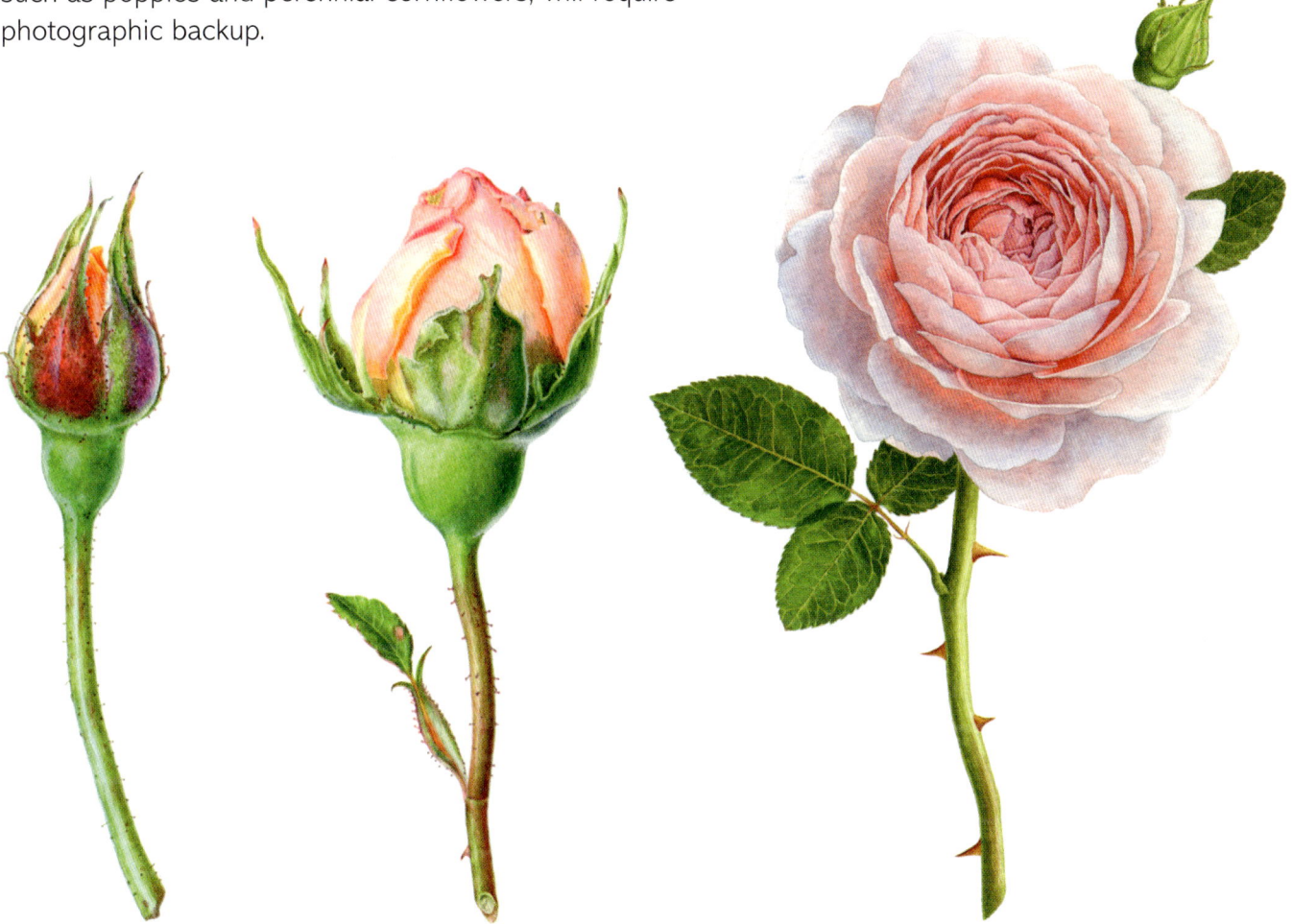

Rosa 'Evelyn' buds – I knew it would take me a couple of days to paint each of these rosebuds and that during that time they wouldn't change too much. This meant that painting them from life worked well.

Rosa 'Scepter'd Isle'. This was a lovely subject to paint. I was drawn to the multiple layers of soft petals, their subtle shades of pale pink, and the light blue shadows.

Rosa 'Scepter'd Isle' is a really pretty light-pink cup-shaped rose bred by David Austin. This painting has less detail than usual as I painted it only from life and I had to work fast to get it onto the paper before it faded. I do quite like the looser style.

TEXTURES

There are a variety of methods that can be used to create the impression of texture in watercolour paint.

Leaves

The leaves of the sage (*Salvia officinalis*) are an example of multiple textures in one specimen. Most leaves, in fact, have two quite different surface textures. Sage has a rough upper side and a contrasting soft, downy or woolly underside. Both surfaces are matt with no shiny highlights.

To paint the surface of the upper side of the leaf, I washed the whole area with a subtle greyish shade of green made from a light mix of Winsor Blue and Winsor Yellow and a small amount of red to dull down the vibrancy of the colour. I then dropped a deeper shade of the same mix into the areas that were shaded while the paint was still wet.

The detail of the tiny round bumps and subtle veins were added later, filling in the spaces in between the bumps with darker paint and leaving the bumps lighter so that they gave the impression of standing proud.

To create the much paler, downy underside of the leaf, I dabbed small dry-brush strokes over the surface – darker where the shadows appear – and used a circular motion with my brush in some areas to create a woolly effect.

Left Sage (*Salvia officinalis*). A strongly scented aromatic herb widely used in cooking and for its healing properties. It belongs to the mint (Lamiaceae) family.

Fruit and Petals

Dahlia 'Karma Choc' is one of the darkest dahlias available. Its masses of dark-red velvety petals appear almost black at their shadowy centre. It belongs to the 'Karma' collection, which was bred to produce especially long-lasting cut flowers. The irony is that I chose to paint this flower when it was past its best, the petals starting to curl up and crinkle at the edges. (See also Using Imperfections, page 111).

Using masking fluid works well to help create the appearance of a dimpled surface (see No. 9 on the grid, page 77). I don't often use it but it's perfect for depicting the texture of citrus fruit peel. I first paint the whole fruit with a very pale wash of the predominant colour then wait for it to be absolutely dry before dotting the very lightest areas with the masking fluid. Once that is dry, I add a darker wash over the top. I repeat this process, working outwards from the lightest area three or four more times, adding more dots of masking fluid and progressively darker washes, making sure everything is completely dry between applications. I then gently rub off the masking fluid and move on to adding the much darker textures over the top.

To depict pale surface bloom on fruit (see No. 10 on the grid, page 77), and occasionally petals, I mostly use the white of the paper. For these very light areas I usually apply a very pale wash of blue, and then work the colour of the fruit or petal in layers around the bloom in tiny dots. Alternatively, I sometimes use a small amount of white paint where the bloom is very powdery, dotting the white paint on the surface.

Above *Dahlia* 'Karma Choc'. This decorative dahlia is near black in parts with fully double flower heads.

Texture Guide

Some fruits display a real variety of textures. The pomegranate, for instance, has a hard and shiny outer skin (see No. 3 on the grid), an interior containing shiny and wet seeds (No. 4) and a spongy pith (No. 5). I liked working on the tiny faults on the skin, showing the bruises and scratches (No. 12).

1. Smooth and shiny – Mexican orange leaf and ivy leaf
2. High gloss – chilli
3. Hard and shiny – apple, acorn, pomegranate
4. Shiny and wet – pomegranate seeds
5. Spongy / pithy – pomegranate
6. Downy / woolly – underside of sage leaf
7. Matt – sage, lichen
8. Powdery – pollen on helenium
9. Dimpled – citrus
10. Bloom – fig, grapes, dahlia petals
11. Velvety – roses, pansy, dahlia petals, peony petals
12. Bruised / scratched – pomegranate skin
13. Translucent and veiny – hellebore petals
14. Fuzzy – magnolia cone
15. Rough – sage leaf upper surface
16. Dry and woody – cassava
17. Contrasting – sage leaf rough upper surface, downy or woolly underside
18. Papery – hydrangea, allium skin
19. Feathery – peony petals, fern, Irish moss, marigold, carrot leaves
20. Spiky – acorn cups
21. Bristly – cornflower bud
22. Ridged or bumpy – surface of cabbage
23. Dry and brittle, crispy – oak leaf

Above Bergamot. Most citrus fruits have a hard deeply dimpled textured outer skin and at the same time a glossy sheen. It can be difficult to capture this bumpy surface but masking fluid can be a useful tool to use here for the highlighted areas.

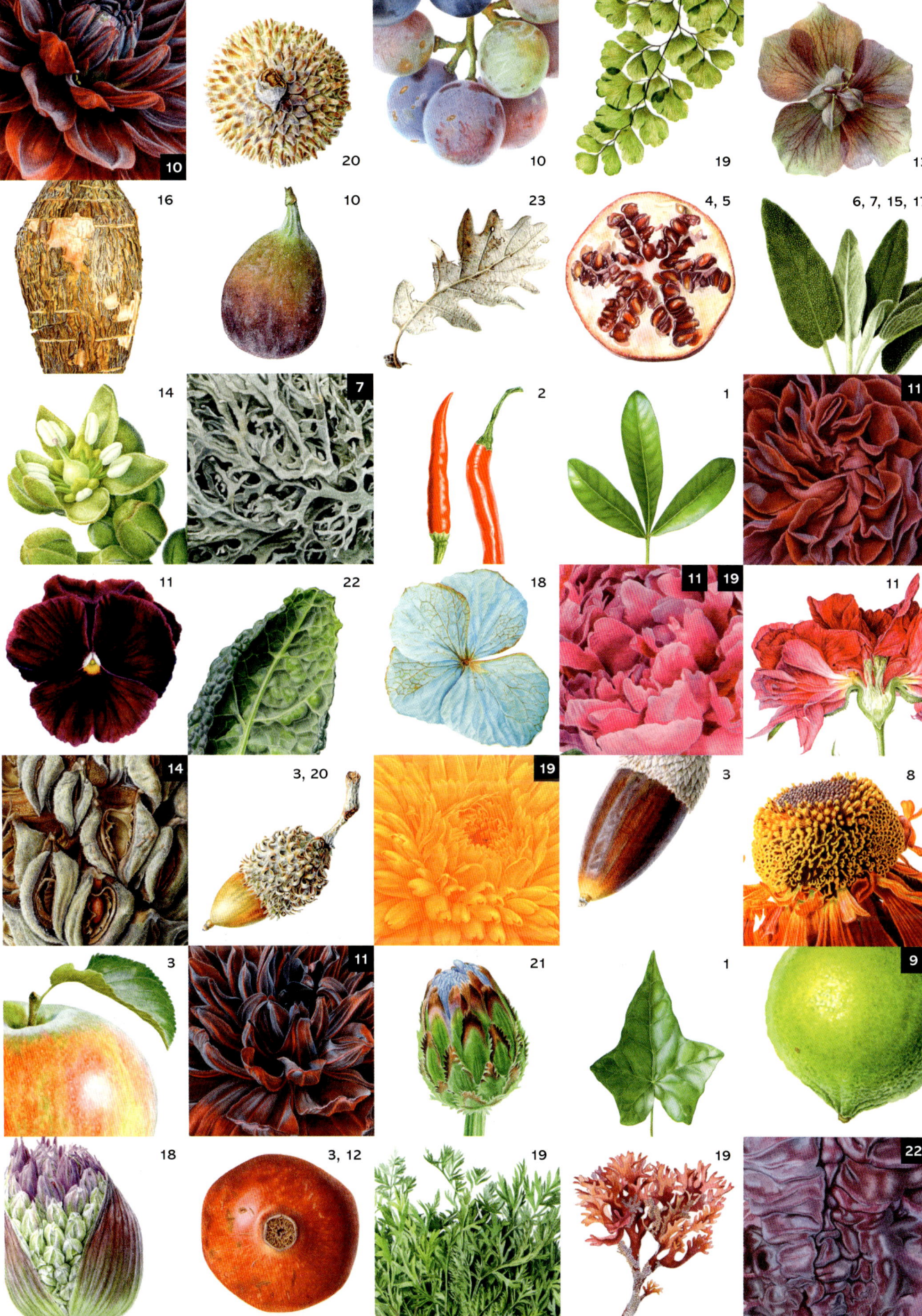

10

20

10

19

13

16

10

23

4, 5

6, 7, 15, 17

14

7

2

1

11

11

22

18

11   19

11

14

3, 20

19

3

8

3

11

21

1

9

18

3, 12

19

19

22

COLOUR

I think about colour in terms of how it will impact a painting, maybe adding some drama using vibrant or contrasting colours, or using colour combinations to create harmonies.

I am especially drawn to subjects with intense or vivid shades and less so to pale colours. However, I like to try to find colours within a subject that go unnoticed and particularly enjoy doing this with dried specimens (see page 71). At first glance they might appear to be brown or grey, but consist of so many other colours if studied very carefully.

I'm currently working on a very simple piece of dried garlic skin that initially appeared to be a very light shade of grey. But when I actually looked at it in detail it revealed a huge variety of colours: blues, yellows, browns, pinks and greens. I'm painting it at six times its actual size with the aim to clearly reveal its subtle colours and details.

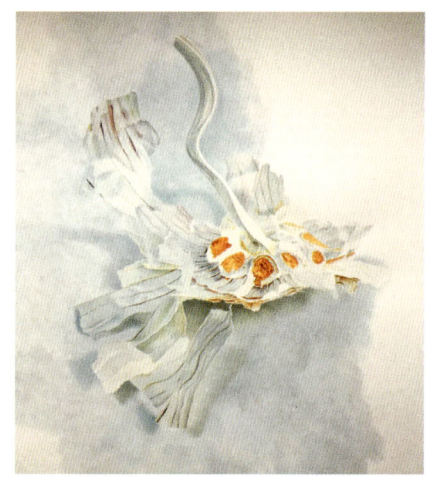

Above Garlic skin, work in progress.

Below Studying the colours of hydrangea petals using a painted colour chart for reference.

Colour Prep

I make lots of colour swatches before starting, to make sure I get all the right paints on my palette ready for a painting. These are sourced from my specimens and from the many photographs I take of them. Colour-matching is often done directly from a monitor if I am happy with the photographic result.

I will also try washing out the paint swatches to see how easy it is to lift colour out in case I want to remove it to create highlights later on. If the paint is very staining I'm careful not to build up the layers too deeply.

I find the deeper the colour of a plant or flower, the easier it is to paint – starting quite pale and building up the colour in layers. It is much easier to add colour with watercolour paints than to take it away or try to wash it out. There is a danger of spoiling the surface of the paper if it is wetted and dabbed too often.

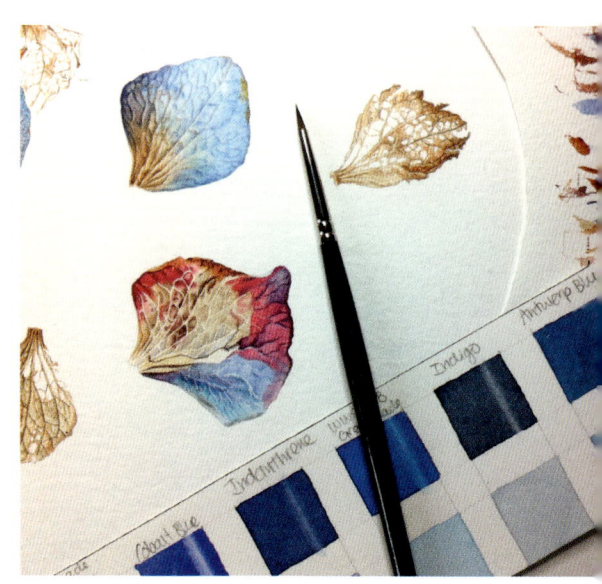

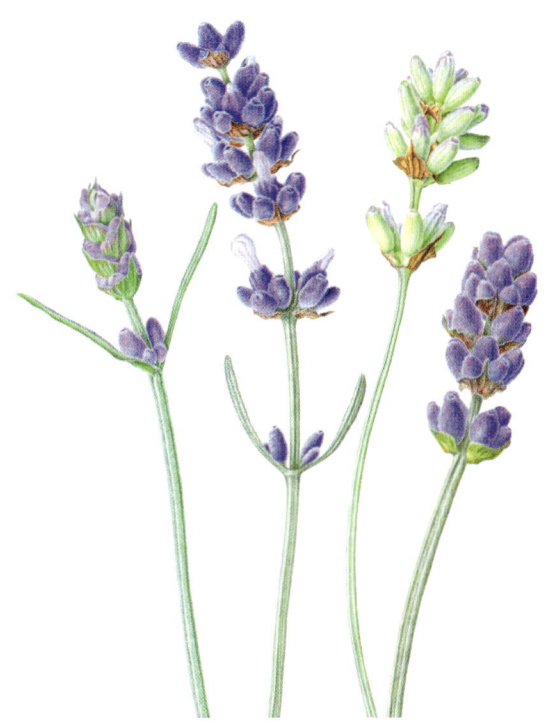

Marigolds and lavender

I tend to favour growing flowers that are blue, pink and green, or deep red and purple. Choosing colours that are adjacent to each other on the colour wheel creates a feeling of harmony in a garden.

When designing a garden scheme I have normally tried to steer clear of yellows because of how they can clash with my favourite colours. However, I have had to concede with our garden in France, as yellow-flowered plants such as Turkish sage (*Phlomis*), cotton lavender (*Santolina*) and Yarrow (*Achillea*) seem to thrive in the climate and actually look stunning against their greyish, silvery leaves.

I'm not completely averse to using contrasting colour in my planting schemes: I do love the striking combination of orange and blue together, and like to plant marigolds near lavender. Together they're also a perfect feast for the bees. It's said that marigolds deter insects, but in my experience bees love them as much as they love the lavender.

Above Lavender (*Lavendula angustifolia* 'Munstead'). Various stages of the flower's development with the colour ranging from pale green to deep blue.

Right Marigold (*Calendula officinalis*).

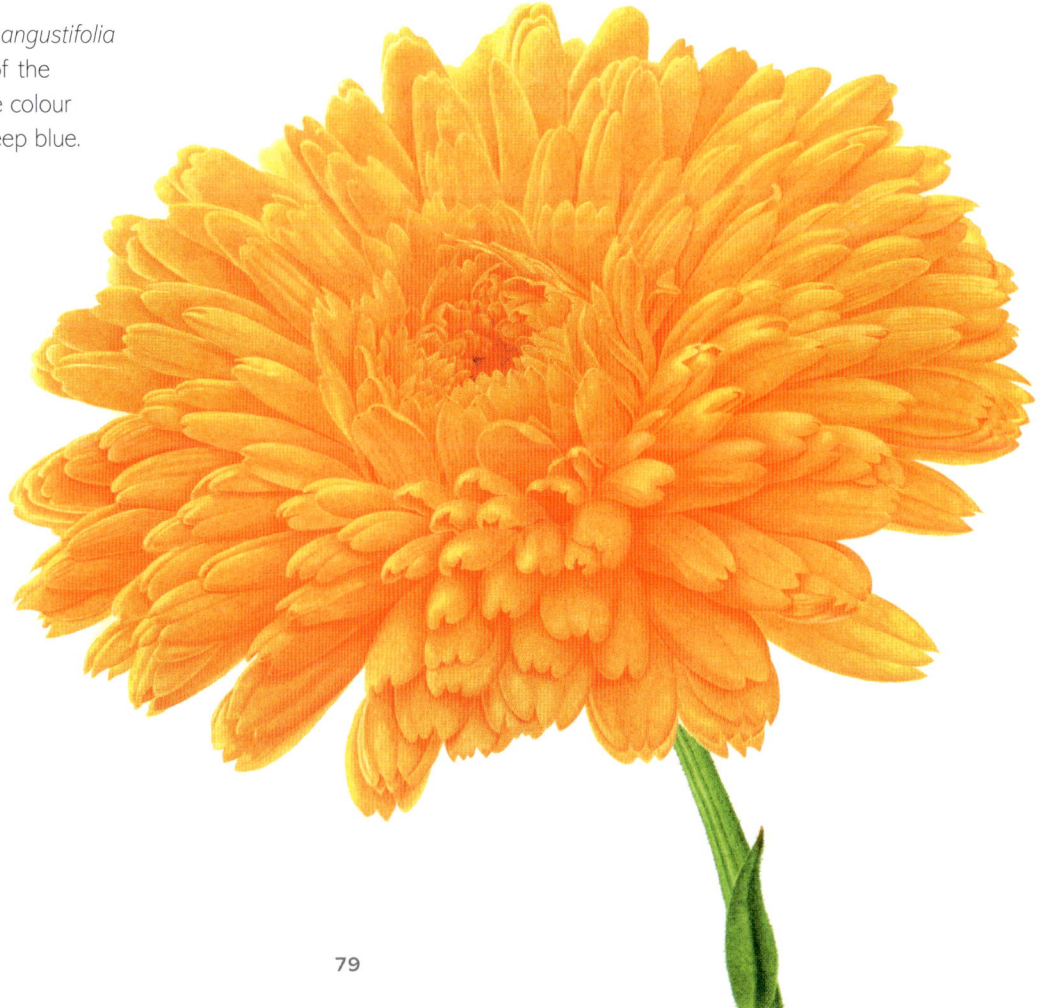

Complex Colour

The painting of the *Hydrangea macrophylla*, with its complex clusters of multicoloured flowers, was definitely a challenge. The colour variation in one head might range from deep crimson to blues, purples and bright greens. The black-edged leaves are interesting too. With so many dramatic colours within each separate flower and a huge variety of colour within each petal, I was worried that the colours could get mixed together and end up looking muddy.

It's a good idea to make sure your brush isn't too wet. This makes it easier to stop the colours next to each other bleeding together and making a mess. Also, if the brush is drier, you can overlay colours without them mixing too much, or lifting the layers below.

Below Something as complex as this mophead hydrangea (*Hydrangea macrophylla* 'Pimpernel') is worked up from close to a hundred reference photographs that I take from different angles and at several different focal lengths.

Right Grapes painting in progress and my painted colour chart to work from.

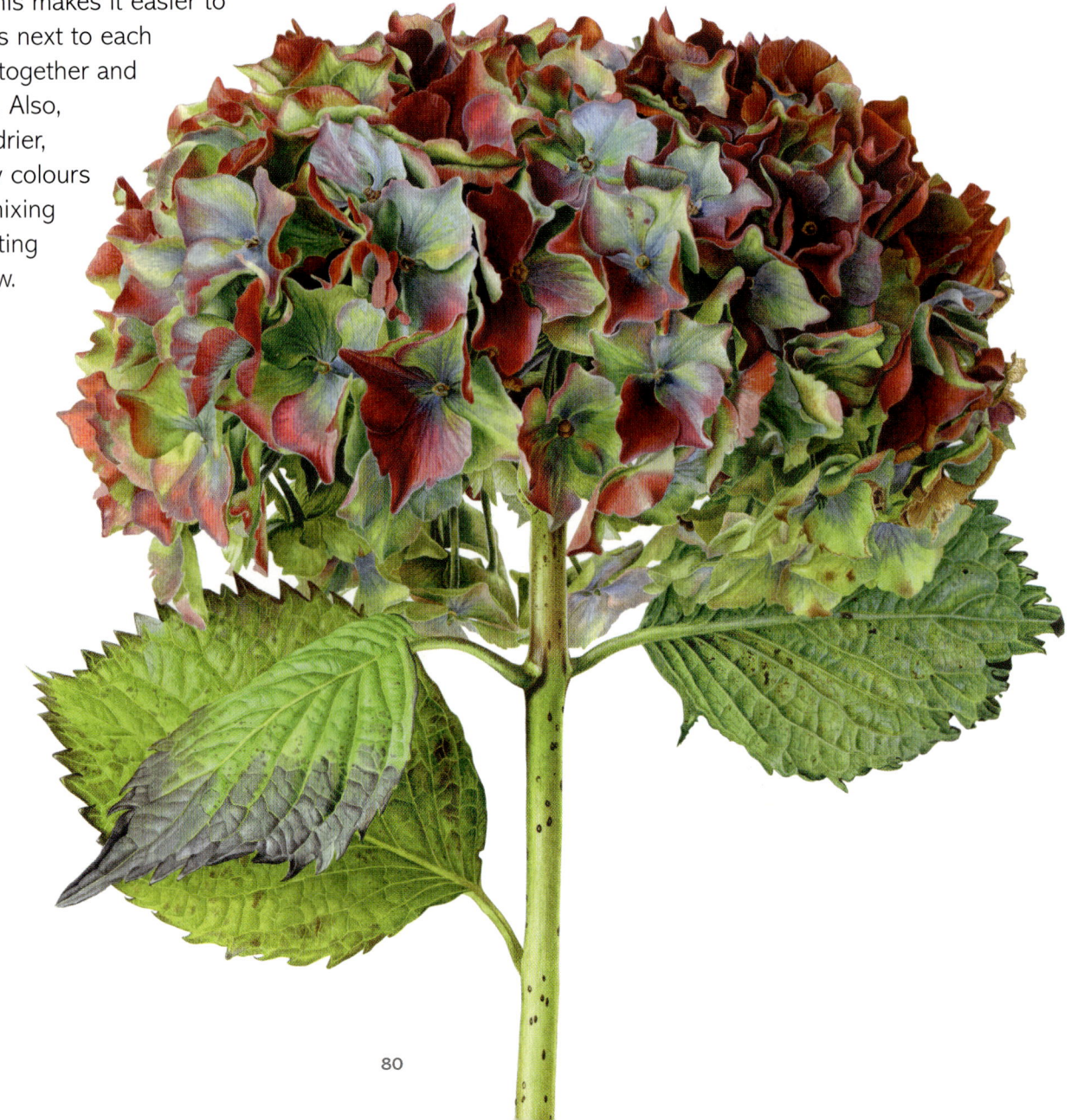

Inspirational Colour

I recently planted a vine in France and was amazed to see how quickly it began producing grapes. I thought they were so beautiful. The variety of colours on one small bunch of fruit was incredible. It was exciting to watch them grow and ripen and I knew I wanted to paint them. I managed to pick this bunch just before the birds got to it. Initially I was annoyed that I'd managed to ruin the bloom on the fruit by touching the grapes – my fingerprints were all over them! But I then decided that it added more interest to the surface texture, so I kept the fingerprints and all the scratches on the bloom and included them in the finished painting.

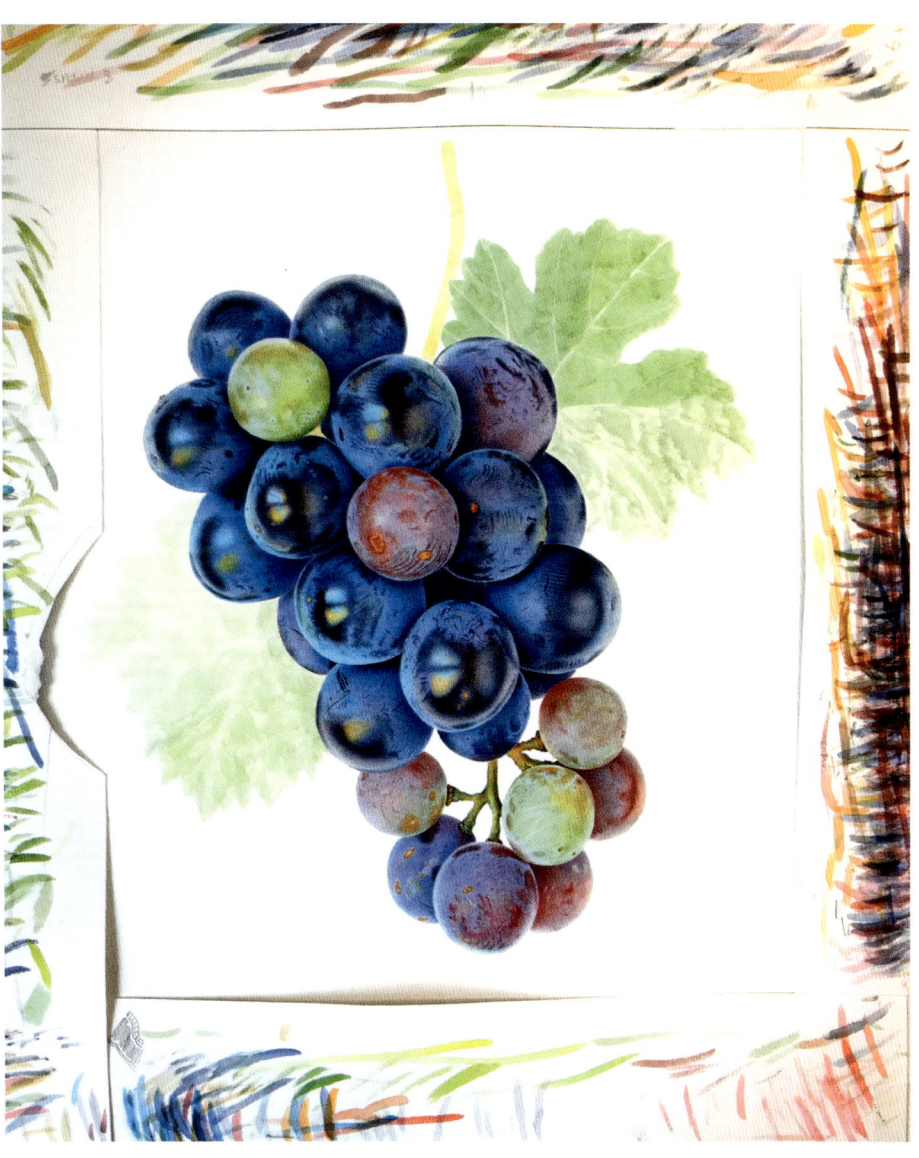

The intense blue of the bloom was what fascinated me when
I saw this plum growing in a friend's garden in France. I then
noticed all the additional colours: yellows, reds, oranges and
hints of green, all within a small fruit. This was painted about
three times larger than life, as I wanted to illustrate the numerous
shades and the details of the varied markings.

I had to build up layers of paint carefully, leaving
parts with just pale washes to show the bloom
and areas of light. This plum had no leaf
when I first painted it but I realized that it
was crying out for some green contrast,
so added the leaf later.

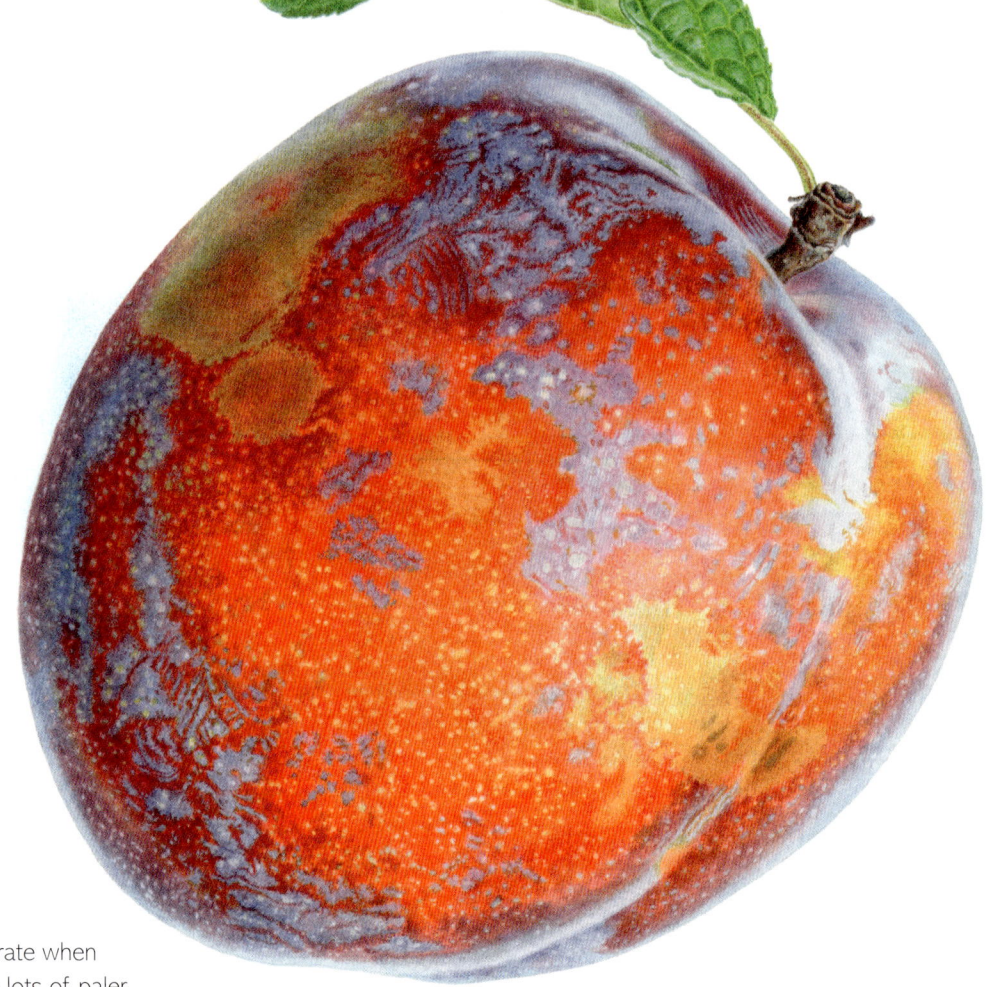

Above I had to really concentrate when
painting this plum. There were lots of paler
yellow markings and patches of bloom on the
skin's surface. I had to be careful to paint around these parts
in darker shades of orange and deep red as no white paint
was used in this illustration.

Background Colour

The pattern of this wallpaper is comprised of a collage of parts of several of my paintings. Essentially it is the same design but with two different backgrounds – one dark, one light – each influencing the character of the finished design. They show how important the background colour is for mood and impact.

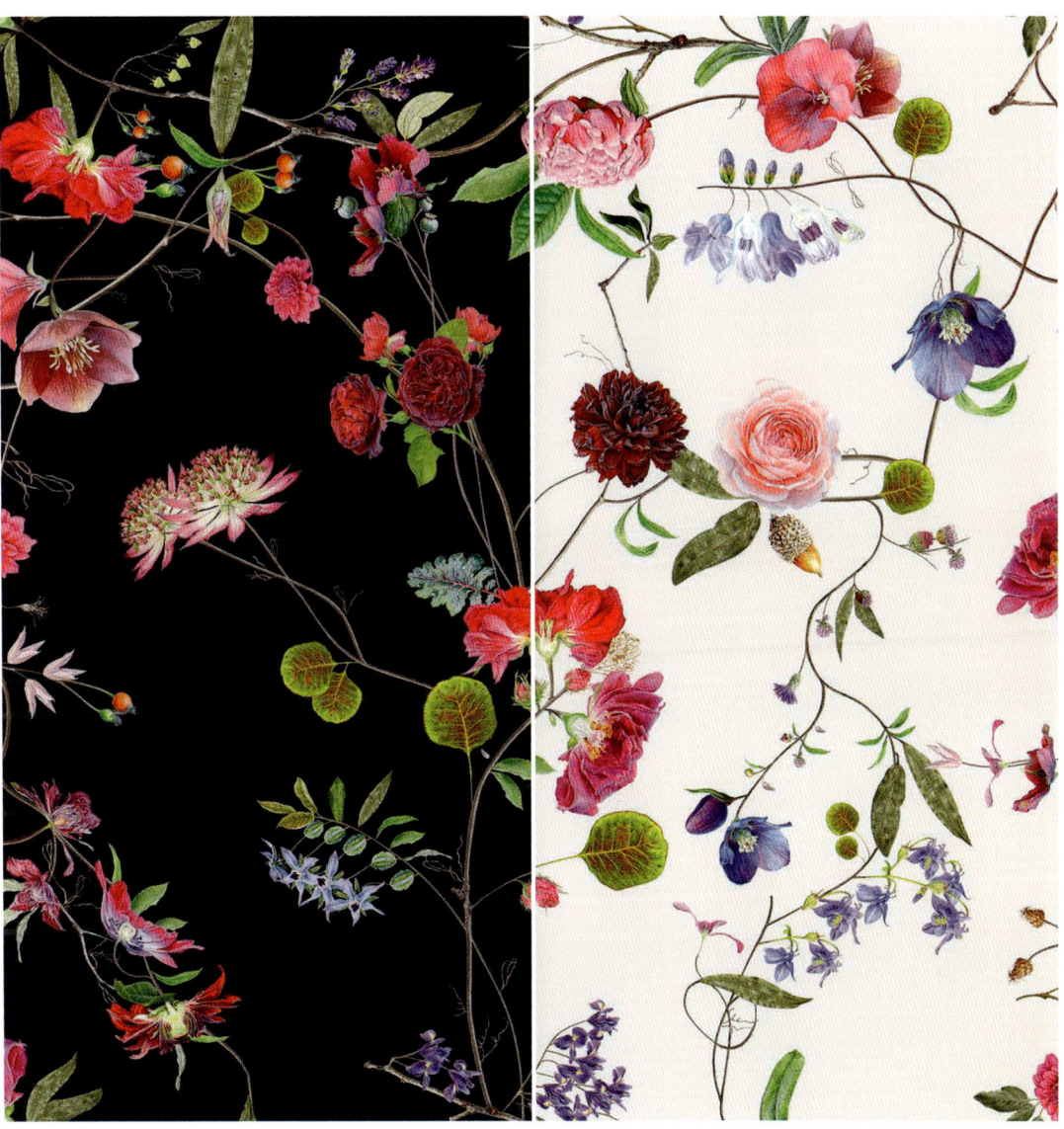

Above Beautiful design of botanical chinoiserie shown in both black and white palettes. Pattern design by Mineheart using several of my watercolour paintings.

Green Leaves and White Flowers

Leaves

The flower is most often the main focus of my painting, but leaves can be just as fascinating. I find if a flower doesn't have enough variety of colour, adding green will normally bring the composition to life. The greens of leaves, stems or bracts create a good contrast.

It's a good idea to do lots of watercolour swatches before starting a painting – to hold up against the leaves you are illustrating. It might surprise you how many variations of colour there are within a single leaf.

I tend not to use green paint straight from the tube as it has a rather artificial look. Like all botanical illustrators, I have my own palette for mixing greens. I use a mixture of Winsor Blue (Green Shade) with Winsor Yellow for a very bright apple-green (which is actually too saturated for the natural shade of most leaves). By adding small amounts of Quinacridone Gold or some red, I add warmth and 'knock back' the brightness to create a much more realistic shade of green. For a greyer green or olive-green I will use French Ultramarine as the blue in the mix, which contains more red than Winsor Blue.

Top Muted grey-green of dried Syrian laurel. For very dark areas I use Indigo as the blue.

Centre Kiwi (*Actinidia arguta*) have green leaves with a prominent pattern of veins. I used Quinacridone Gold for the initial layer to highlight the veins and edges of the leaves. Basil leaves are a really lush, lively green, while the maidenhair fern (*Adiantum*) has warm green leaves with lots of tiny veins fanning out to the edges.

Bottom Cotinus is one of my favourite plants, mainly for the seasonal changes. The leaves aren't green for very long as a lot of varieties emerge red, turn green and then back to brilliant reds or oranges in the autumn.

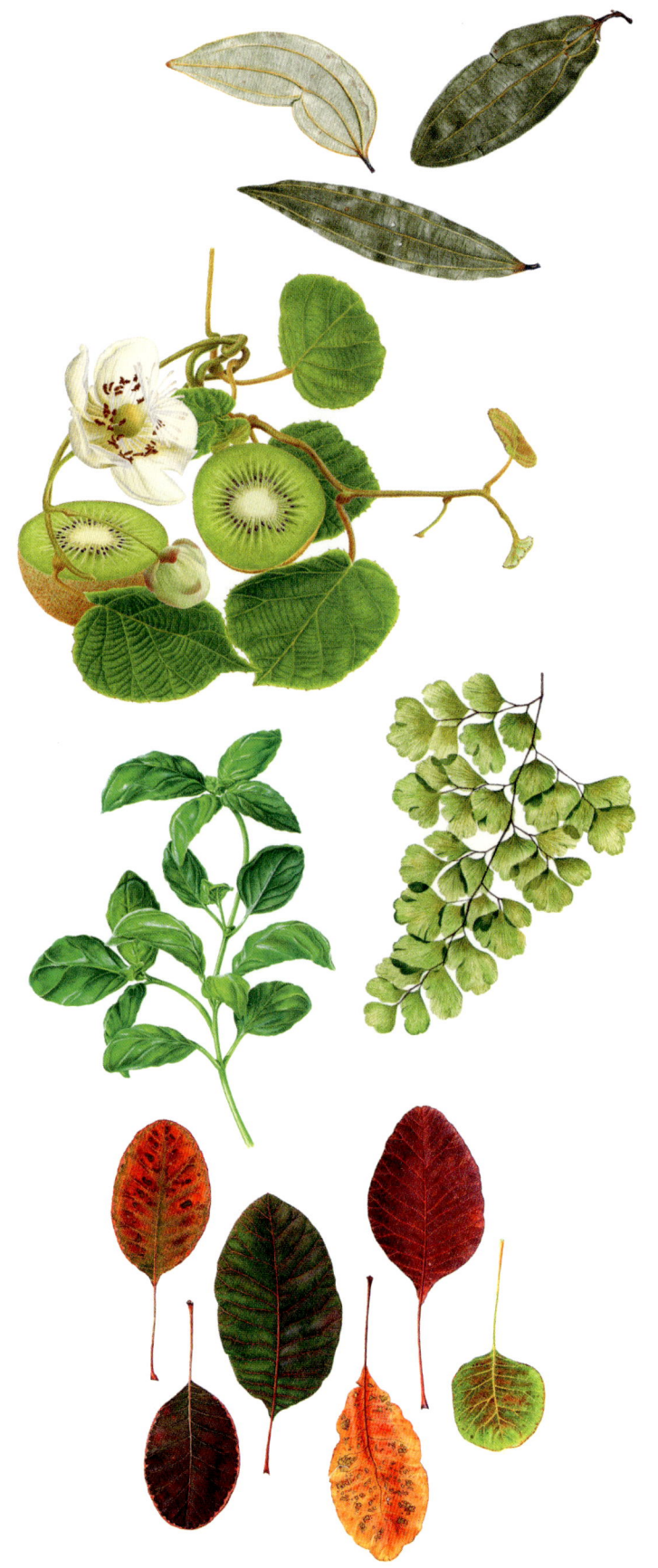

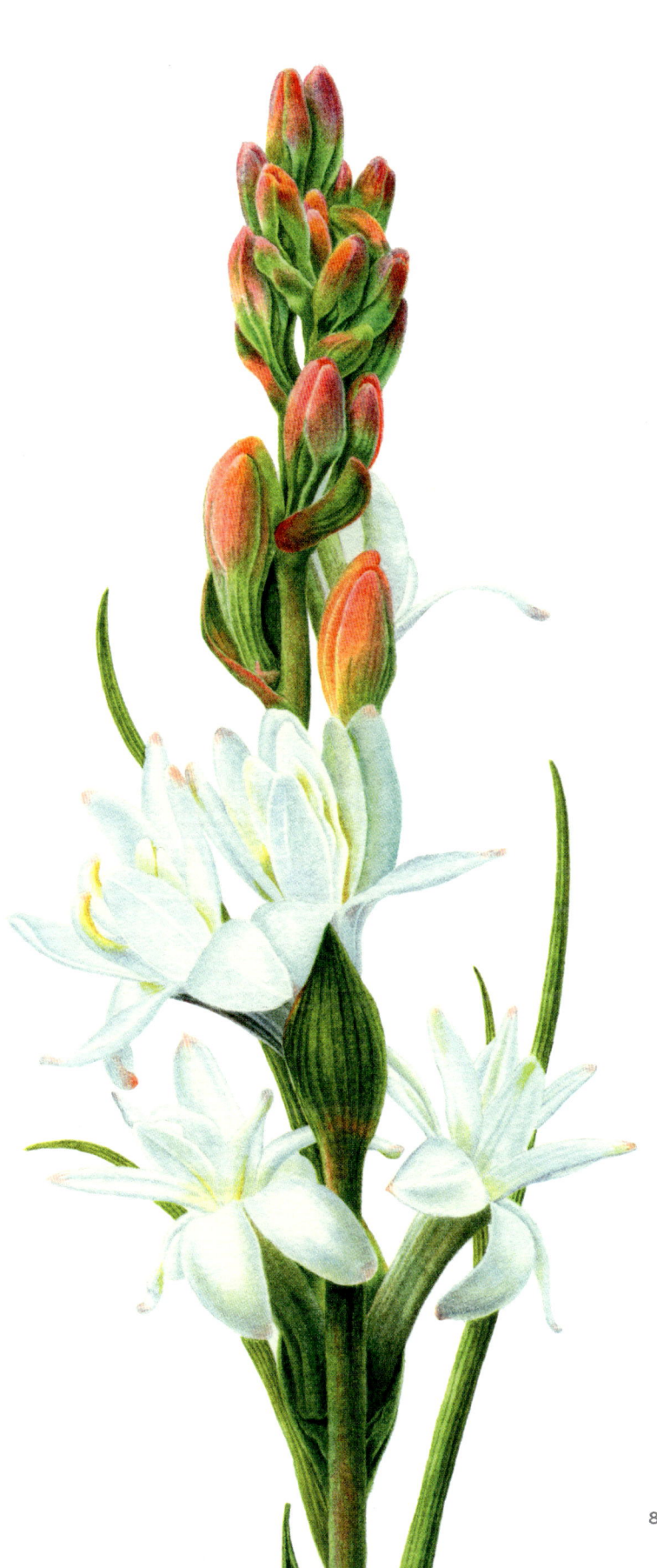

White – the challenge of 'no colour'

The most challenging paintings are the ones where there is very little colour or the subject is white.

Working up a white subject on a white background means there is no holding shadow to define the edges. In reality, even a white flower isn't really white – there is normally some very pale colour in there – apart from the highlighted areas. The edges of a white flower can be defined by adding subtle shading.

It's hard not to make a white flower look boring and grey so you have to really look for some colour within the petals and maybe slightly exaggerate it with very pale blues, ochres or greens.

White paint is occasionally useful when painting the tiny white hairs sometimes found on stems and leaves. For this I use Titanium White. Where the hair overlaps on to the white background, I will finish off the end of the hair with a very pale grey so it can be seen on the white of the paper (a technique I learned from botanical artist and teacher Helen Allen while on the course at the English Gardening School).

Left *Agave amica*. Blues, yellows and greens were used to paint the white flowers of this tuberose. It was a lovely plant to paint as the buds were bursting with colour, rose-pink and green. It made a very nice contrast to the white of the open flowers.

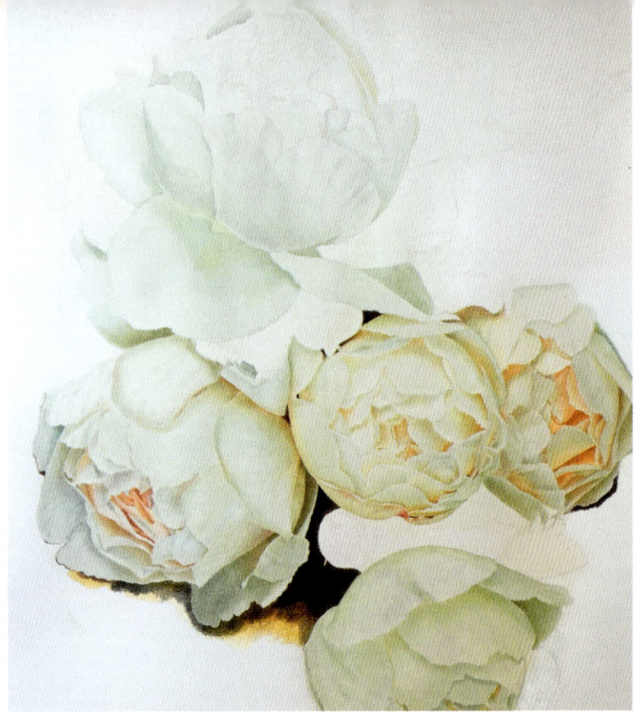

Left and opposite *Rosa* Wollerton Old Hall. The commission to paint these very pale roses was made easier as they were to be shown against a dark colour. This meant that all of the edges were clearly defined by the almost black background.

White flowers

White paint is not often used in watercolour and is not needed when painting white flowers on a white background – the paper is your white.

Once you have decided on a composition, it's important to draw the outlines of your flowers very faintly. The pencil lines shouldn't show on the finished painting.

I use a putty rubber to lift off the drawing until it's barely visible.

It's a good idea to do lots of tests of light paint washes on a separate piece of watercolour paper before beginning and hold them up against your subject to compare colour and tone.

I start painting by using a wash of clean water on a single petal and then drop in incredibly pale washes of whatever colour that I think predominates. Normally this isn't just grey but a subtle variation or mix of blues, yellows or reds. I leave the lightest areas completely clear of paint for the highlights.

When these washes are absolutely dry, I work with a very small brush on the areas that are in shadow – and therefore darker – with a dry brush, using minute strokes and building up tonal layers to create a three-dimensional form. It's a good idea to go lighter than you think you need to. It's easier to add darker shades than remove the paint later on as you progress.

The margins of white petals can disappear against the background, so I improvise here and add very subtle shading at the edges to make them more visible. Another technique to make painting white flowers easier is to add a leaf behind the petal when working out a composition – this will make it very clear where the petal edge ends.

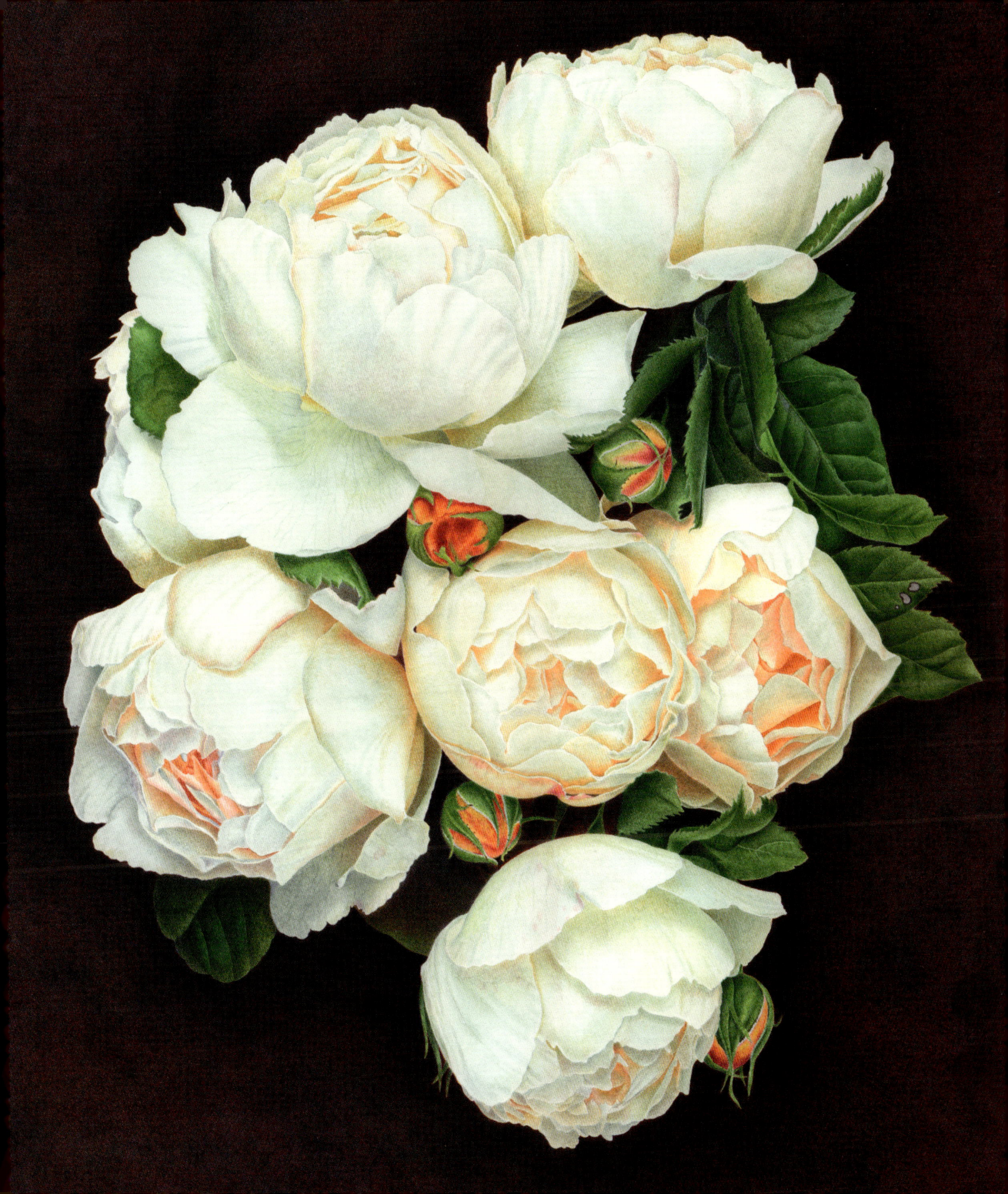

SPECIAL PLANTS

There are a number of reasons that make particular plant specimens interesting enough for me to want to paint them. I like to choose flowers and plants that grab my attention – subjects that generally have distinct characteristics, idiosyncrasies or peculiarities.

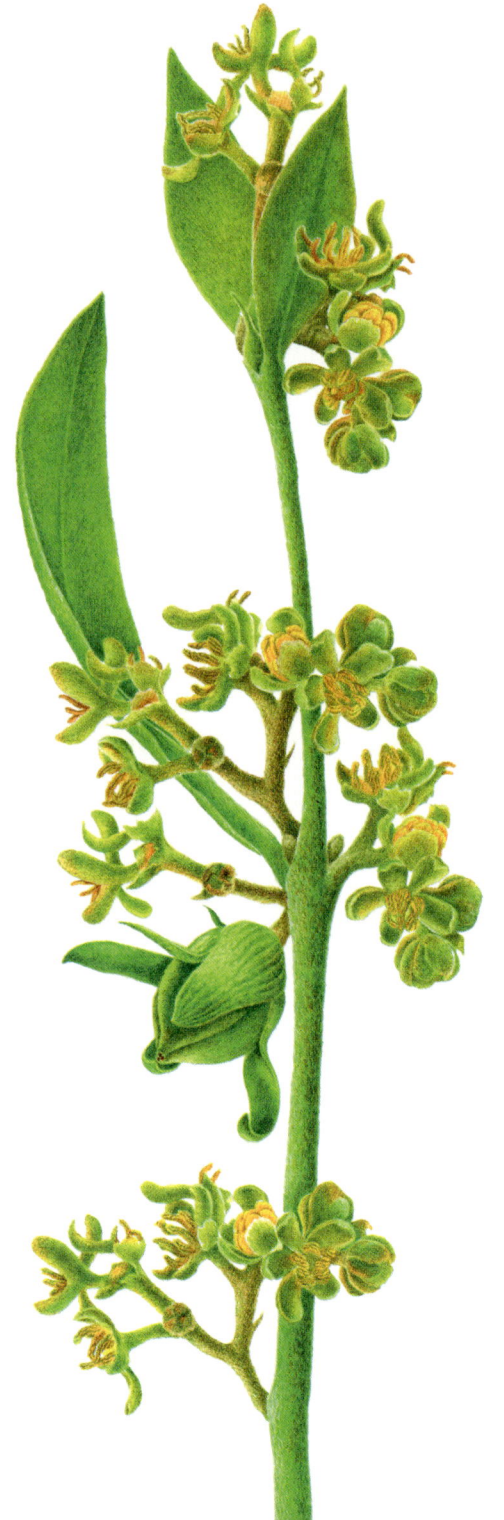

I've grown hundreds of different plants over the years, most of which I'm really fond of. I plan to paint many of these, especially those that have quite unusual characteristics. There are also a small proportion I have already painted but find so irresistible and interesting that I'm sure I will return to them again in the future.

I am usually influenced by colours and textures. Darker colours always seem to attract me to a plant – I love working with the deeper tones. I am especially swayed if the colours I like are combined with interesting textures – whether shiny, smooth, velvety or fluffy. The challenge of getting these different textures successfully into a painting is particularly appealing to me because of the chance to use a variety of techniques. See pages 74–77 for more on textures.

Left Jojoba (*Simmondsia chinensis*). Despite its Latin name, *chinensis*, this plant originated in the harsh desert environment of California not China. It produces nuts that are used to make beauty products and hair oils.

Above right Peony (*Paeonia lactiflora* 'Monsieur Jules Elie'). A beautiful pale pink peony with deeper pink outer petals.

Right Three illustrations of peonies, showing the opening of the flower from bud to full bloom.

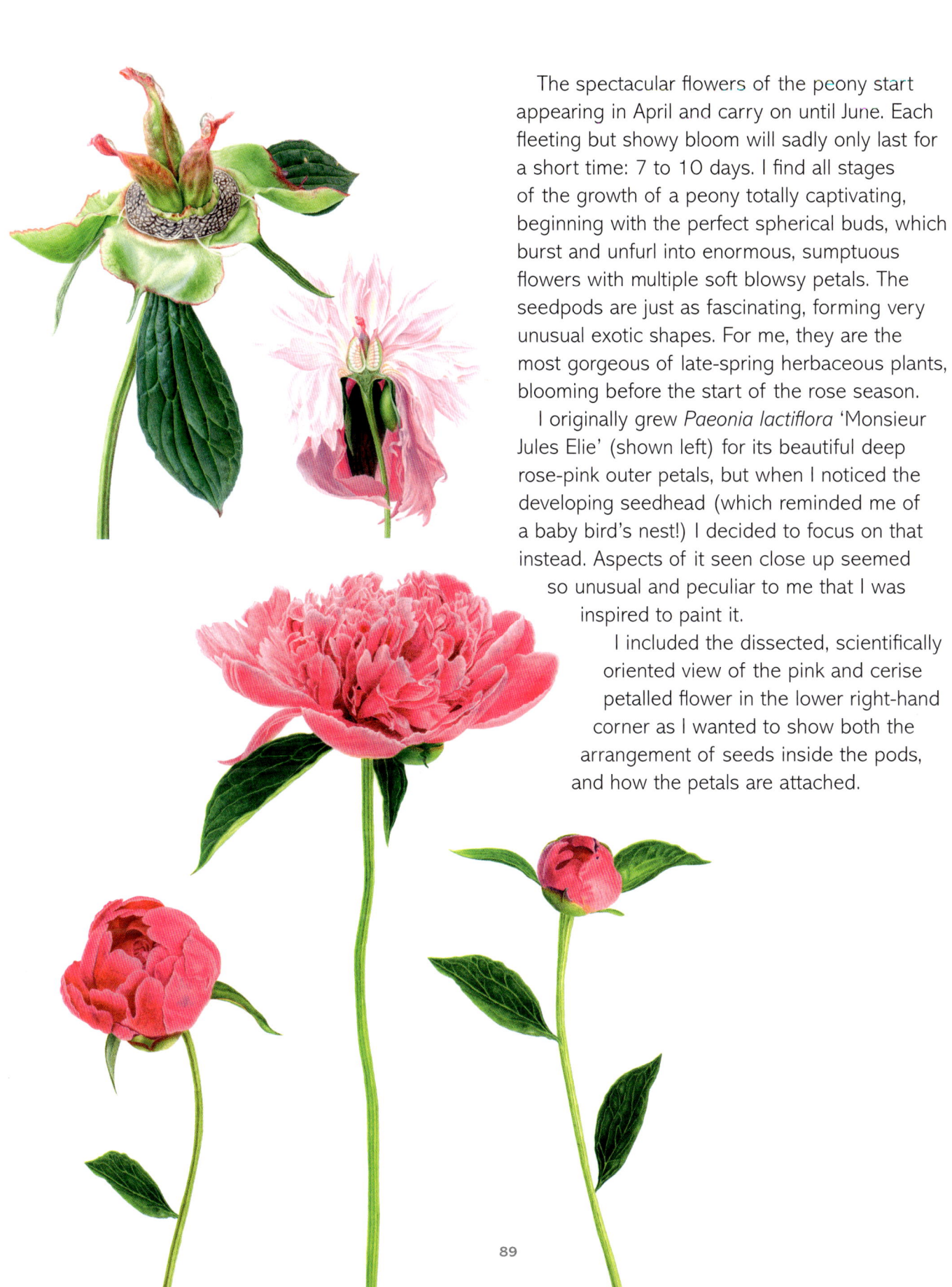

The spectacular flowers of the peony start appearing in April and carry on until June. Each fleeting but showy bloom will sadly only last for a short time: 7 to 10 days. I find all stages of the growth of a peony totally captivating, beginning with the perfect spherical buds, which burst and unfurl into enormous, sumptuous flowers with multiple soft blowsy petals. The seedpods are just as fascinating, forming very unusual exotic shapes. For me, they are the most gorgeous of late-spring herbaceous plants, blooming before the start of the rose season.

I originally grew *Paeonia lactiflora* 'Monsieur Jules Elie' (shown left) for its beautiful deep rose-pink outer petals, but when I noticed the developing seedhead (which reminded me of a baby bird's nest!) I decided to focus on that instead. Aspects of it seen close up seemed so unusual and peculiar to me that I was inspired to paint it.

I included the dissected, scientifically oriented view of the pink and cerise petalled flower in the lower right-hand corner as I wanted to show both the arrangement of seeds inside the pods, and how the petals are attached.

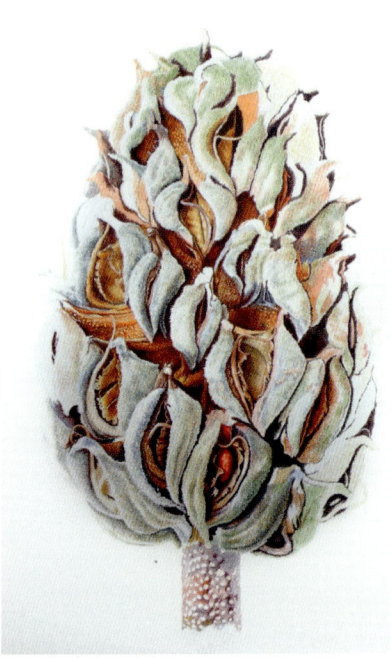

Magnolia have large, showy flowers that are followed by the formation of colourful cone-like fruits called follicles. These are unusual and extraordinary in the way that they open to expose brilliant red berries, covered in a waxy coat, which contain the seed.

By the time I started painting this one, all the berries had dropped out bar one, but I found the shapes, textures and patterns equally as fascinating without them. The striking combination of fluffy, mottled and patterned surfaces make the magnolia receptacle a compelling subject. With its complicated pattern of multiple seedpods, I had to make sure that I did a really careful drawing before applying any paint – it's really easy to get lost further down the line if all the sections aren't in the right place.

I started by painting the predominant background colours of each area in pale washes, and then got straight on with painting in the darkest parts (doing this helps me to know where I am).

No white paint was used here so while painting dark areas I needed to leave the white of the paper to show the fluffy edges.

Next, I concentrated on individual small areas. I quite like to nearly finish one small part at a time so that I can feel some sense of progress.

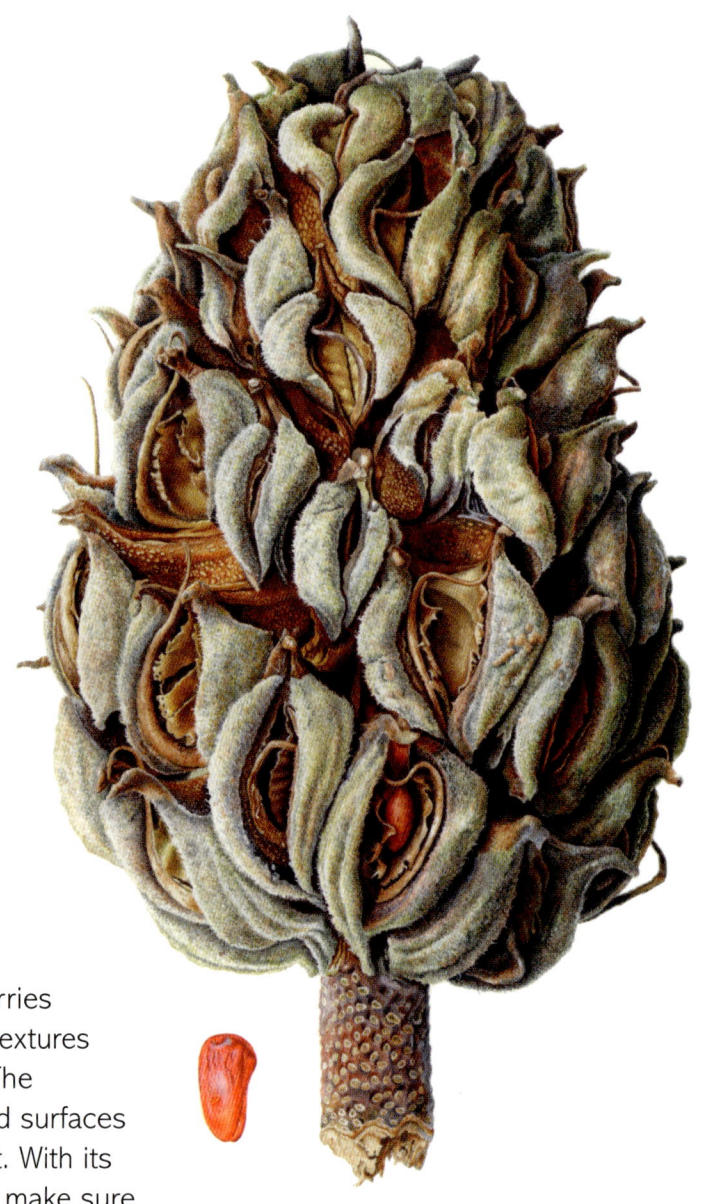

Above *Magnolia grandiflora* receptacle in progress (left) and the completed illustration (right).

I planted this helenium in my garden with the express intention of painting it after seeing heleniums growing en masse in Piet Oudolf's 'Glasshouse Borders' at the RHS garden at Wisley. I love everything about this variety, 'Moerheim Beauty': the beautiful copper-red and rich dark orange velvety petals and a central disk of chocolate brown covered in a dusting of deep golden pollen, surrounded by the downward pointing petals. Heleniums bloom around late summer and make fantastic, long-lasting cut flowers, keeping fresh for over a week – a good amount of time to study and paint them.

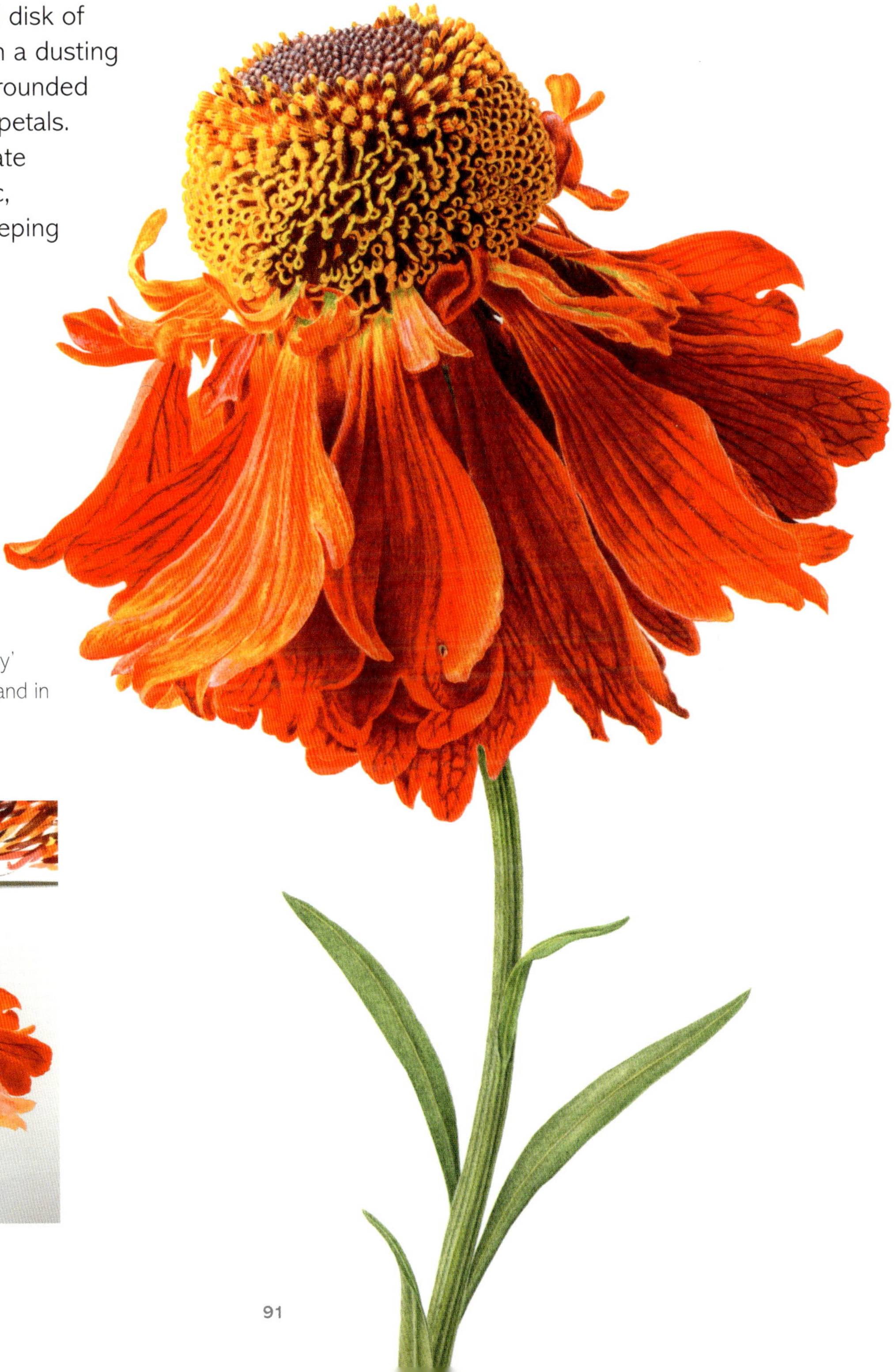

Right *Helenium* 'Moerheim Beauty' the completed illustration (right) and in progress (below).

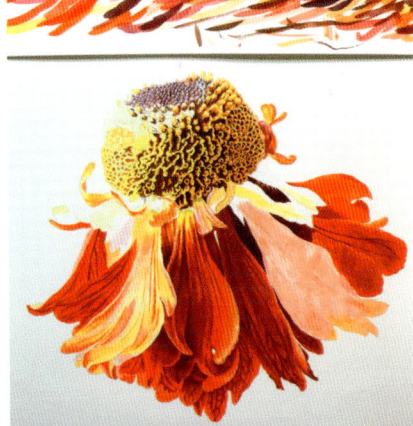

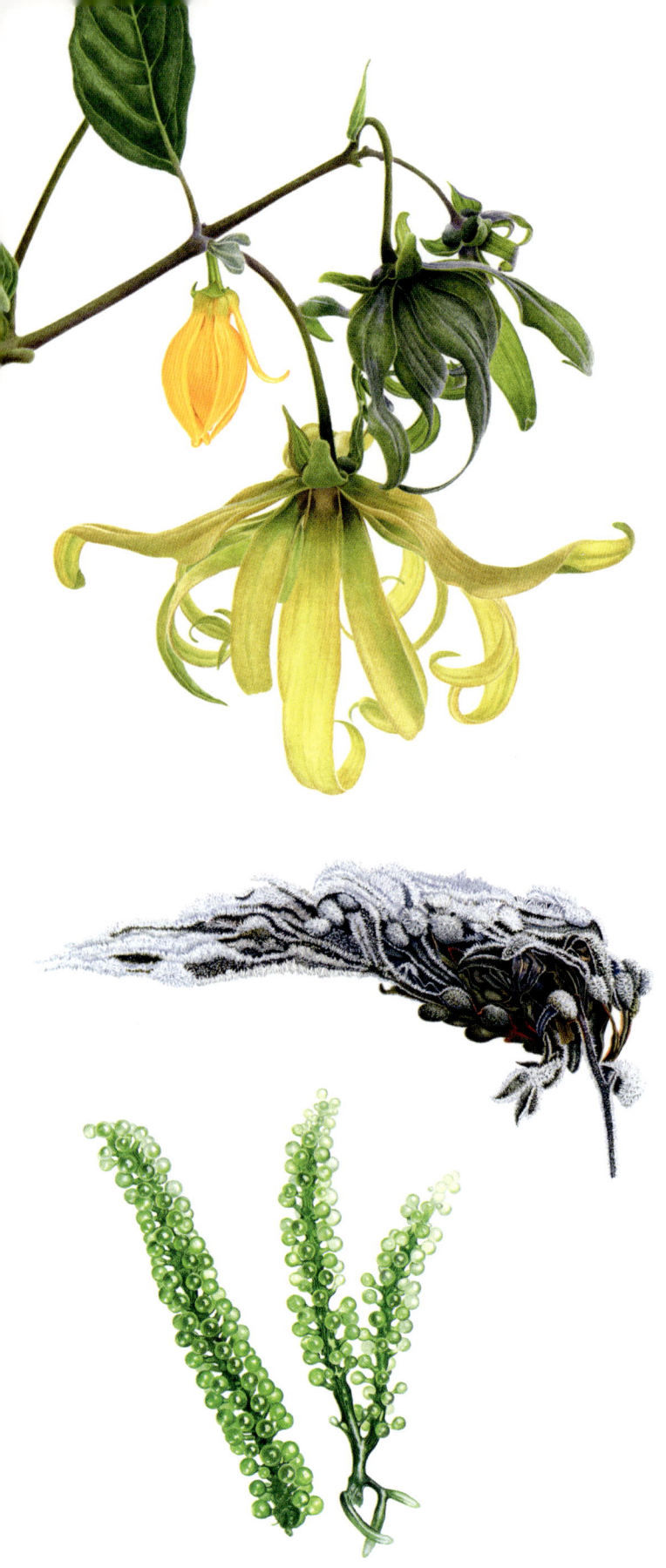

New Favourites

I spend a lot of time illustrating plants I've been commissioned to paint, and so I haven't chosen the subjects myself. This means I am often working on something it might not have occurred to me to paint. I frequently end up being totally fascinated and intrigued by these plants. From knowing very little about them, I gain so much from the research I have to do to understand and better illustrate them.

For example, I had often heard of ylang-ylang used as a perfume or essential oil, but didn't know what it looked like. I'm so glad that I was commissioned to paint it (left), discovering an exotic, unusual, beautiful and quite curious-looking star-shaped flower with greenish-yellow petals that curl inwards at the ends.

Likewise, I would never have considered painting frozen seaweed! I loved doing this one, although it was tricky trying to capture the detail of the white frosted icy parts on a white background. The subject makes this one of my more unusual illustrations but, being a bit out of the ordinary, it makes a welcome and interesting addition to my portfolio.

Another unusal subject was sea grapes (*Caulerpa lentillifera*). This amazing plant, which I had not seen before, is an edible algae also known as 'green caviar'.

Above left Ylang-ylang (*Cananga odorata*). A tropical plant used for its perfume extracted from the flowers.

Centre Frozen seaweed. The extracts from this seaweed are used as an ingredient in skincare products.

Left Sea grapes (*Caulerpa lentillifera*). Traditionally cultivated as a food in East and Southeast Asia but it is also used in skincare products.

COMPOSITIONAL IMPACT

When beginning a painting, I try to keep the design simple, focusing on the graphic shapes of the subject with a clean white background.

I prefer to keep my arrangements straightforward and unfussy, and normally steer clear of washed-out colours. I like to focus on parts of the plant that have unusual shapes, details or textures, and the areas that create the most interest. I will often take out some elements that might distract from the main subject to give an uncomplicated overall look.

Odd Numbers and Asymmetry

Almost all my paintings have an odd number of elements within the composition – something I've particularly noticed when selecting pictures for this book. This has always been an instinctive choice – an uneven number makes for a more natural and informal composition.

When I place the main object of interest in the centre of my painting and I plan on adding more elements, I will try to make sure that they are all at different heights, usually with some overlap on one or both sides. I do like the composition to be balanced, but complete symmetry will look unnatural – some variation in heights and angles is more aesthetically pleasing.

Right French lavender (*Lavandula stoechas*). This lavender is a stunning sight in late spring where it grows wild all along the coastline in the South of France.

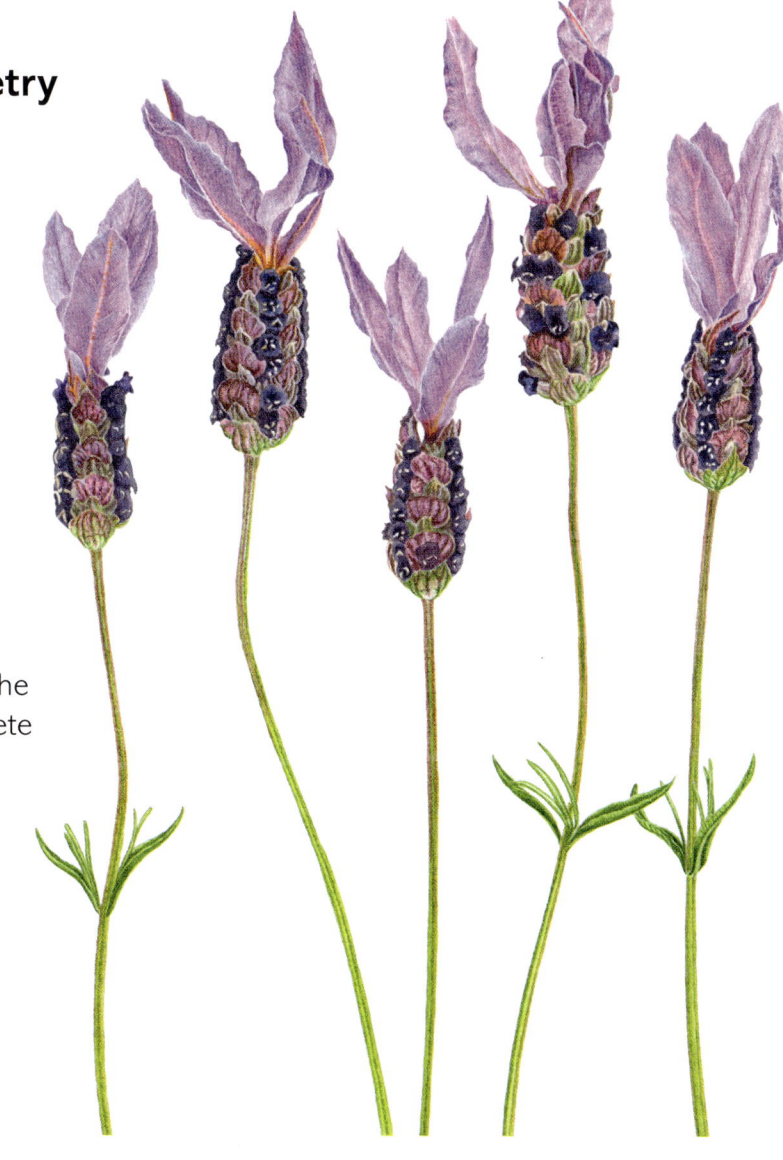

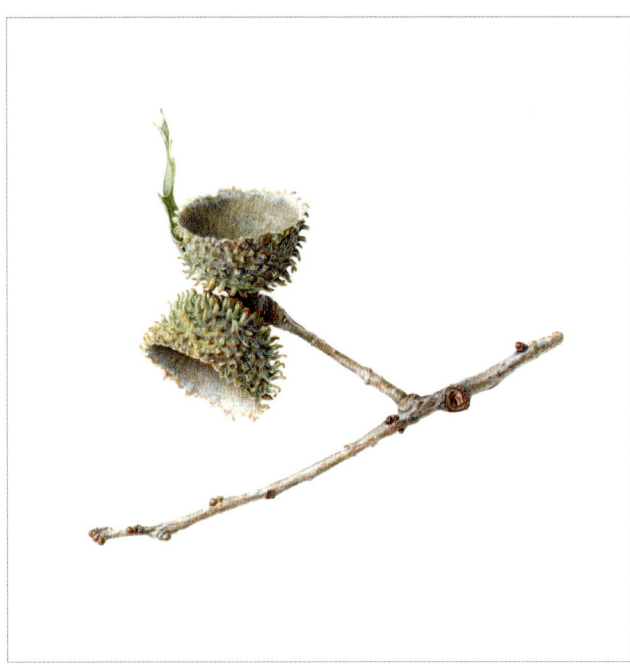

Above Acorn cups from a Kermes oak tree (*Quercus coccifera*).

A Square Format

I tend to work within a square format; I don't know why, but I've been doing it for about 30 years. When I compose an image, I will arrange the subject so that it works harmoniously but interestingly in that space.

Quercus coccifera is one of a series of three acorn pictures all painted within a square format. I liked the negative space being roughly divided into three sections by the placement of the twig and its acorn cups. In life, my whole subject was only 6cm (2½in) long, so the cups were absolutely tiny. Blowing them up and accentuating all the subtle colours added more impact to the design. (See page 71 for more of my acorn paintings.)

Other Formats

I don't always work with a square format. When my work is privately commissioned I will discuss the composition with the client and adjust a piece depending on what they want. The format of the compositions I complete for design companies is nearly always determined by them, because it will have to fit on packaging or around lettering, so I will work to compose within the required format or shape.

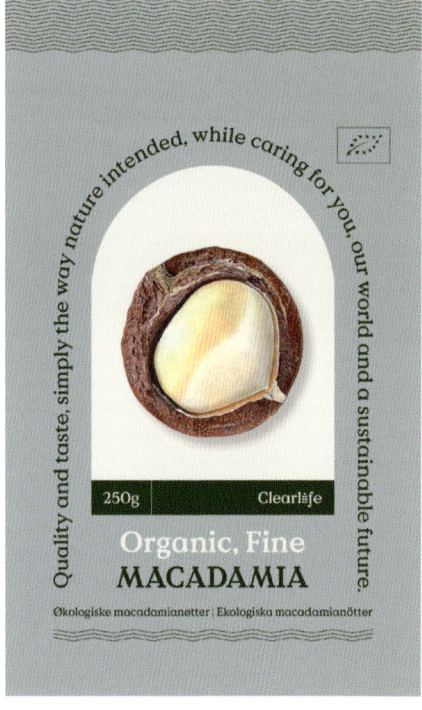

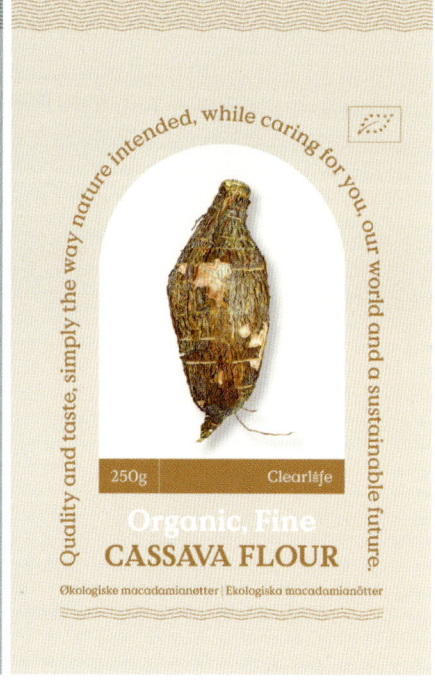

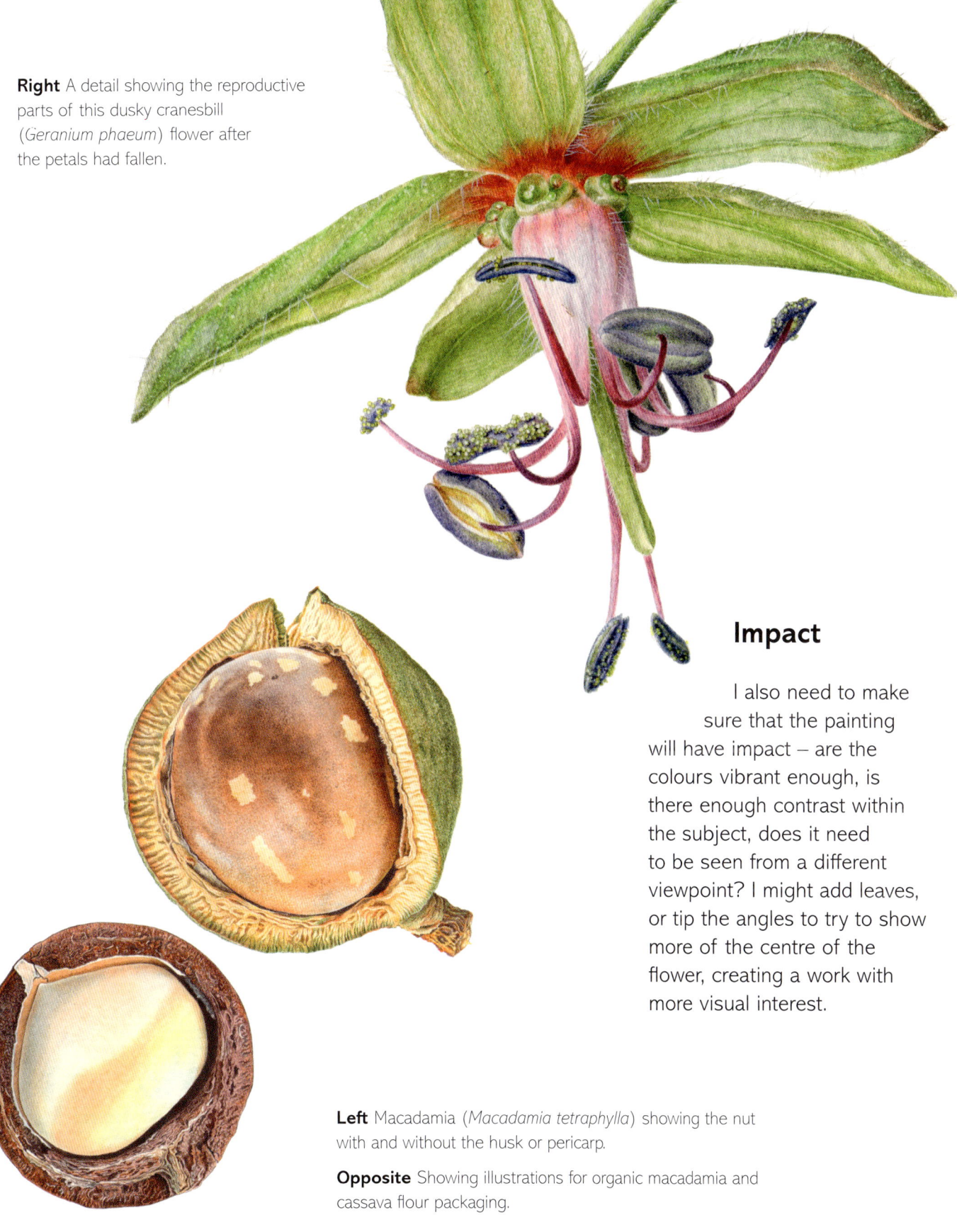

Right A detail showing the reproductive parts of this dusky cranesbill (*Geranium phaeum*) flower after the petals had fallen.

Impact

I also need to make sure that the painting will have impact – are the colours vibrant enough, is there enough contrast within the subject, does it need to be seen from a different viewpoint? I might add leaves, or tip the angles to try to show more of the centre of the flower, creating a work with more visual interest.

Left Macadamia (*Macadamia tetraphylla*) showing the nut with and without the husk or pericarp.

Opposite Showing illustrations for organic macadamia and cassava flour packaging.

Size

The size of my work is becoming more important too. I've started to paint much larger pictures, as they are definitely more impactful and impressive, which means they will work better in exhibitions when viewed from a distance. Painting larger does, however, mean a lot more work. It is technically quite difficult too – if the picture is too big, it's hard for the arm of the magnifier to easily reach all parts of the painting.

I found this emerging allium flowerhead to be extraordinarily beautiful. I was fascinated by the pattern of the unopened flowers emerging from tight, slightly translucent, papery skin and the striking ball shape sitting on top of a very upright stem. This plant really stood out as something unusual at this stage of its growth. I painted it about four times its normal size, partly to be able to show the detail, but also for dramatic effect.

Below *Allium hollandicum* 'Purple Sensation'. Showing the emerging bud, a cross section of a single flower and a flower from above.

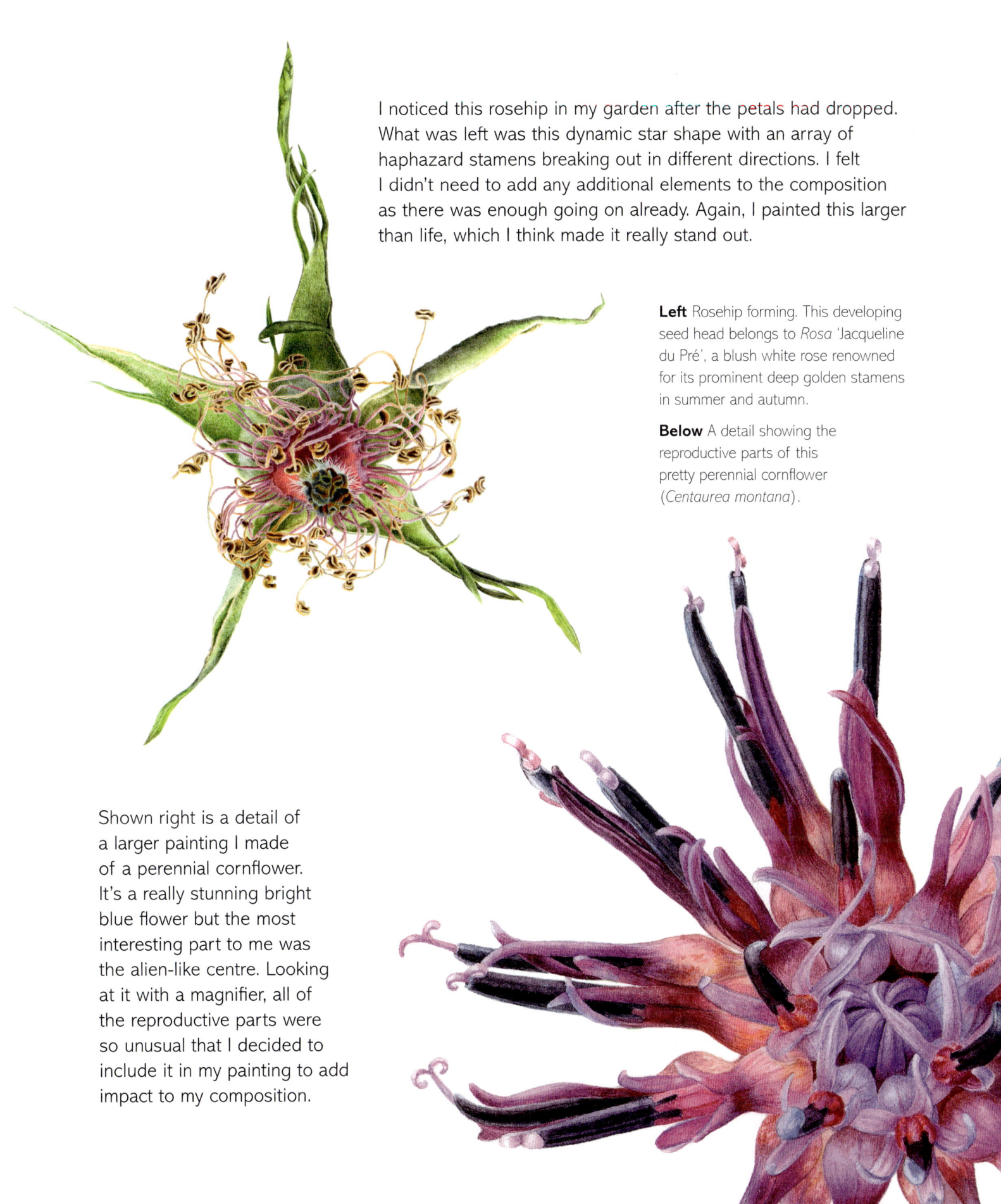

I noticed this rosehip in my garden after the petals had dropped. What was left was this dynamic star shape with an array of haphazard stamens breaking out in different directions. I felt I didn't need to add any additional elements to the composition as there was enough going on already. Again, I painted this larger than life, which I think made it really stand out.

Left Rosehip forming. This developing seed head belongs to *Rosa* 'Jacqueline du Pré', a blush white rose renowned for its prominent deep golden stamens in summer and autumn.

Below A detail showing the reproductive parts of this pretty perennial cornflower (*Centaurea montana*).

Shown right is a detail of a larger painting I made of a perennial cornflower. It's a really stunning bright blue flower but the most interesting part to me was the alien-like centre. Looking at it with a magnifier, all of the reproductive parts were so unusual that I decided to include it in my painting to add impact to my composition.

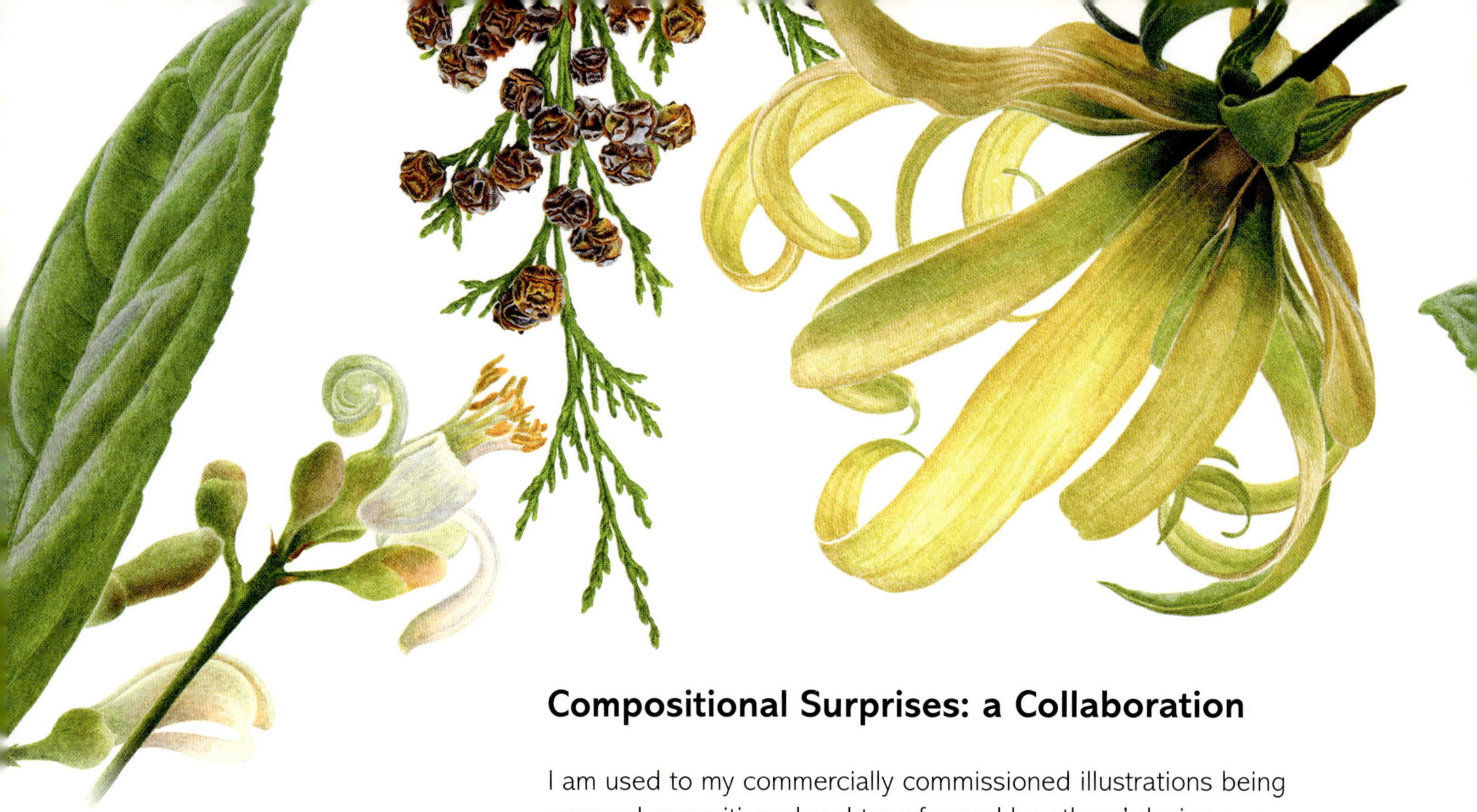

Compositional Surprises: a Collaboration

I am used to my commercially commissioned illustrations being cropped, repositioned and transformed by others' design eyes into something else. Sometimes my original paintings are used in campaigns in ways I could never have imagined – for instance these landscape format panels, which also became animated panels for retail areas.

Above Ylang-ylang (*Cananga odorata*), cedarwood (*Cedrus atlantica*) and neroli (*Citrus aurantium*).

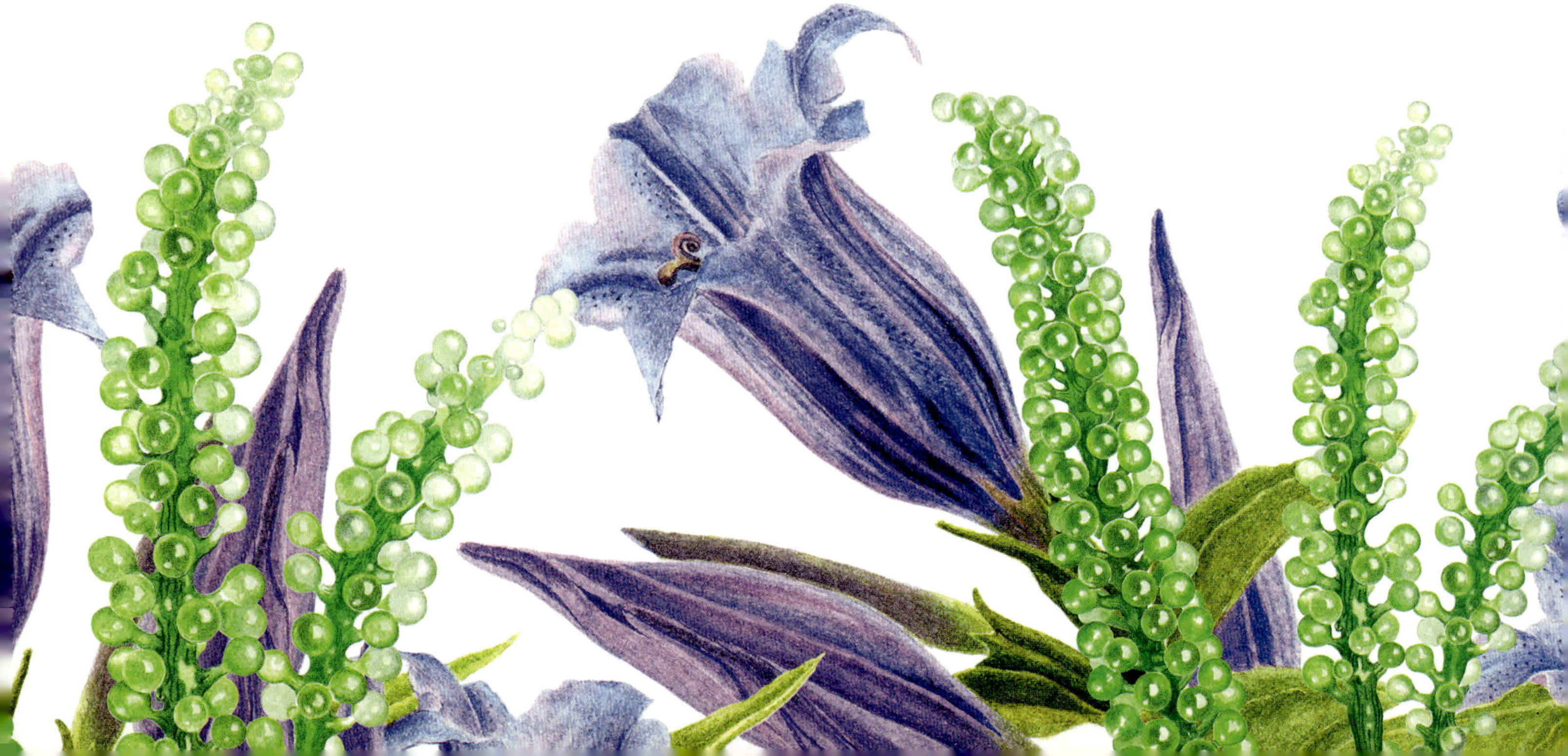

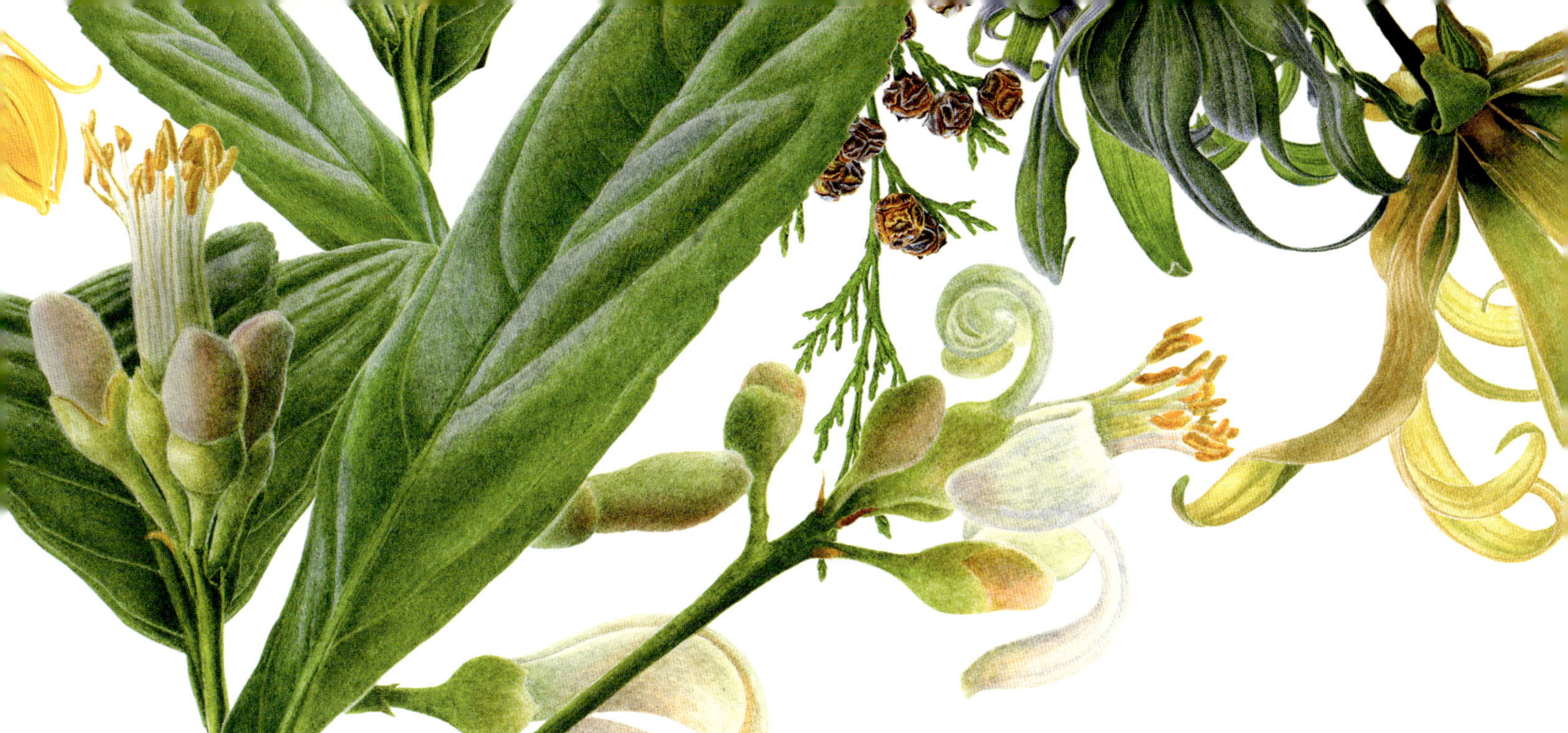

I loved the way that the creative director Matthew Axe has used my illustrations for a skin-care product campaign, placing them into a series of horizontally oriented compositions. He has positioned the flowers in a really clever way: making the elements work so well together by repeating them but changing their scale, flipping their direction, and overlaying them.

Below Gentian (*Gentiana* 'True Blue') and sea grape (*Caulerpa lentillifera*). The two elements are repeated and repositioned here to create a harmonious composition.

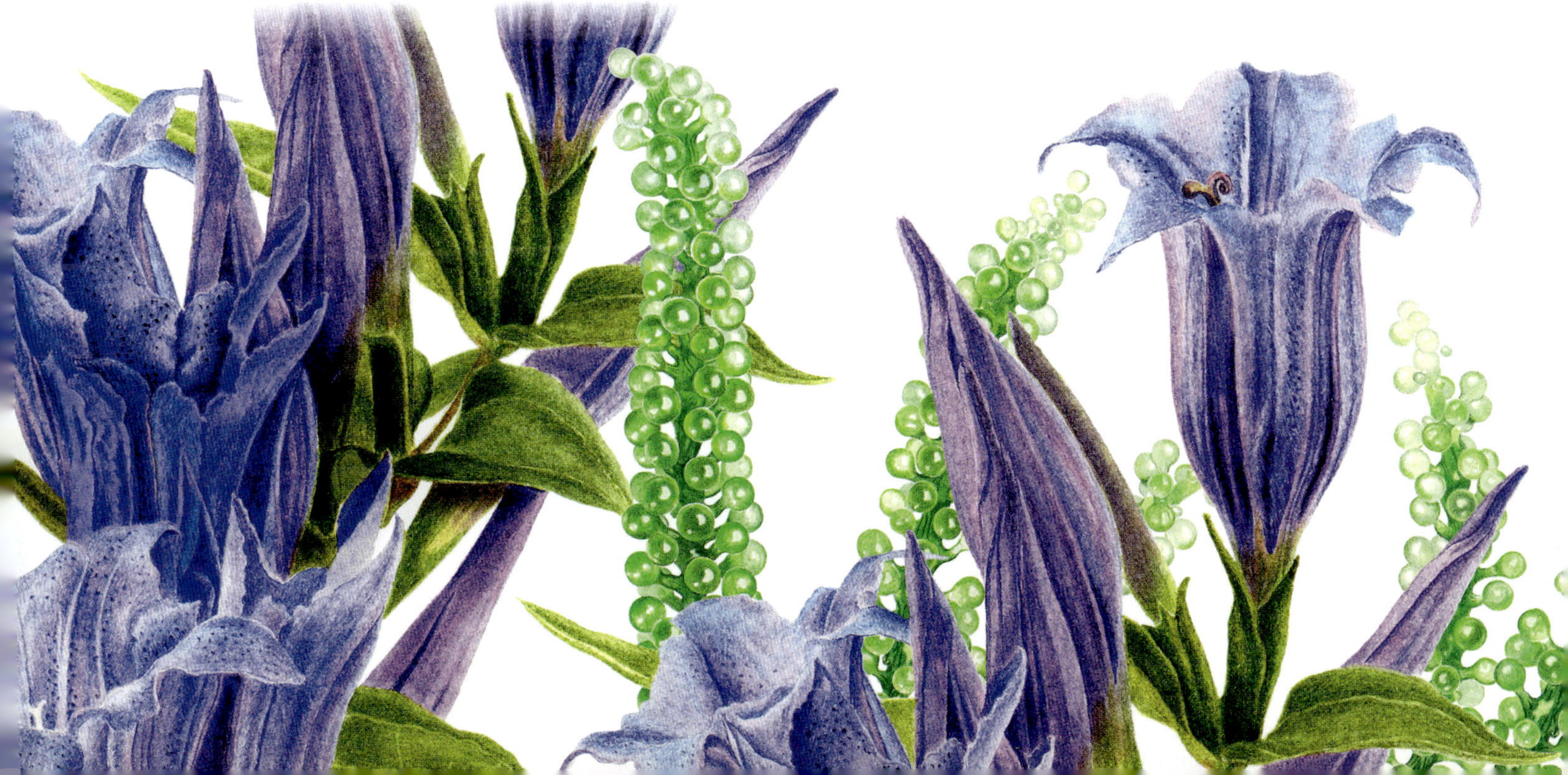

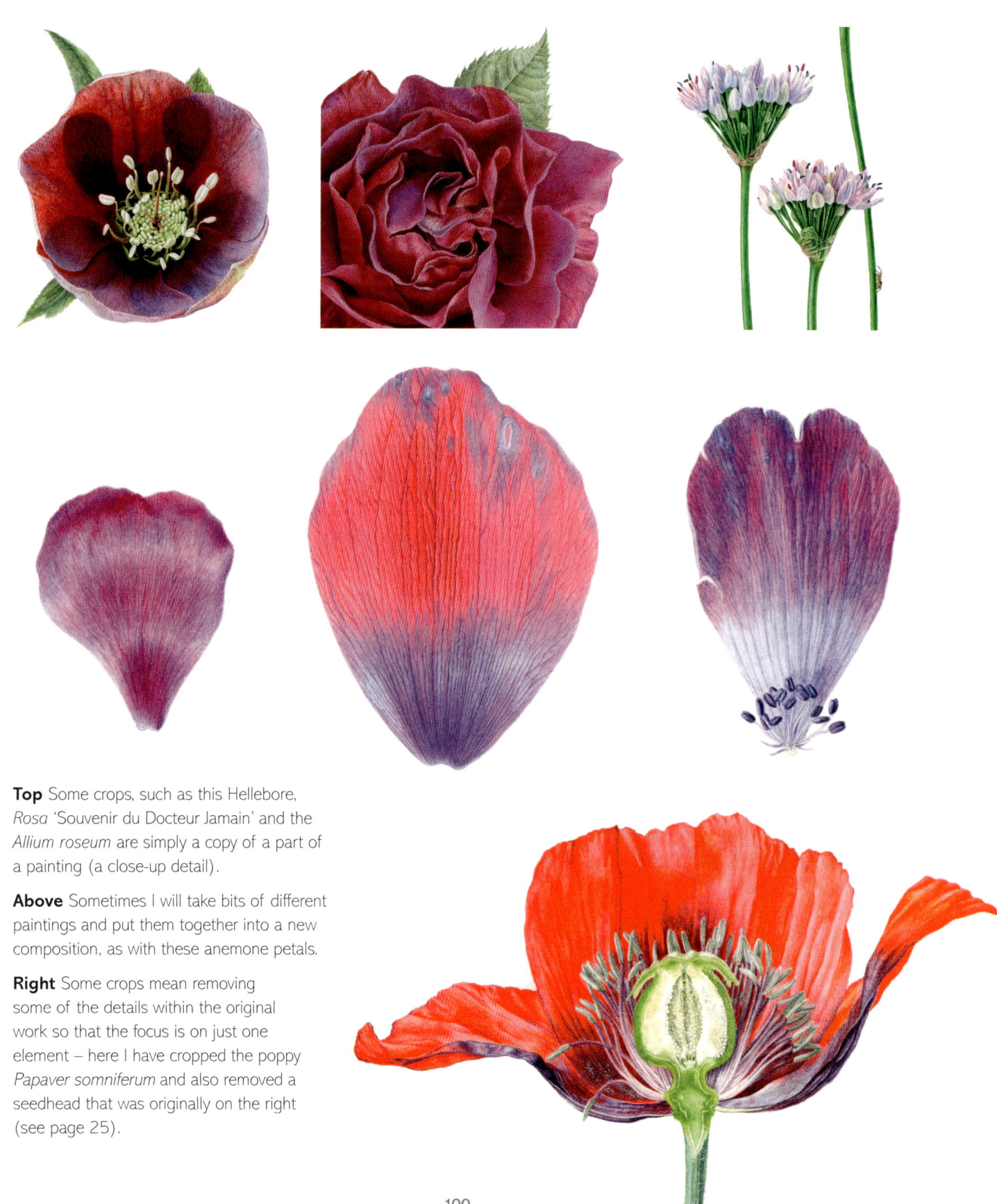

Top Some crops, such as this Hellebore, *Rosa* 'Souvenir du Docteur Jamain' and the *Allium roseum* are simply a copy of a part of a painting (a close-up detail).

Above Sometimes I will take bits of different paintings and put them together into a new composition, as with these anemone petals.

Right Some crops mean removing some of the details within the original work so that the focus is on just one element – here I have cropped the poppy *Papaver somniferum* and also removed a seedhead that was originally on the right (see page 25).

Crop and Enlarge

I wouldn't usually want my paintings blown up much bigger than I originally painted them. However, there are often new compositions to be found within my work. The detail I paint in means I can sometimes afford to select a certain part of a painting, focus in on it, and crop a new close-up. I'm always careful about the magnification of this cropped work so there is no loss of quality. Occasionally, these rules aren't always possible to follow. For instance, if I'm illustrating for a shop window or retail display, I will paint as large as is practical within the time I am given to do the job.

It is usual practice to paint an illustration a bit larger than is actually needed. Reducing the size of an image to fit an end product – for example, for packaging – always looks better than blowing it up, especially if the product requires sharp detail.

I keep all of my work in a photo library on my computer. I will often return to paintings to edit them into new compositions in Photoshop. This gives me the flexibility to try all sorts of different image crops. I work with two screens: a monitor and a laptop. This doubling up gives me space to view and compare the results.

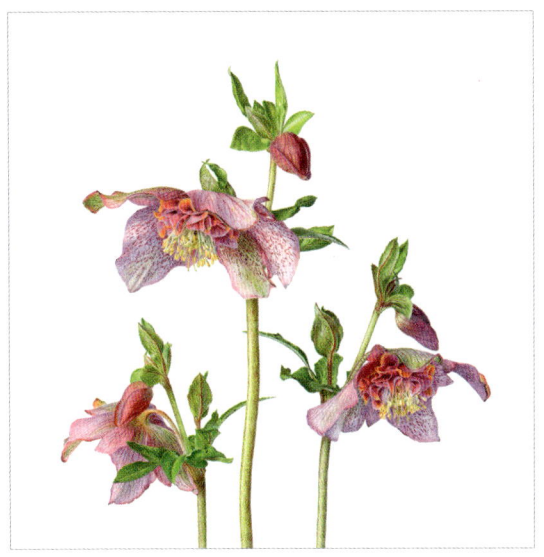 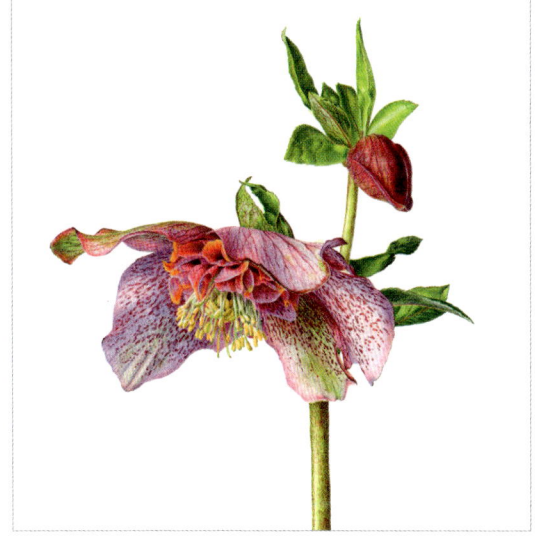

Above *Helleborus* x *hybridus*. The complete painting.

Above right The painting cropped and a part of a leaf removed from behind the stem.

Social media

It's lucky that the square format I often work in is perfect for Instagram, which is the social-media platform that works best for me. I use it solely as a portfolio. I like that it is a quite easy to use, well designed, visual space. Interestingly, any work I share there seems to receive more likes and positive feedback when cropped than when it's posted 'in full' (i.e. as the original composition). I suppose this is because most people are looking at my work on a smartphone screen as a small, quick, instant view, where these crops fill the screen and grab attention more readily. This discovery has made me change my mind about compositions in general. I plan to try out working at a much larger scale in the future, with just a single element in a simple composition. Obviously I wouldn't be doing this just to post on Instagram! But via this social-media route I have learned that bold, close-up images do seem to work very well.

When uploading work to social media it is important that the digital quality of my images is good enough to be seen on a computer screen as well as a smartphone. I scan my work at a high resolution (800dpi), so when I crop any of it there is no loss of quality.

I never used to scan my work at a high enough resolution and I regret this now. There is work I have done in the past that doesn't have the picture quality for me to be able to use it for other purposes, such as for prints or for relicensing.

Cropping for print design

I have designed my own sets of cards from a catalogue of my paintings. A lot of these I crop for the 'wow factor'. They need to be eye-catching enough to stand out in the retail setting of a shop's card display.

I was fascinated to find out that large card companies are most interested in the top half of a card's image, because when they are stacked on shelves the bottom half is not in view. Since making this discovery I have designed my cards accordingly – making sure there is enough to attract attention at the top of each design.

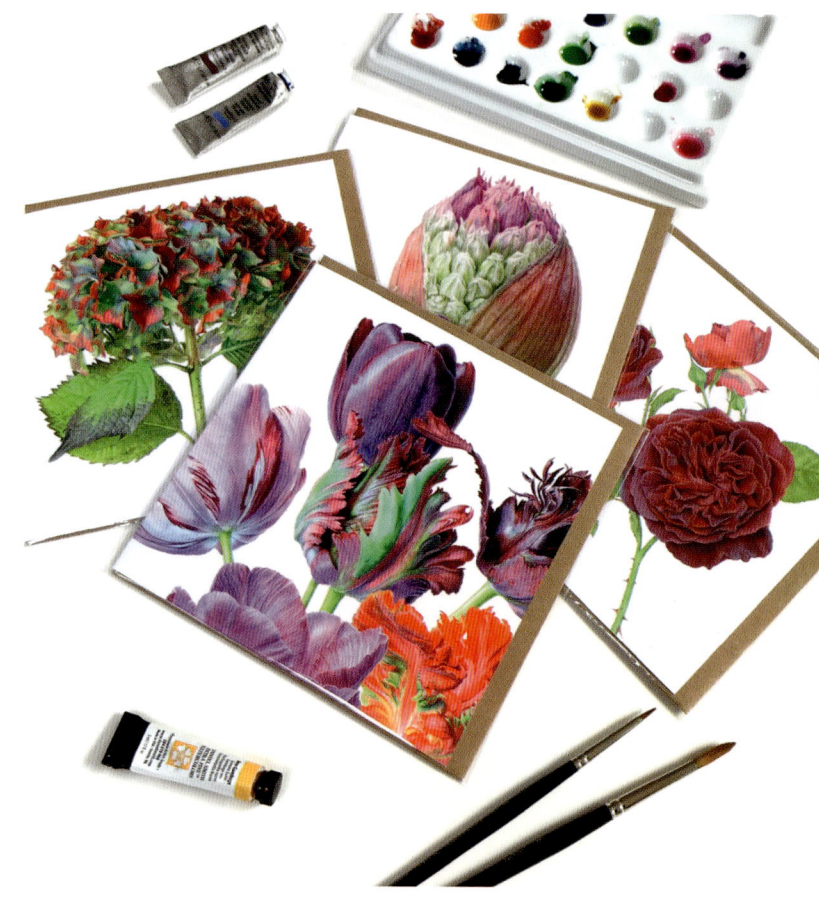

Above Cropping illustrations for card design. For the full, uncropped illustrations, see pages 33, 80, 96 and 107.

PHOTOGRAPHY AND PHOTOSHOP

Use of the camera and computer screen are intrinsic parts of my practice. I find that the highly detailed nature of my work means that working from life needs to be supported by sequences of photographic and digital back-up.

I never work from just one photograph because there will always be a part of the plant that is out of focus. I take several photographs of all parts of the plant at different focal lengths. This also ensures that I don't get the problem of distortion at the outer parameters of my subject. If I am working from life I don't have the problem of areas being out of focus. As I turn my specimen around, observing it from different angles, my eyes will deal with that!

Working in minute detail from photographs is different in that I will need to keep flipping from one shot to the next when painting. For instance, a single tulip flower in a photograph can be in focus at the front but the petals at the back blurred. In this case, I will paint one petal at a time to avoid having to constantly switch the image on my screen.

Right Working from a monitor. I enlarge the image on the monitor that I am working from to get the maximum amount of detail from the photographs I have taken.

Occasionally I have to work from stock photos – photographs I haven't taken myself. This usually depends on the demands of a client's brief. Some clients require very specific plants – for instance when the genus, species and variety have to be exact to match an ingredient in their product. Some commissions are less strict about being botanically accurate: a generic pink rose might be acceptable, its variety not essential but the openness of the flower, angle of the stem or amount of leaves can be especially important. I might have to collate multiple images from different sources into a visual whole – piecing together, gradually building my composition.

When I take my own pictures, I can keep the light constant and observe the relevant parts of the plant from my chosen angle. I do, of course, have to source the right plant to begin with though.

Once I have a series of photographs, I put them into Photoshop. I create a blank file and add the photographs in layers. This means

Below A view of a folder in my photo library showing how many pictures I take for one painting, with lots of different focal lengths and lighting, at different times of day, and both cool and warm lighting.

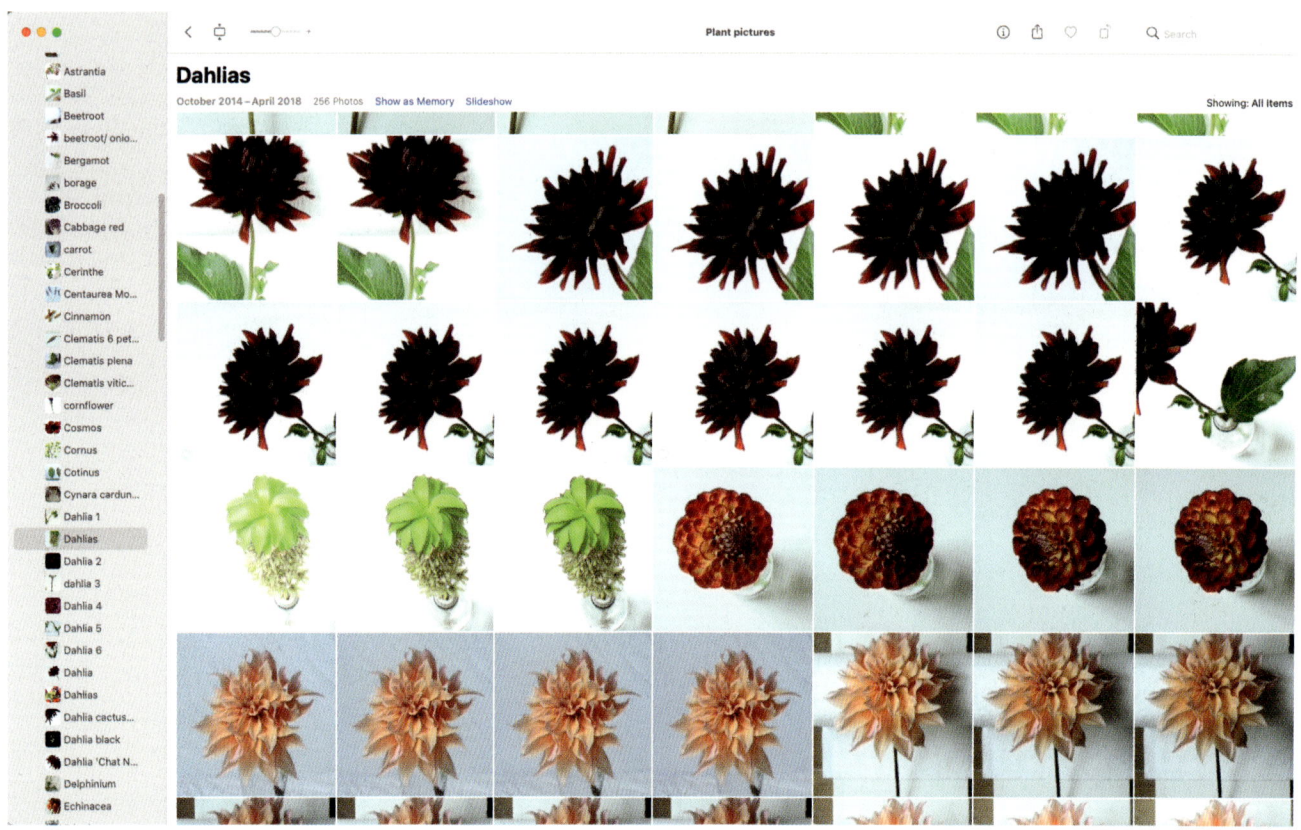

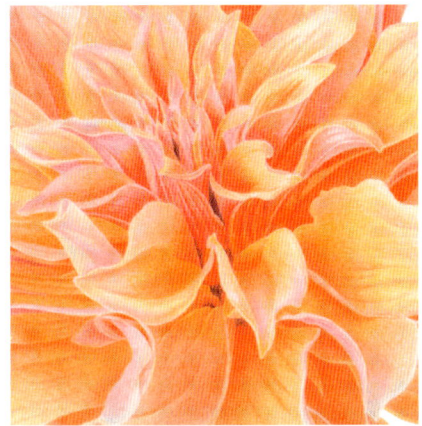

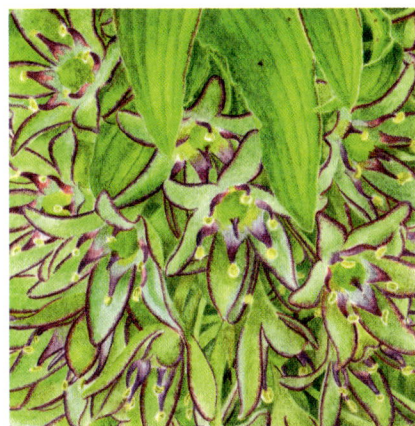

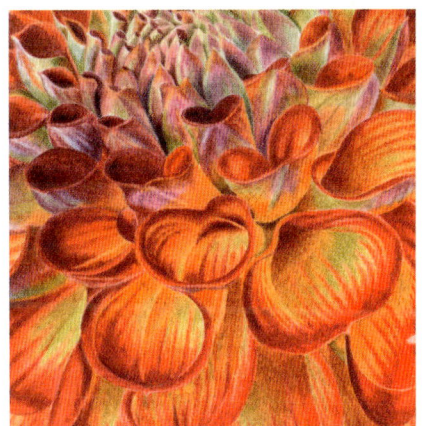

I can move them around and try lots of different compositions, turning layers on and off to see which elements work best, and where. I work on colours, brightness, saturation levels and so on before I start painting. This preparation helps me to decide how I want my painting to look – which may not be necessarily exactly botanically correct. This process usually takes me a couple of days and almost always I find I need more photographs to get the right elements for the composition I want.

Careful planning of the composition is very important. I do several different compositions using Photoshop and put them all up on my screen. I look at them from a distance, make my choices, then leave it and come back to it several times.

With commissioned pieces I am much more nervous about getting this process right – what if my client doesn't like the work after I've spent six weeks or so working on a painting? In practice this rarely happens because I usually send 'painted roughs' – line drawings with back-up photographic reference I've put together in Photoshop prior to the painting process – to make sure the client is happy with how I am approaching the composition. I will often provide three or four alternatives.

I spend more time getting the composition right before I start a private commission or an illustration job. When I paint for myself I'm probably less careful about that aspect. If I'm painting a self-directed piece, working from something I absolutely love, I'm occasionally a bit overenthusiastic, don't give things enough consideration and have to start all over again.

Above Three close-up details of dahlias and eucomis. Painted from several photographs I took of these plants.

Case Study – Tulips

1 Composing using Photoshop Elements: I add layers to a blank file using my chosen tulip photographs.

2 Using the Magic Wand tool to highlight the backgrounds and then the eraser tool to delete them.

3 The backgrounds of individual layers are now transparent, revealing the white of the main background.

4 Moving and tilting the layers to create a composition: I do several different compositions, save them to my desktop as jpg files, and look at them side by side to see which one works best. If I don't like any of them I'll go back and try more arrangements.

5 When the layers are how I want them I flatten the image (choose *layer, flatten image*). This means that the layers are combined and I can work on the lighting, contrast or colour of the overall picture. Here, I chose *enhance, lighting, brighten*.

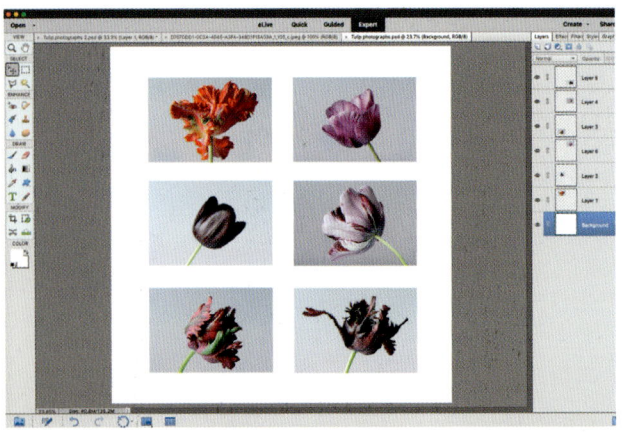

1

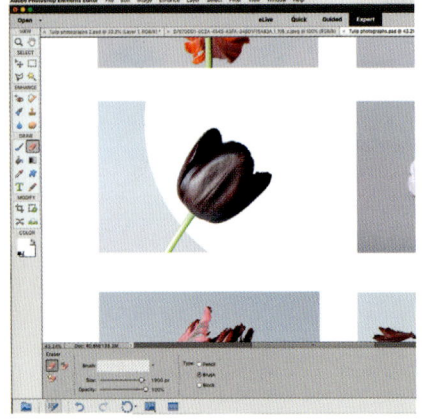

2

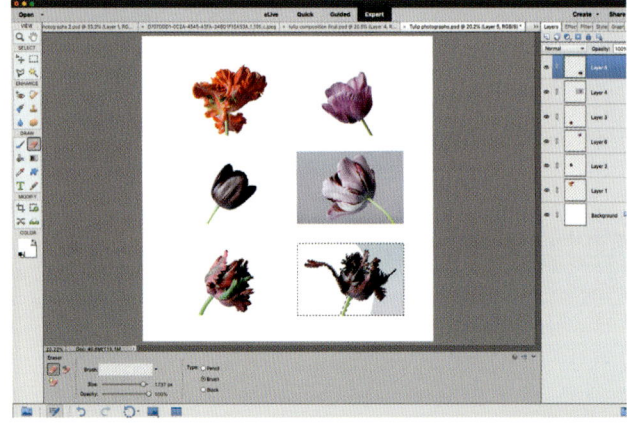

3

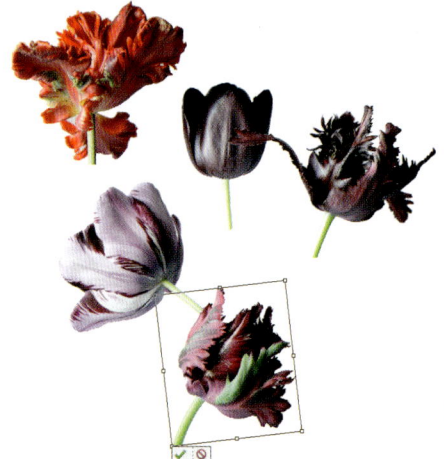

4

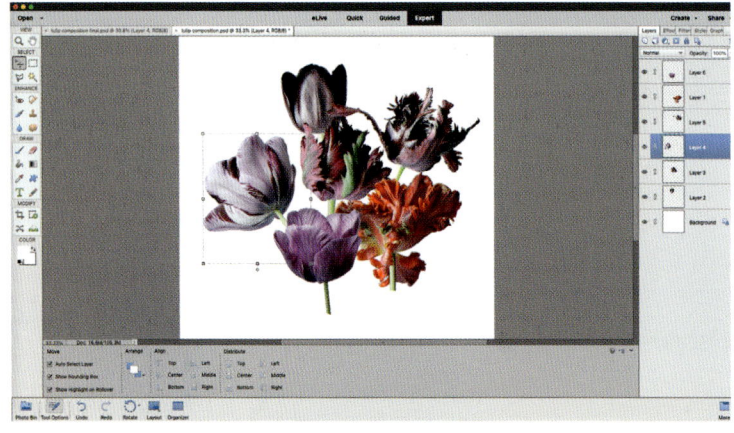

5

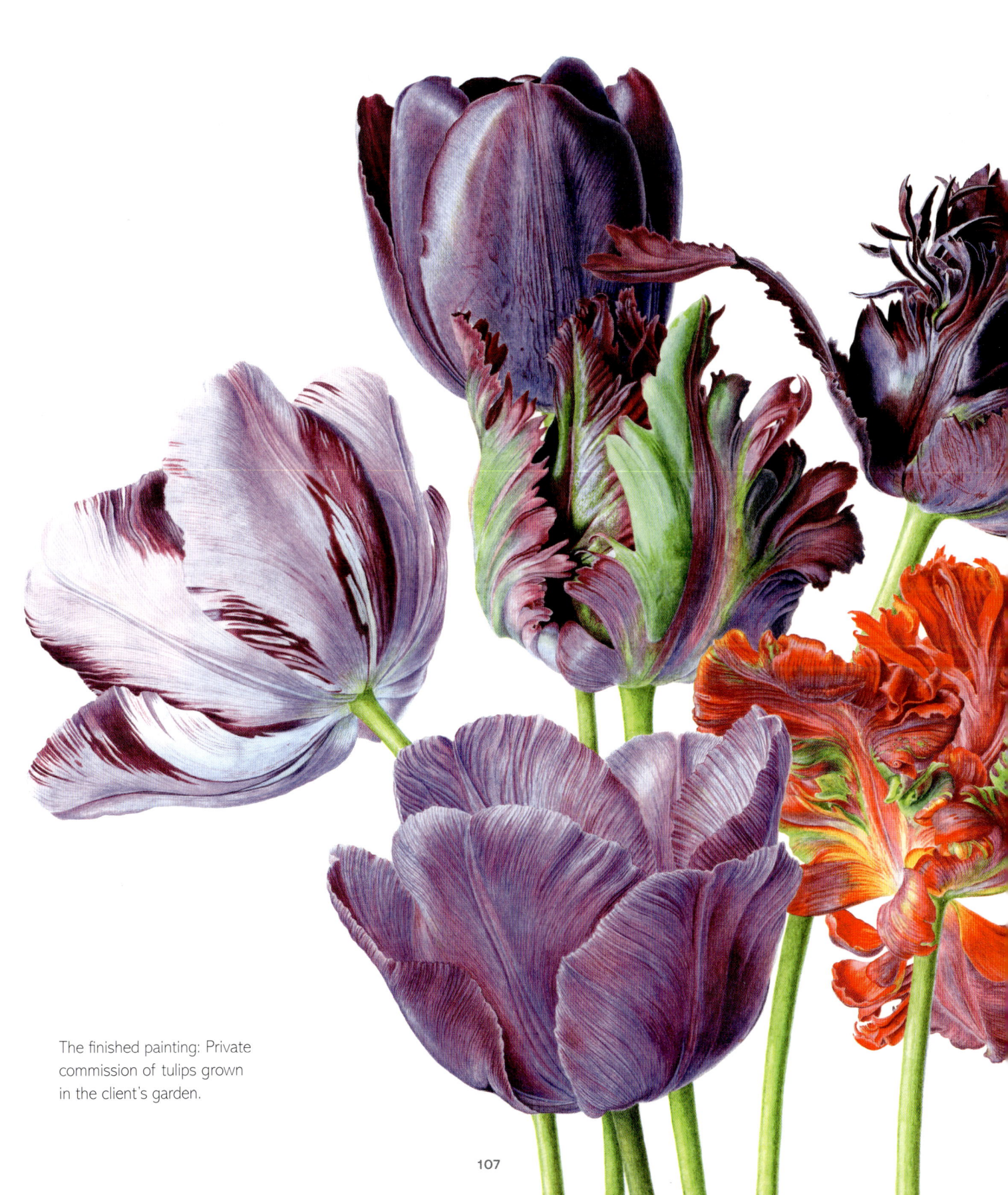

The finished painting: Private
commission of tulips grown
in the client's garden.

WORKING UP A DESIGN

When I'm finally happy with one of the arrangements I've created in Photoshop, I flip the image horizontally and print it out.

Transferring Images to Paper

I trace the printout with a fine HB pencil. At this point the image is back to front, so I turn the tracing paper over, making the image the right way around again. This is attached to my watercolour paper with masking tape, which is then secured to a drawing board, again with masking tape at the edges.

Using an HB pencil, I go over the drawing, rubbing gently along all the lines. This transfers the image on to the watercolour paper. Next, it's important to remove the masking tape and tracing paper carefully without touching the transferred image too much. The marks made by rubbing the tracing paper will be very powdery and will disappear very easily if touched.

Finally, trace back over all the lines very gently and lightly with a sharp pencil.

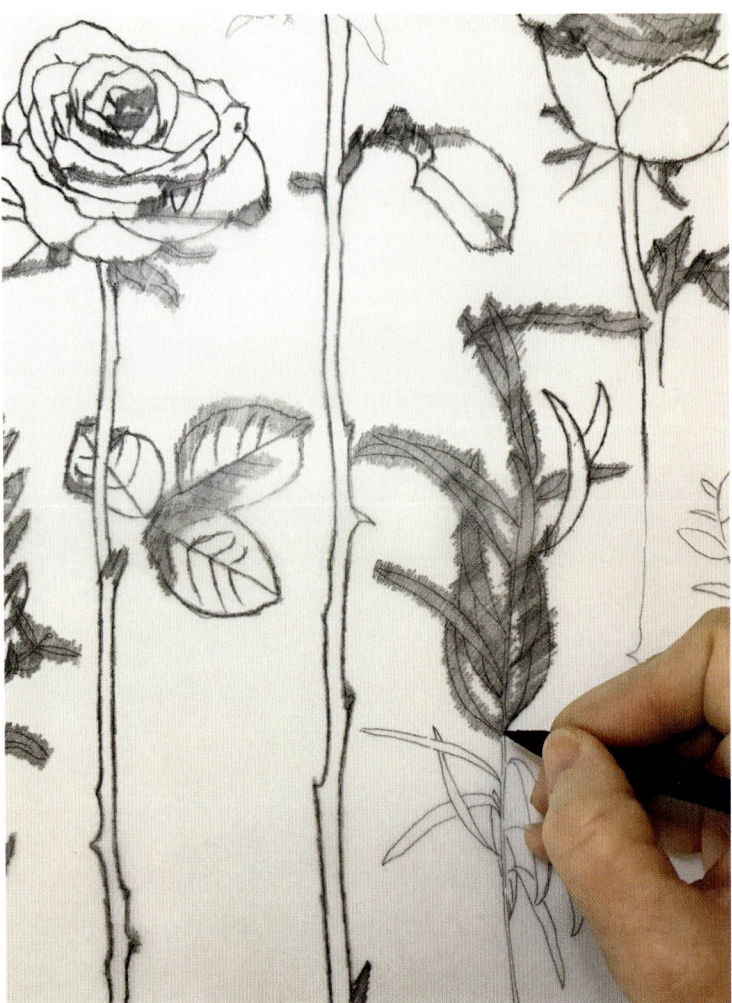

Left Transferring an image from tracing paper to watercolour paper.

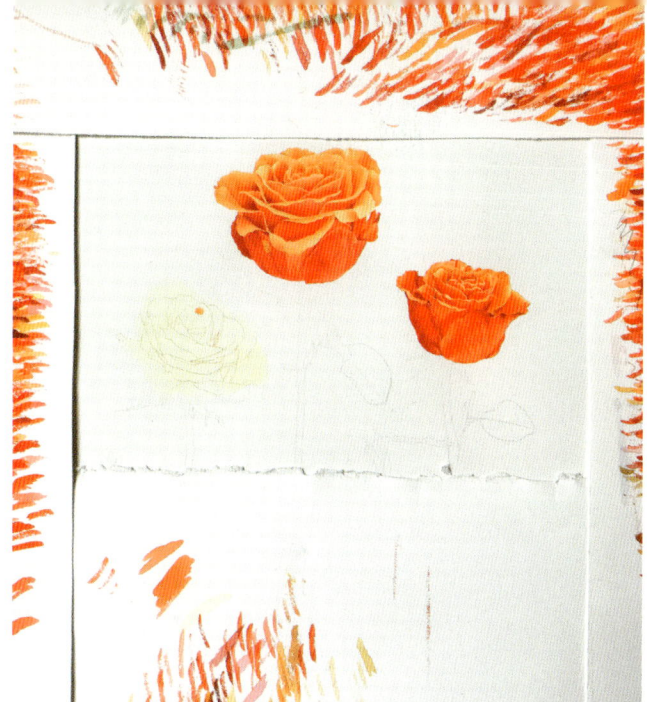

Left Mask off the areas of the painting you are not working on. Use watercolour paper so you can test the colours as you work.

Below A single rose and stem. A detail from the complete painting shown on page 120.

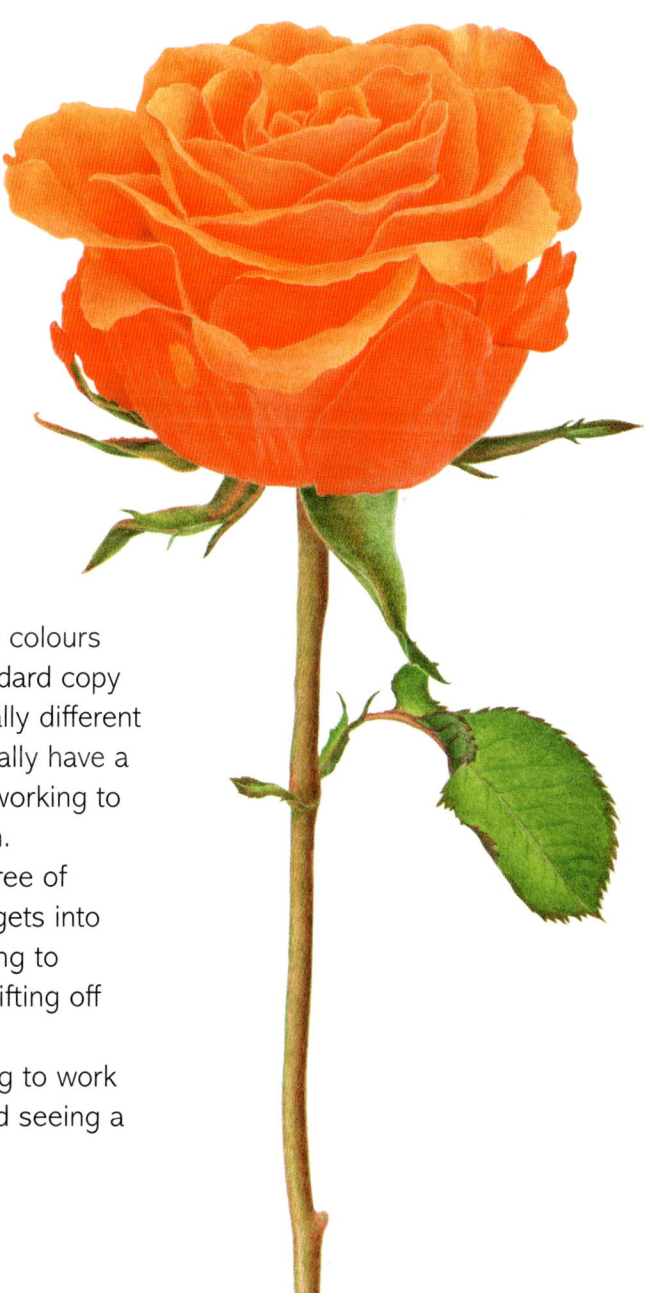

Preparing the Paper for Drawing

Use a putty rubber to dab all of the pencil lines carefully, lifting off the powdery pencil and lightening the pencil marks. Once watercolour paint goes over pencil marks, the line work or residue is very difficult to remove. Outlines should be as faint as possible while still being able to see them as a guide.

I mask off all the edges of the paper that won't be painted. Most people use tracing paper for this but I always use watercolour paper. It allows me to test my colours right next to where I'm working. I have tried using standard copy paper for this, but it doesn't work: the colours look totally different when they are painted on to the wrong surface. I normally have a sheet of watercolour paper that I move around as I'm working to lean my hand on and also to protect the paper beneath.

It's really important to try to keep the working area free of clutter and clean. Dust can be a real nuisance when it gets into the wet paint on the paper; I can drive myself mad trying to pick up a speck of dust with a paintbrush and end up lifting off previous layers of paint.

I usually work on one area at a time rather than trying to work on the whole picture. By finishing one small section and seeing a result, I'm encouraged to continue with other areas.

'Roses and Eucalyptus'

For this painting, shown on page 120, I started with the central flower and painted a pale wash of Indian Yellow over the whole area of the rose. I gradually built up thicker layers of the same yellow to create the darker areas, but each time mixed it with some Daniel Smith Transparent Pyrrol Orange (a wonderful deep, slightly rusty orange) to lay over the top with fine, light brushstrokes. I also used Yellow Ochre and Quinacridone Gold, a very rich yellow. As the painting advanced, I used a progressively drier brush, to avoid pulling off the layers of paint beneath. The deeper orange areas were created by mixing in scarlet-red, and finally Permanent Alizarin Crimson along with Winsor Blue and Transparent Pyrrol Orange, for the very darkest areas.

The rose stems, leaves and eucalyptus were painted last. For the greens I used mostly Winsor Blue (Green Shade) mixed with Winsor Yellow. I added Quinacridone Gold to knock back the brightness and to add some warmth – more for the rose leaves and less for the eucalyptus.

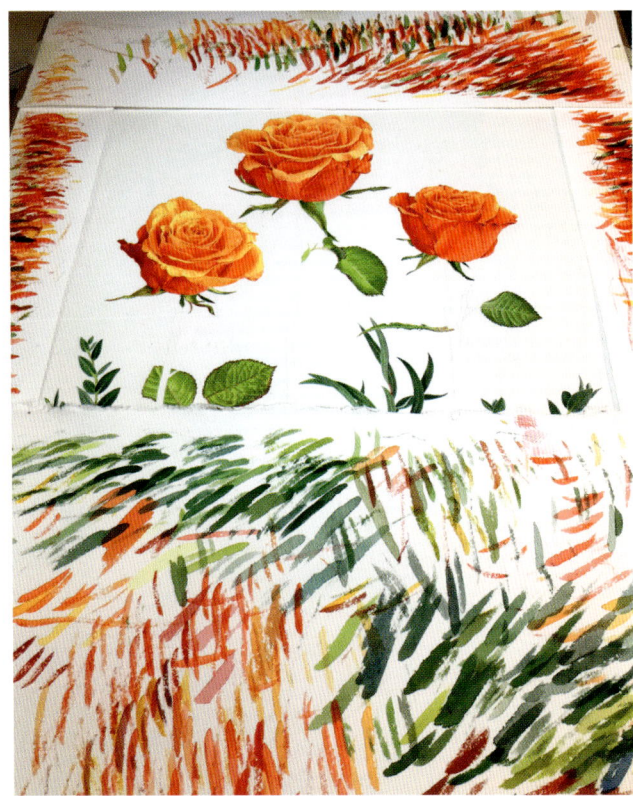

Far left A painted chart for colour reference.

Left Painting of roses and eucalyptus in progress. I always test my colours on spare watercolour paper so I can be sure it is exactly what I want.

(UN)USUAL SUBJECTS

I use the word 'unusual' to refer to ordinary subject matter as well as exotic, rare or expensive specimens. It is often the ordinary and everyday that we take for granted and overlook.

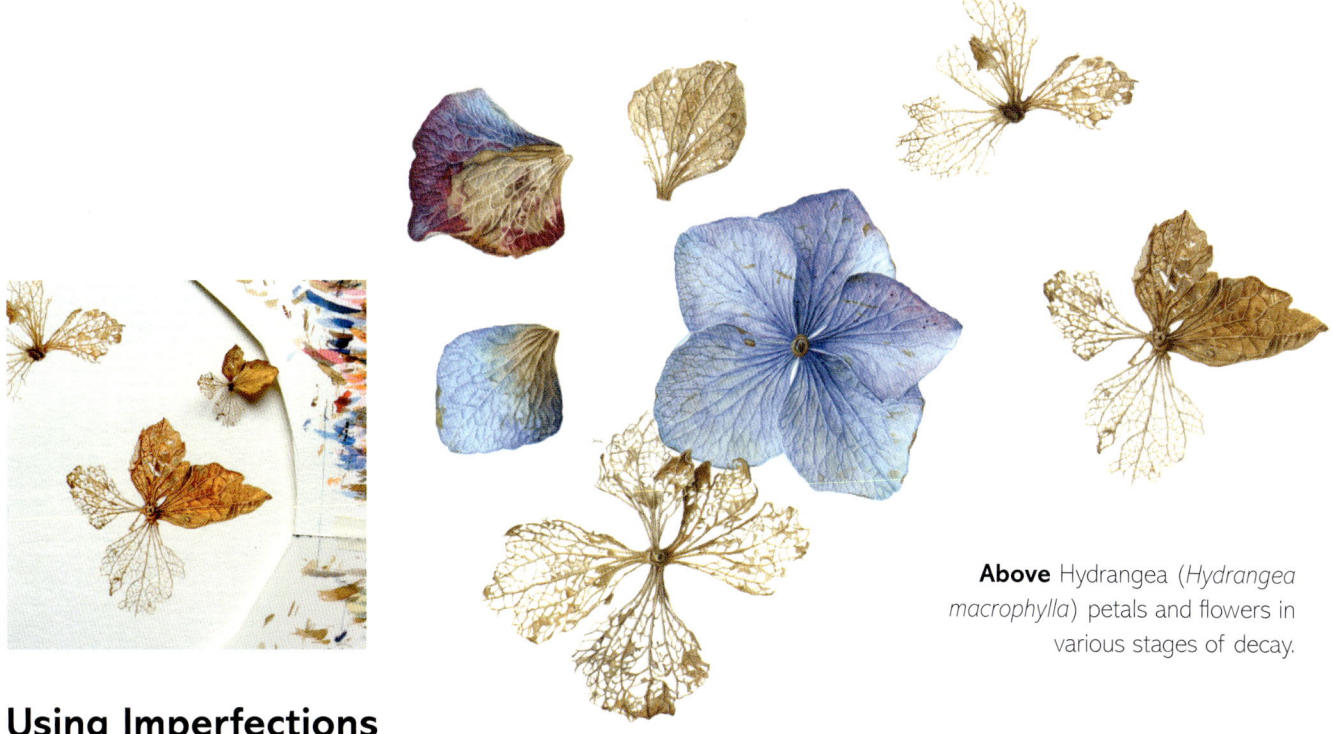

Above Hydrangea (*Hydrangea macrophylla*) petals and flowers in various stages of decay.

Using Imperfections

The idea of a perfect plant specimen makes me think of the amazing plant and flower displays of specialist growers at the elite botanical exhibitions, perfect vegetables grown by competitors at county or even local village shows, and the beautiful blooms found in flower markets and good florists' shops.

When a botanical illustration focuses on the recording of imperfect specimens, not just flawless ones, the resulting painting is often more interesting. Perhaps these works could be thought of as plant portraits because they allow us to see a subject's 'real' life. For this reason I will often use the loose, dropped parts of a dying specimen in a composition to emphasize a plant's life cycle and mortality.

The painting above is a deconstruction of a mophead hydrangea's multiple flowerhead into its constituent parts. Seeing it like this can help us understand some of the complexity of the parts that make up one of the dramatic blooms. The composition also reveals a gradual change of colour – from bright blue to brown – as the plant dries out, until eventually a skeletal veined structure is revealed.

I tend to paint what I find. If something is starting to fade or is past its best but looks good to me, then I want to paint it. Occasionally I dry things on purpose: for example, heads of hydrangea flowers (single and whole), seedheads of poppy and magnolia, as well as many acorns, their cups and rosehips.

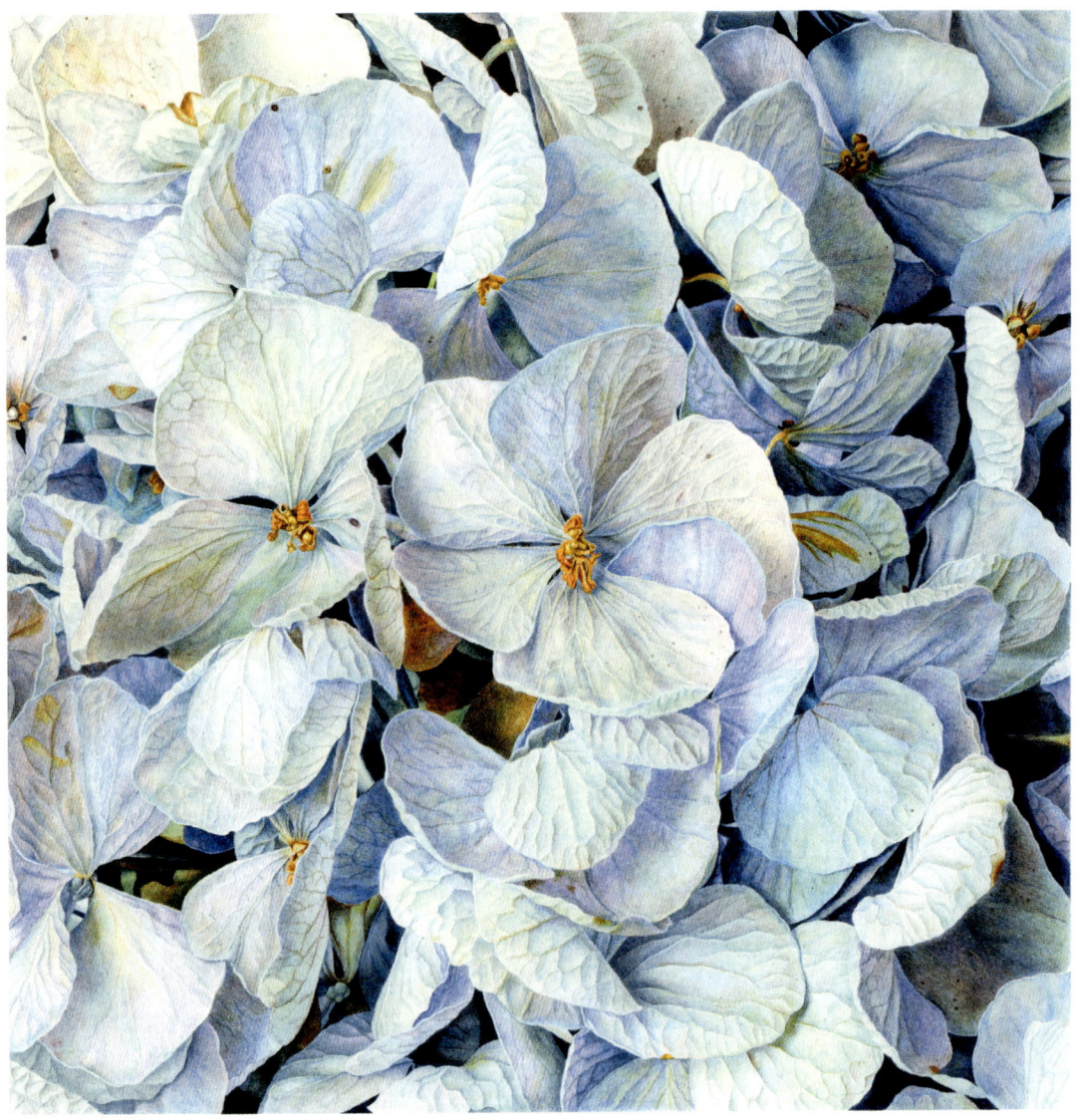

Mophead hydrangeas, like *Hydrangea macrophylla* 'Blue Danube', can be almost too perfect so I like to show the colour variations and changing textures of decay creeping in; I purposely waited for this flower (shown above) to dry out. I preferred it when its vivid blue faded and some warm colours crept in during the process of drying. I maybe waited a little too long, as the specimen I was working from lost most of its colour. It became such a pale blue as to be almost white. I enhanced the blue in my painting to liven it up again and also accentuated the golds and burnt siennas to create some interest and colour contrast.

Hydrangeas dry beautifully, which means they can be used as plant studies one intends to take time over. After drying they have stabilized, so there will be no more wilting. No more watering is necessary either.

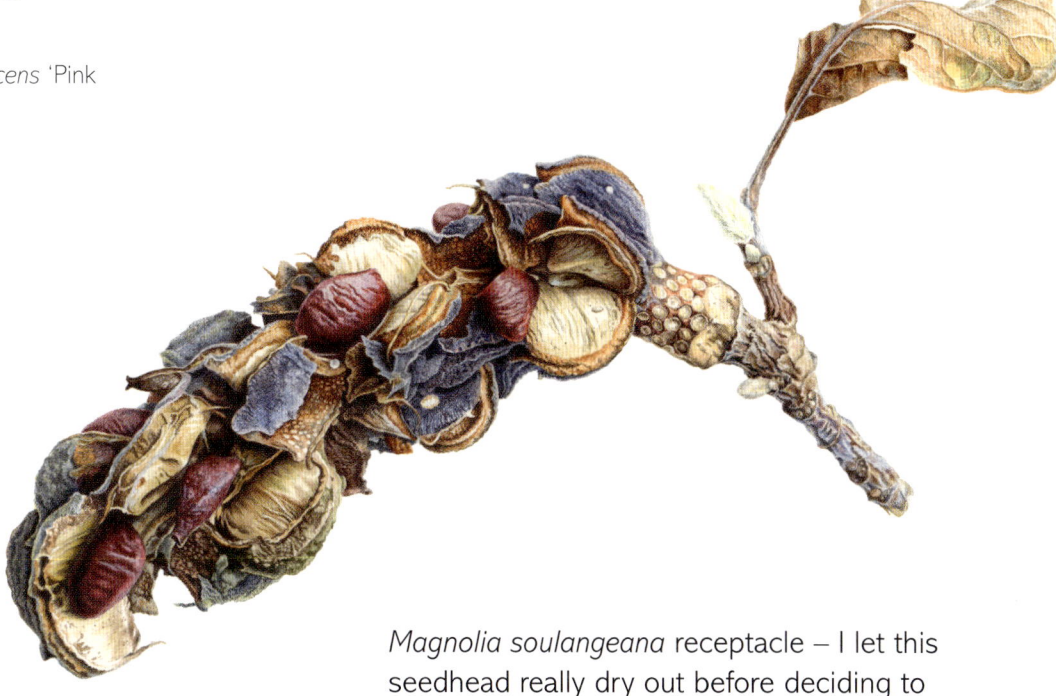

Magnolia soulangeana receptacle – I let this seedhead really dry out before deciding to illustrate it, liking the way the brilliant red berries faded and other more muted colours appeared. The textures of this magnolia seedhead are so varied: smooth, suede-like, wrinkled, and with incredible surface patterns. I found it a more interesting subject to paint like this than when it was fresh from the tree.

Hydrangea arborescens is normally less regular in shape when compared to the *macrophylla* (mophead) variety. It is less dense and you can see space through the small flowerheads. This one (shown left) was painted as the flower was 'going over' so there were some subtle shades of gold creeping in as it decayed – some small seedheads were forming too. I liked including another imperfection – the crispy texture of the withered, dying leaf.

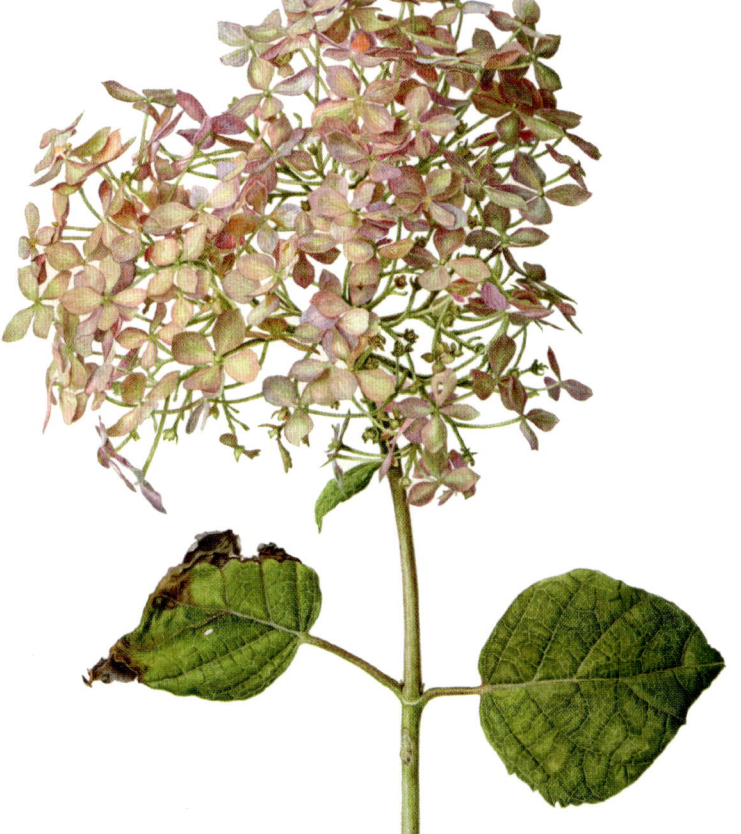

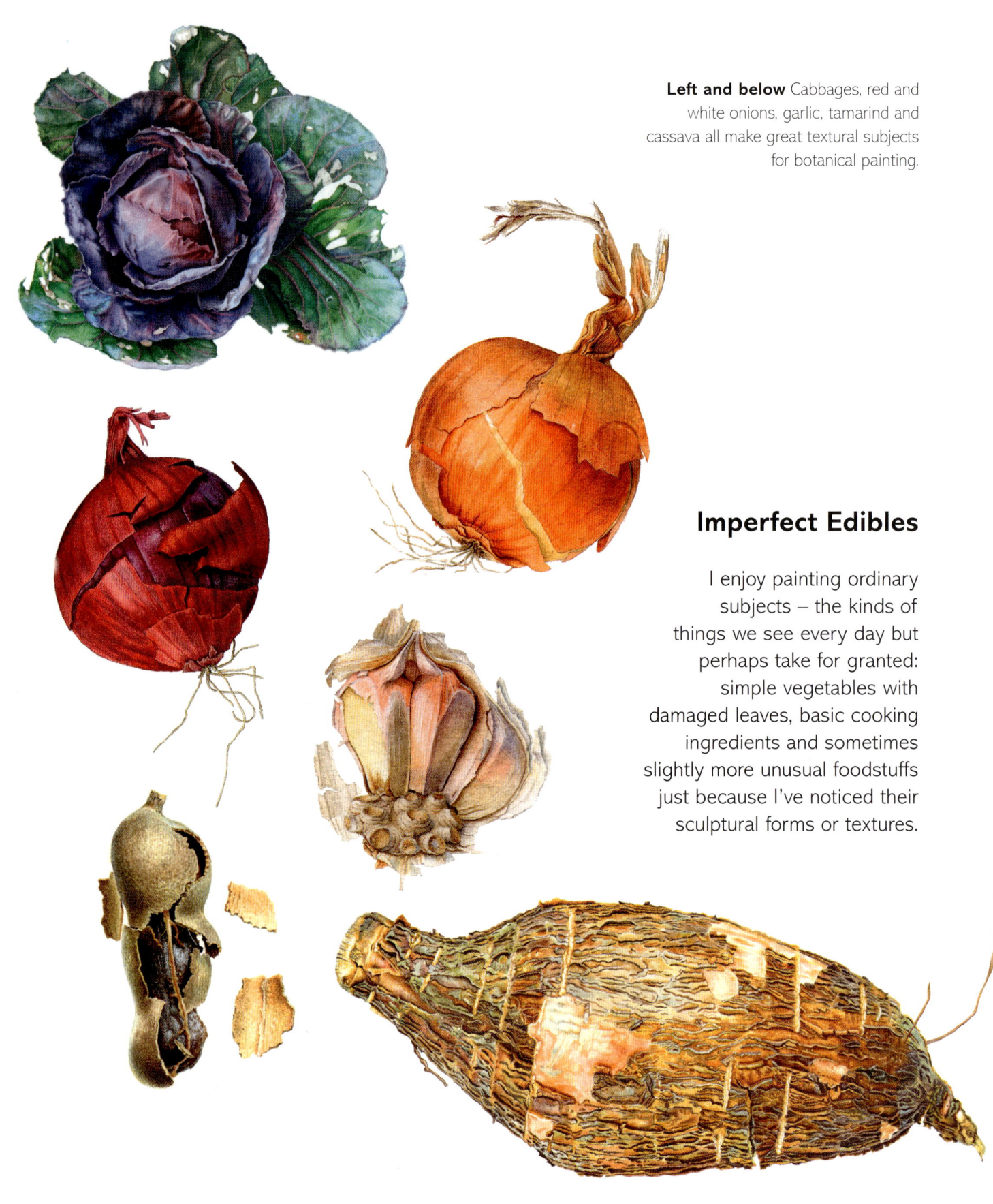

Imperfect Edibles

I enjoy painting ordinary
subjects – the kinds of
things we see every day but
perhaps take for granted:
simple vegetables with
damaged leaves, basic cooking
ingredients and sometimes
slightly more unusual foodstuffs
just because I've noticed their
sculptural forms or textures.

Fruit and Vegetables

When I first started becoming interested in botanical subjects, I seemed to paint a lot of fruit and vegetables. I think that was mainly because I didn't have my own garden and also because the subject matter is relatively easy to find and is fairly stable: it takes a while before most fruit and vegetables dry up and change their appearance. This gave me plenty of time to study and paint them. It was very satisfying to paint something so 'everyday', take the time to really look at it, and find so many colours and interesting details to illustrate.

Alliums are really easy plants to grow, most producing lovely bold, pompom-like flowers in the spring and summer — the bees absolutely love them. They also go on to produce wonderful ornamental seedheads. The allium family consists of hundreds of species. Many are cultivated edible bulbs that we are all familiar with, including onions, garlic and chives.

Alliums (shown right) is a very early work of mine. Looking at the painting I realize that right from the beginning I was interested in different textures although I would work in more detail if I was painting them now.

Fresh purple garlic (centre right) is sold in huge bunches in the markets of France in April and May. Passing the stalls I genuinely love the overpowering smell of the garlic and it really is a truly wonderful sight.

The cabbage, again, is a very early piece of work. Here, I was fascinated by the variety of colours and the surface patterns on the leaves made by the bumps and veins. I used three different cabbages for this painting and started working at the centre so that as the outside leaves wilted I could replace them with fresh leaves from a newer cabbage.

Above Alliums of all kinds — from garlic (*Allium sativum*) and round-headed garlic (*Allium sphaerocephalon*) to chives (*Allium schoenoprasum*) and onion (*Allium cepa*) —provide interesting colour and texture.

Right January King Cabbage.

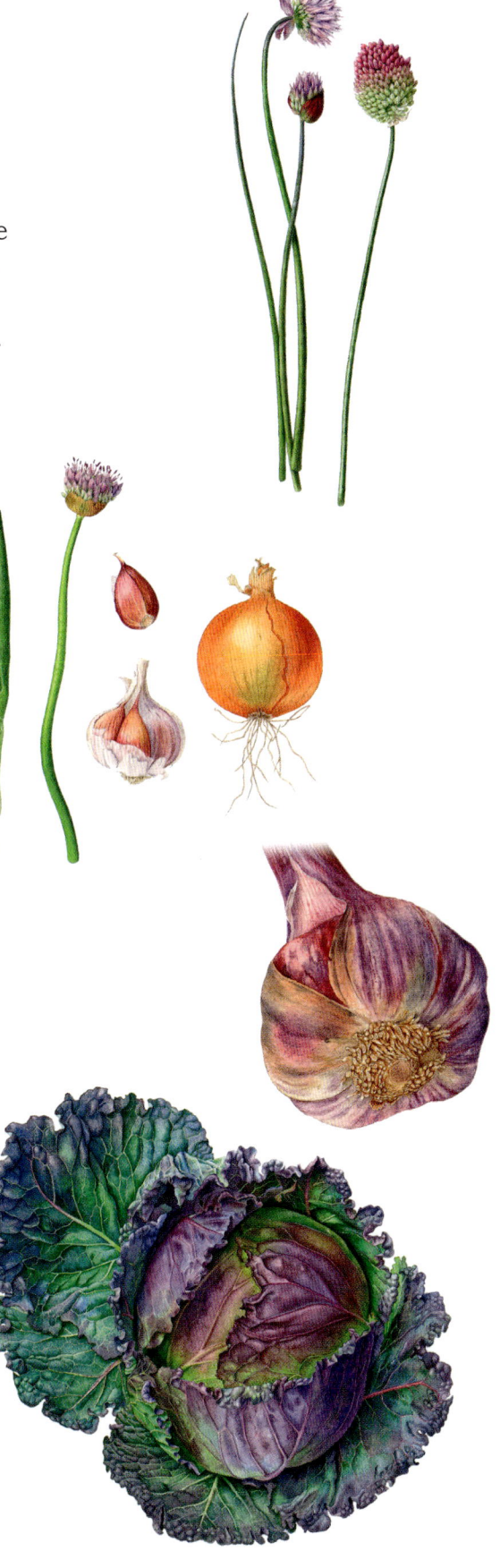

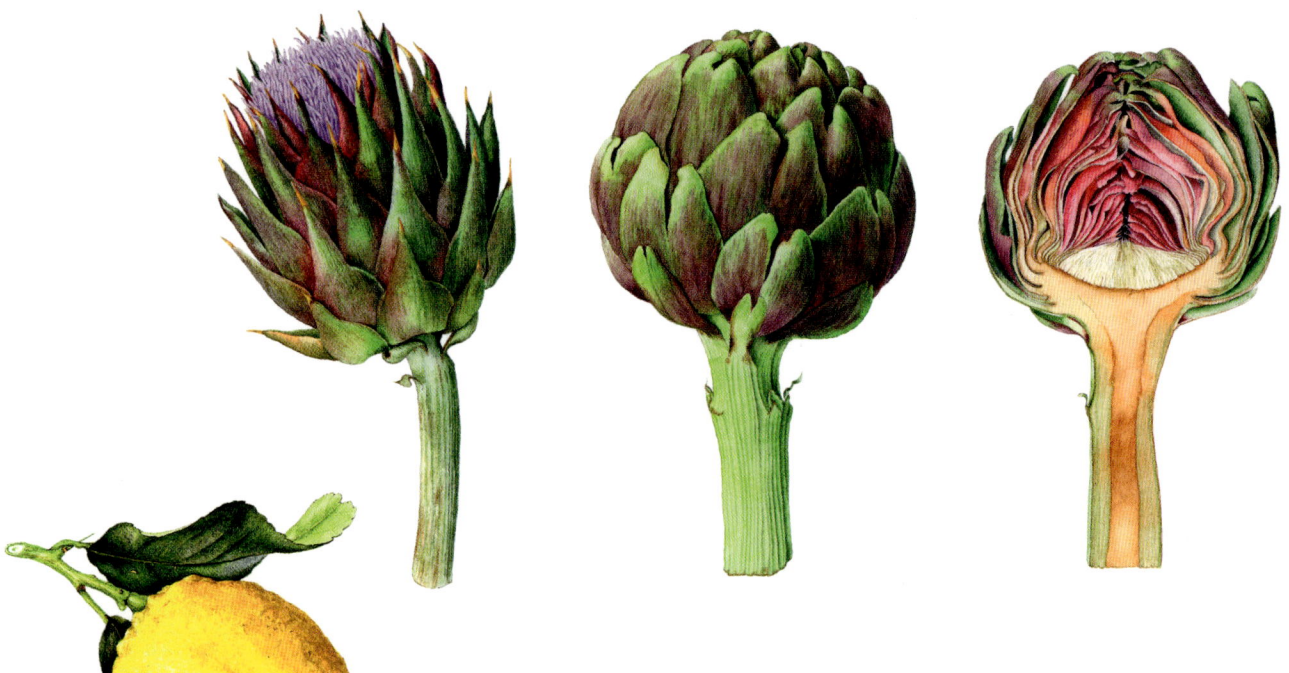

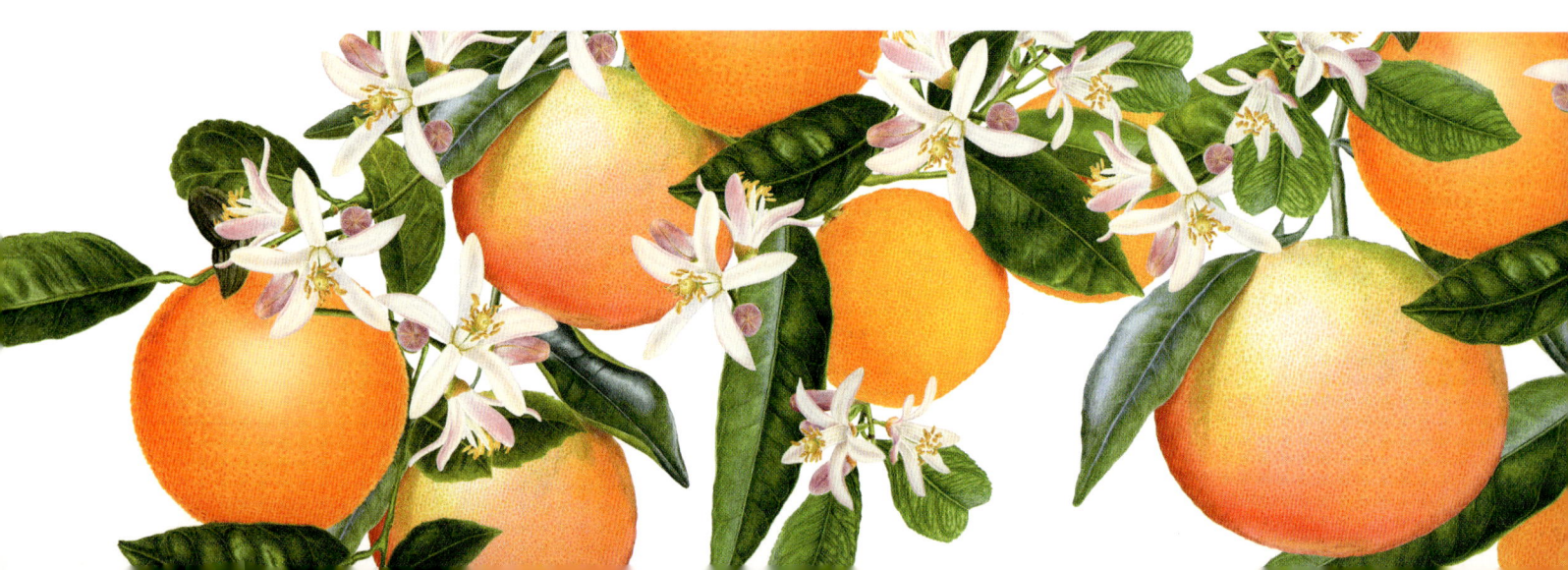

Above Lemon (a commission for Petersham Nurseries Café) and a globe artichoke and pomegranates, showing different views and cross-sections.

For the globe artichoke (*Cynara scolymus*) above I examined pattern, texture and other colours emerging from the greens. This was probably the first time I cut a plant in half to show the interior workings. It's interesting to see the cream-coloured feathery hairs inside (the choke), which eventually become the beautiful purple florets of the artichoke flower.

The early painting of a lemon (left) is in a much looser style. It was painted for the Petersham Nurseries Café business card. All the ingredients used at the restaurant were of high quality and mostly organic. This beautiful Italian lemon was given to me to paint by the then chef, Skye Gyngell. I used to work in the plant nursery at Petersham under Lisette Pleasance, an amazing plantswoman and

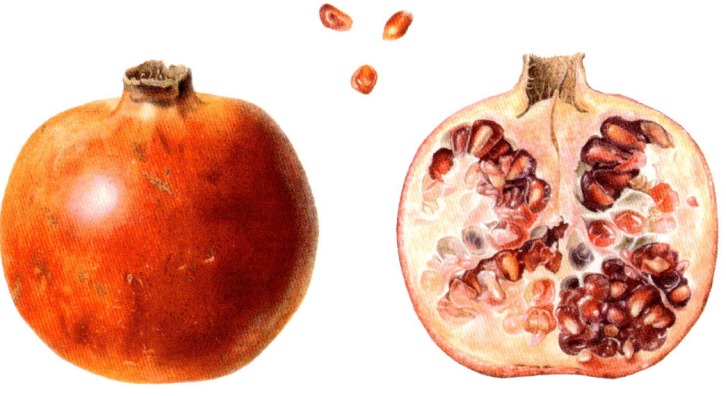
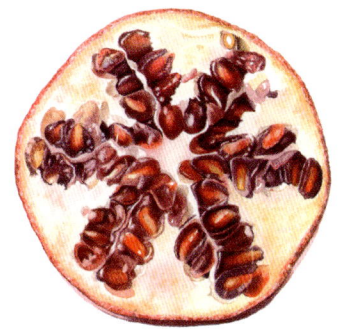
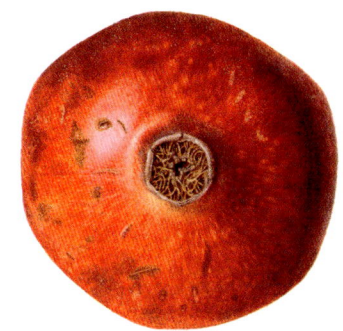

garden designer who I learned so much from, especially about using colour and form for designing planting plans.

The bergamot (*Citrus bergamia*) is thought to be a hybrid of a bitter orange and a lemon. It is used as the flavouring in Earl Grey tea and is also used as a perfume.

The pomegranate fruit (shown above) is so interesting to paint as it has a variety of surfaces and textures: sharp glistening highlights on the wetness of the seeds, a less harsh highlight on the smooth, slightly waxy surface of the outer skin, and softer shadows and highlights on the matt surface of the pith to show the hollows where the seeds once were.

I painted all of the elements in the image below separately: the orange, tangerine, pink grapefruit and neroli flowers. They have been put together beautifully by designer Matthew Axe into a really energetic and vibrant composition, with the fruits, leaves and flowers cleverly positioned and overlaid.

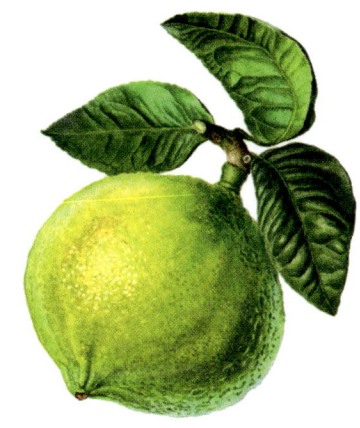

Above Bergamot (*Citrus bergamia*)

Below Tangerine, orange, pink grapefruit and neroli. A composition of repeated and repositioned illustrations form a stunning design.

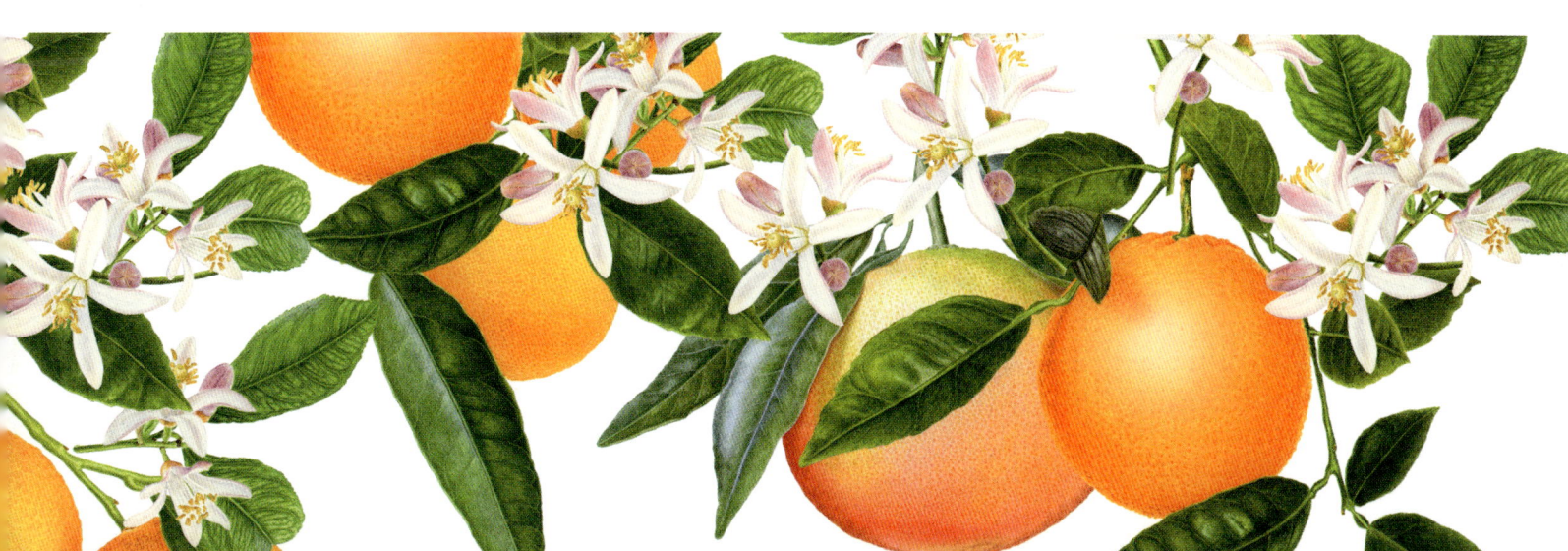

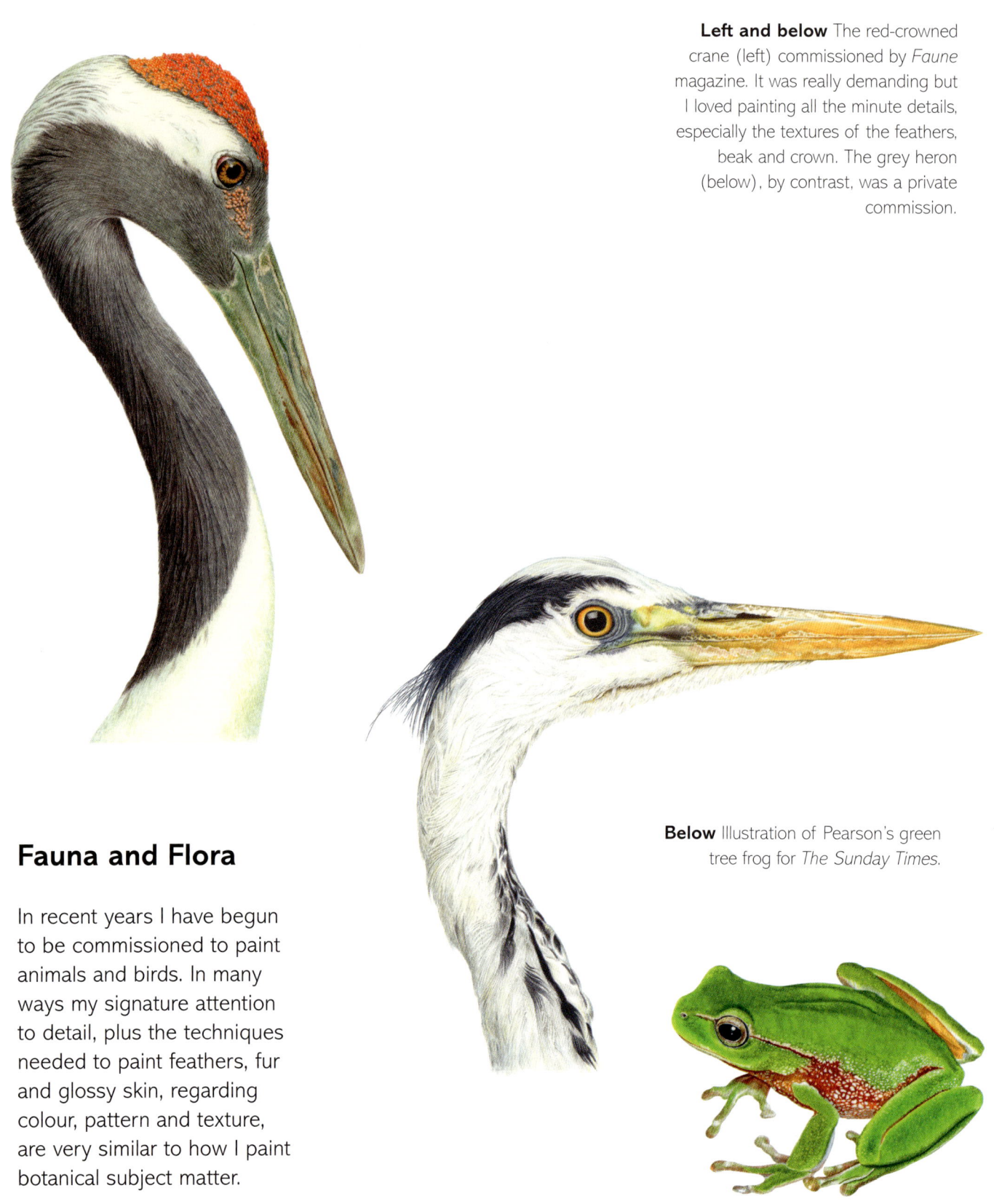

Left and below The red-crowned crane (left) commissioned by *Faune* magazine. It was really demanding but I loved painting all the minute details, especially the textures of the feathers, beak and crown. The grey heron (below), by contrast, was a private commission.

Below Illustration of Pearson's green tree frog for *The Sunday Times*.

Fauna and Flora

In recent years I have begun to be commissioned to paint animals and birds. In many ways my signature attention to detail, plus the techniques needed to paint feathers, fur and glossy skin, regarding colour, pattern and texture, are very similar to how I paint botanical subject matter.

COMMISSIONS AND COMMERCIAL: A DIVERSE PORTFOLIO

I am regularly commissioned to produce paintings. The requests for these are equally divided between commercially oriented illustration work, which comes via my agent, and private painting work commissioned by individuals. I don't have a preference for either and I'm happy to paint any plant as long as I can get some good reference to work from. For private commissions it is nice to be able to broadly choose the type of composition.

Like many artists who take on commissioned work, I necessarily have parameters for the kind of work I tend to do. For instance, a client will probably want to hire me because of my detailed style of painting – being asked to imitate someone else's work wouldn't work for me. Trying to execute a more simplistic style with much less close scrutiny just wouldn't be an authentic reflection of my style of painting.

It is hard to sell your own work, so I am glad to have an agent acting as a middleman. I'm represented by the illustration agency Folio Art, an established agent with a good network of clients that they can show my work to. They also deal with the negotiation of fees, contracts, invoicing and so on, which allows me to get on with my painting.

When I take on botanical painting commissions I sometimes consider the visibility and kudos they might bring me as well as any financial reward. For instance, I might take on lesser-paid work if it is something that really interests me, or that I think will be good for my portfolio.

Commercial illustration for advertising or for use as botanical imagery on a product usually pays relatively well. If an illustration is used in a publication, it tends to be the case that the more prestigious it is, the smaller the fees.

Below Peony, chamomile and hawthorn.

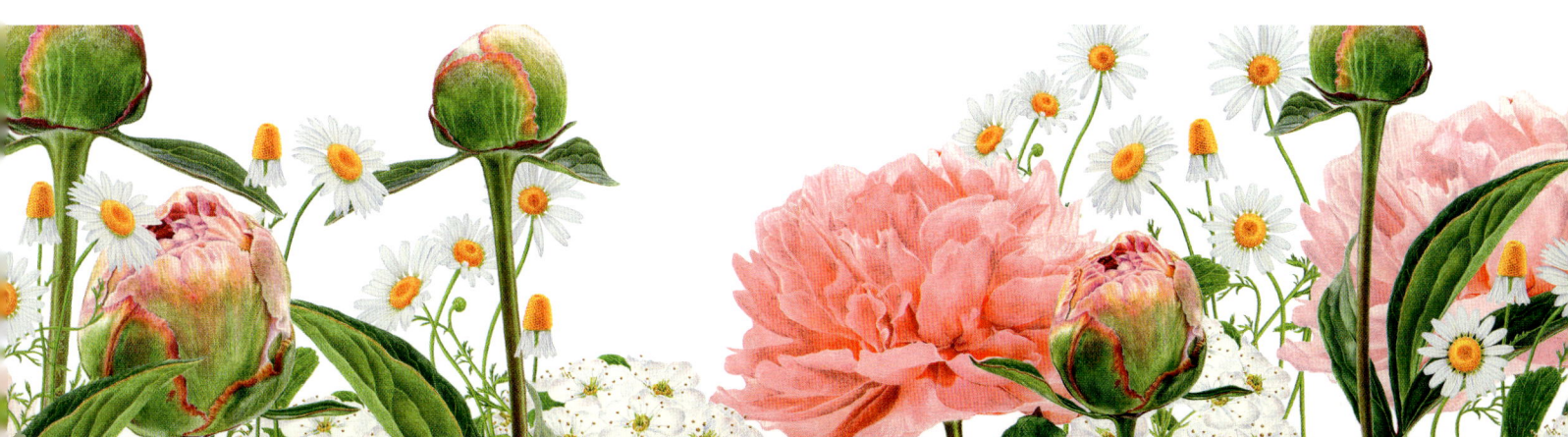

Non-commissioned Work

In addition to commissioned work, I produce my own portfolio of non-commissioned work. At these times I paint whatever I wish without the input or influence of others. This personal work is usually done from plants in my own garden and occasionally from something interesting I might spot in a florist's shop or garden centre.

I have sold these paintings through exhibitions such as the annual RHS Botanical Art Show and via private galleries.

Social media is becoming an important part of raising awareness of my work. I've been approached through this route regarding both illustration and private work. A lot of my sales simply come from being contacted for any paintings that are available.

Orange Roses and Eucalyptus – Preparing for a Commission

One of my most recent commissions was for a friend as a 30th wedding anniversary present. He sent me an image of their original wedding posy of orange roses and eucalyptus, asking me to design and paint a contemporary version of it. He was happy with my idea of the elements of the posy laid out in a more graphic manner (shown right).

It took several days to source plants that were as close a match as possible. I bought bunches from various florists and market stalls before I was happy with the variety and different stages of maturity of the roses. (Most roses I found were too yellow, rather than the deep orange needed, and too tight in shape.)

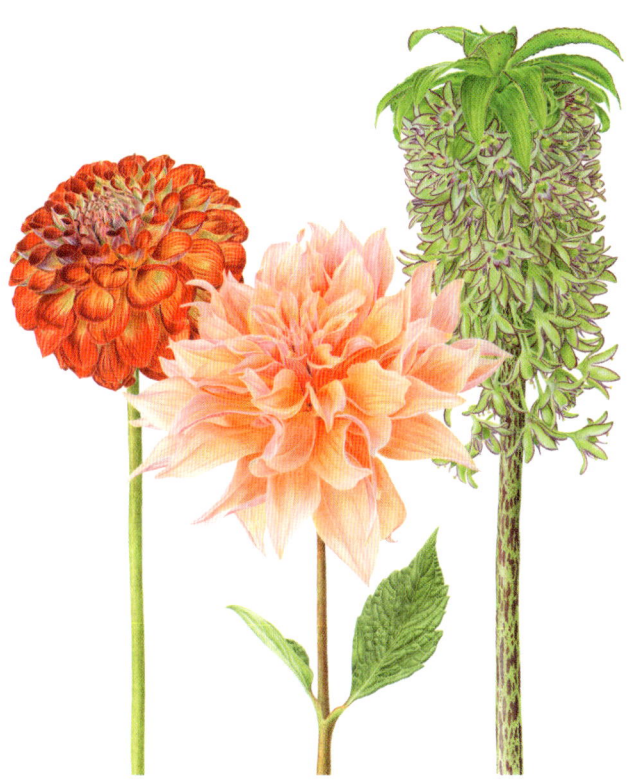

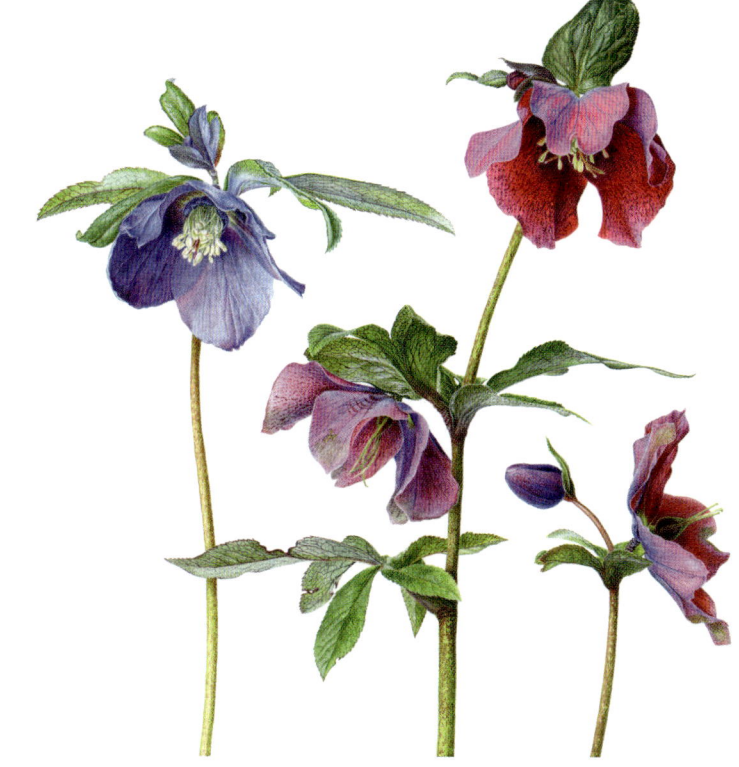

Commissioned Paintings from Clients' Gardens

These were all commissioned by the same couple. They have an exquisite and extremely large garden in London, full of the most interesting and wonderful plants. The first painting of hellebores was commissioned by the husband as a birthday present for his wife; she then went on to commission more paintings from me. I was able to choose and collect a huge range of stunning fresh flowers from their garden for each picture and take them back to my studio. It really was the perfect job.

Clockwise from top left *Dahlia* and *Eucomis*, *Helleborus* x *hybridus* and *Rosa* 'Munstead Wood'.

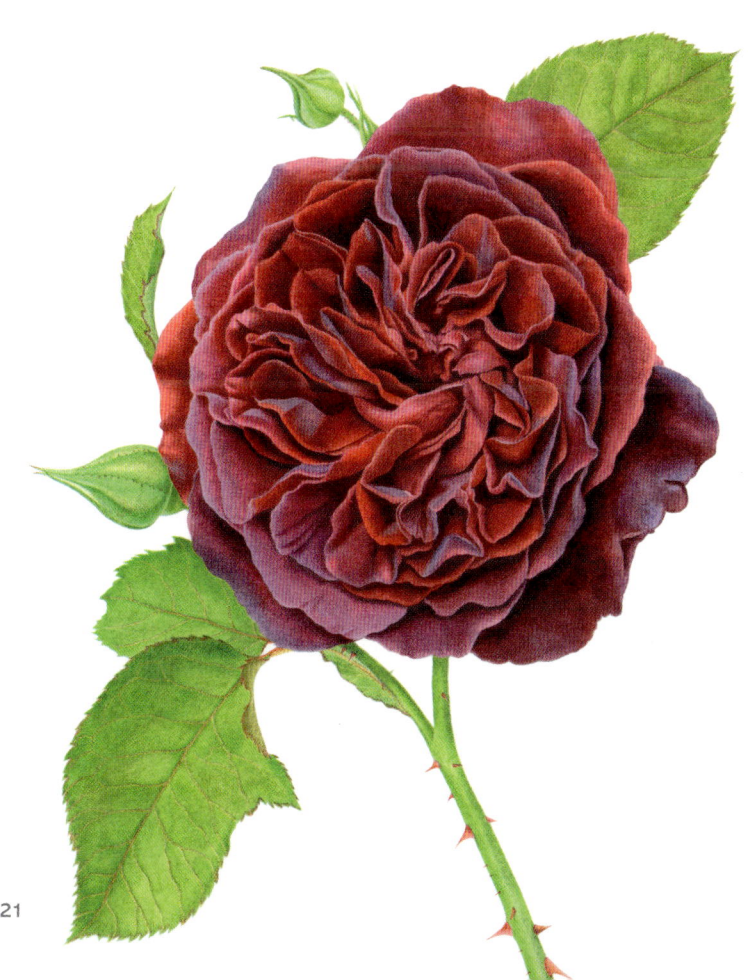

Rosa Wollerton Old Hall was commissioned by a friend; it is her favourite rose, a stunning David Austin-bred climber. It has the most perfect large cupped, almost white flowers, with subtle shades of very pale yellow and apricot. It is renowned for its strong myrrh scent. Oddly, I really don't like the smell and found it quite hard to have to sit with it in my studio for so long! Part of the brief was that the background should be dark, as it was to hang alongside other paintings with blackish backgrounds. I normally leave the background white, but I did think that the contrast of the pale rose against the dark tones worked very well.

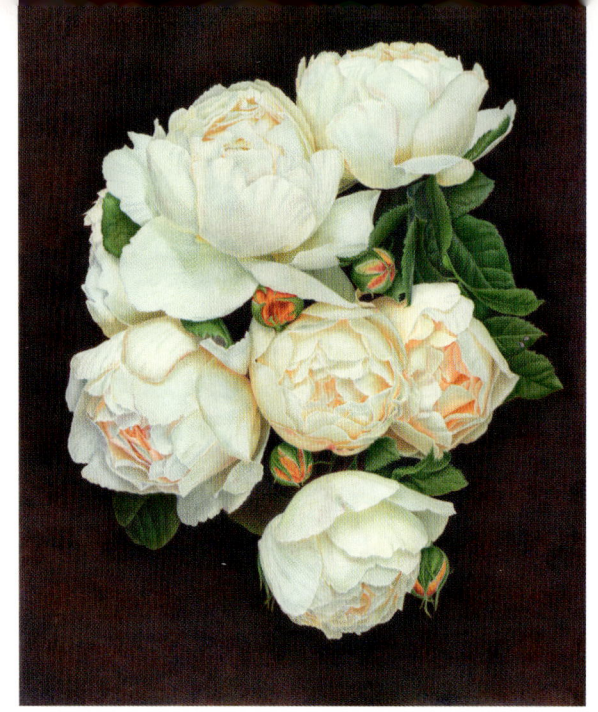

Above *Rosa* Wollerton Old Hall. See pages 86–87 for an earlier stage of the painting and a closer veiw of the detail involved in capturing these beautiful flowers.

Below *Rosa* 'Souvenir du Docteur Jamain' One of my sister Nathalie's favourite roses.

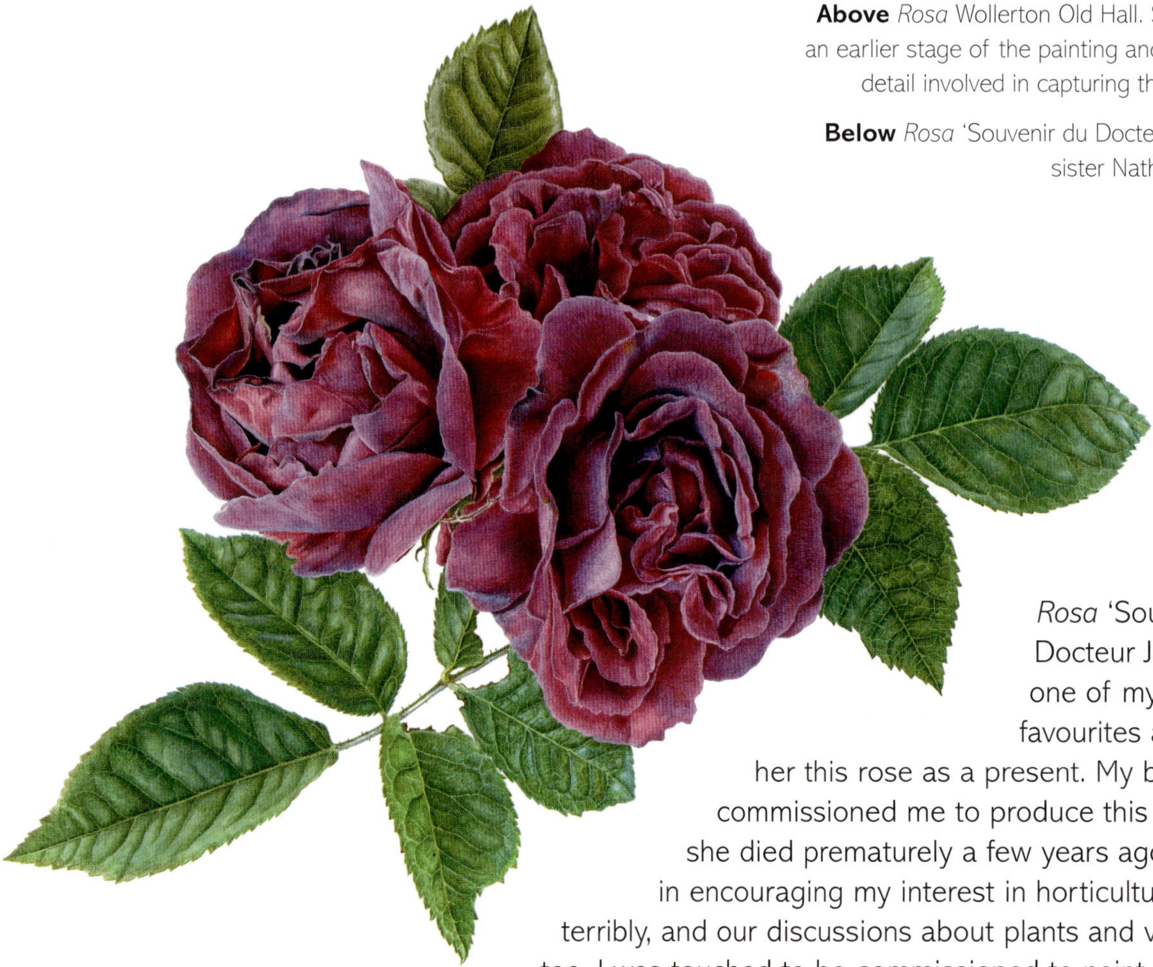

Rosa 'Souvenir du Docteur Jamain' was one of my sister's favourites and I had given her this rose as a present. My brother-in-law commissioned me to produce this picture after she died prematurely a few years ago. She was key in encouraging my interest in horticulture. I miss her terribly, and our discussions about plants and visits to gardens too. I was touched to be commissioned to paint this picture.

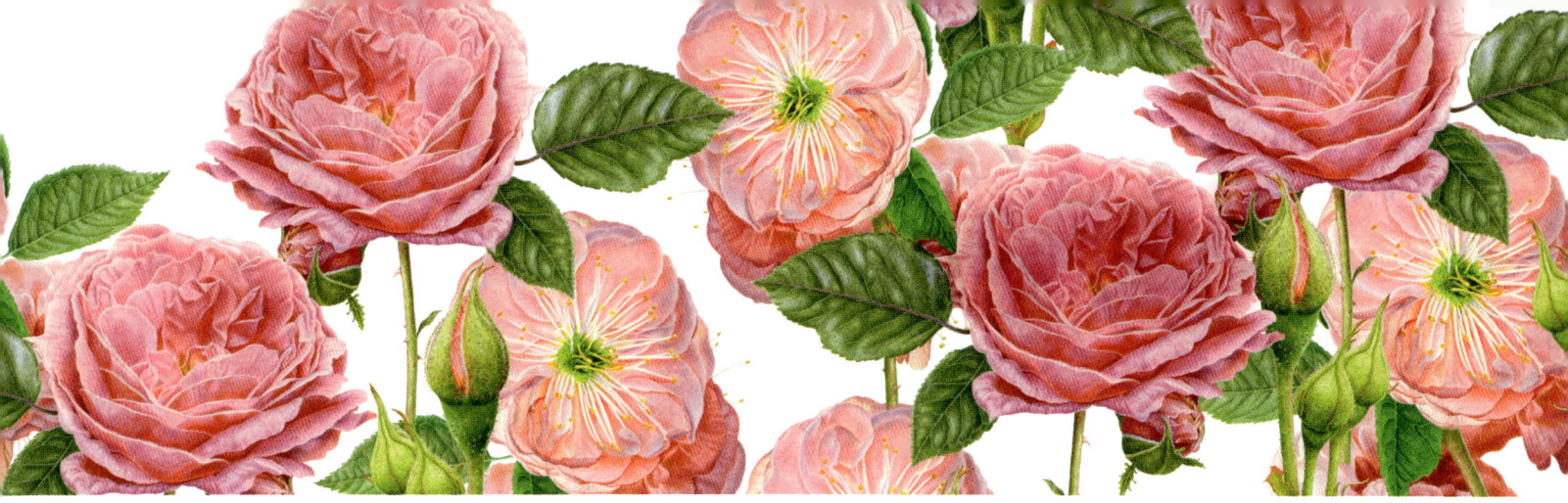

Commercial

These images were painted for a company producing skincare products made from natural botanicals: one for the olfactory senses as well as the visual.

Above Highly scented old variety Damask and Centifolia roses.

Below Rosewood, sage and vanilla flowers.

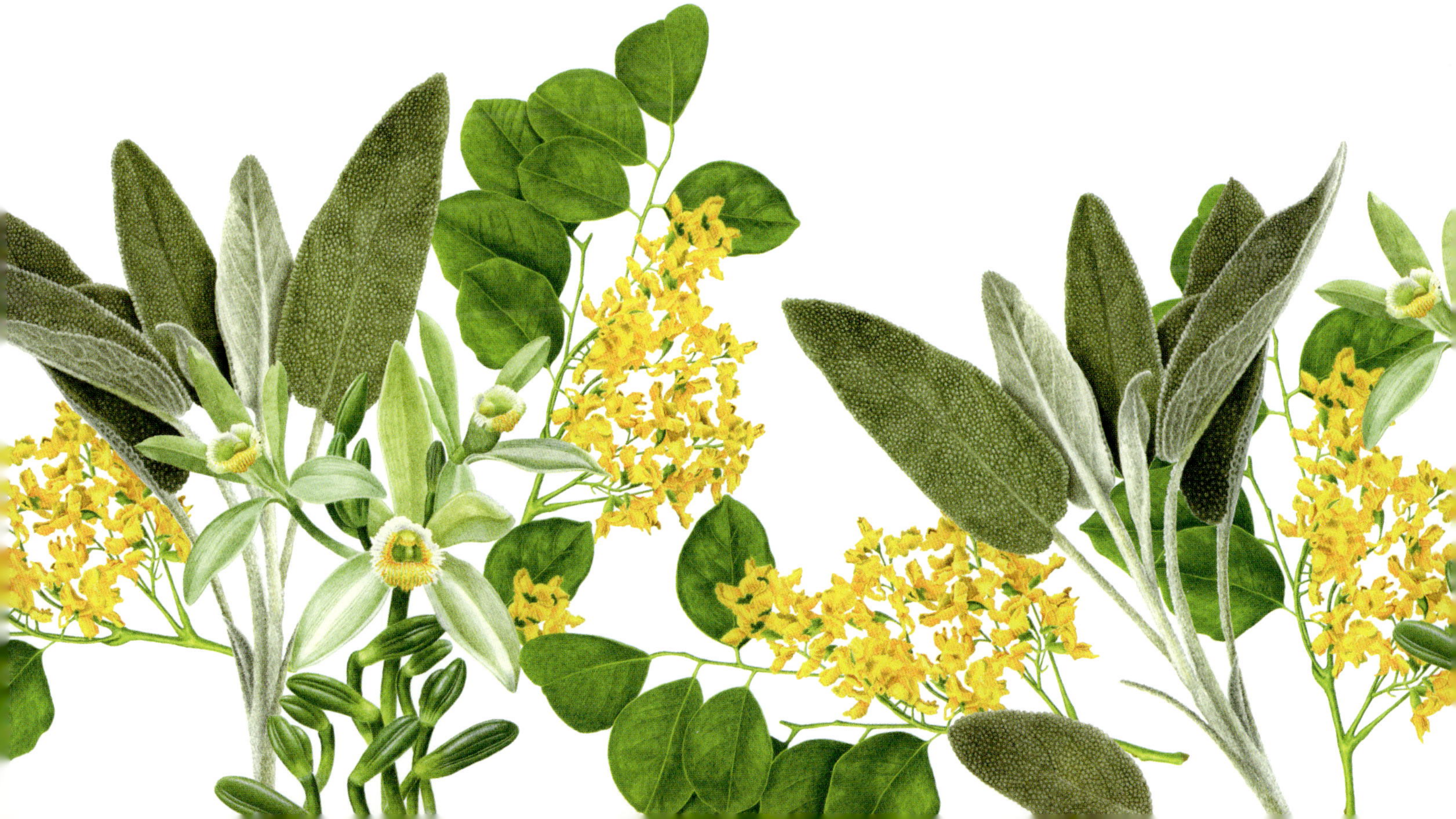

RESOURCES

English Gardening School
I am pleased to be one of the school's alumni society, Amicus Botanicus. Its aim is to act as a supportive, creative and interactive platform for the graduates and to enable us all to continue to exhibit work as a group, actual and virtual.

Association of British Botanical Artists
I am a member of ABBA, an association for aspiring botanical artists with a love of native plants.

Exhibitions

The Anatomy of Flowers, The Royal Horticultural Society Botanical Art show (London, 2011).
14th International Exhibition of Botanical Art and Illustration, The Hunt Institute for Botanical Documentation (Group show, Pittsburgh, Pennsylvania, USA, 2013).
'MOR.PHOL.O.GY': Five Botanical Artists, Sunbury Embroidery Gallery (Surrey, 2013).
'The Art of Cultivating Hope': Amicus Botanicus, 54, The Gallery, Shepherd Market (London, 2014).
Hydrangeas, The Royal Horticultural Society Botanical Art Show (London, 2016).
Worth a Thousand Words, The Royal Horticultural Society Lindley Library (Group show, London 2018).
Worth a Thousand Words: Gold Standard Botanical Art, The Royal Horticultural Society Lindley Library (Group show, London 2020).

Work in Collections

Helleborus x hybridus and *Dahlia* 'Arabian Night', The RHS Lindley Library.
Holm, Kermes and Pyrenean Oak – The Hunt Institute for Botanical Documentation, Pittsburgh, USA.

Publications

RHS Botanical Illustration: The Gold Medal Winners, Charlotte Brooks, 2019
Just Draw Botanicals, Helen Birch, White Lion Publishing, 2020
Highgrove: a Garden Celebrated. H.R.H. The Prince of Wales & Bunny Guinness.
    Weidenfeld & Nicolson.

Bibliography
Books I admire on artists (botanical painters and photographers)
who have inspired me:

Cedric Morris: Artist Plantsman, Andrew Lambirth, the Garden Museum
Rory McEwen: The Colours of Reality, Martyn Rix, Royal Botanic Gardens
Flora, Nick Knight, The Natural History Museum
Seeds: Time Capsules of Life, Rob Kesseler & Wolfgang Stuppy, Papadakis
Art Forms in Nature, Ernst Haeckel, Dover
Rosie Sanders' Roses: A Celebration in Botanical Art, Rosie Sanders, Batsford

Further Reading

Contemporary Botanical Artists: the Shirley Sherwood Collection, Shirley Sherwood,
    Weidenfeld & Nicolson
The Art of Botanical Illustration, Wilfrid Blunt and William T. Stearn, The Antique
    Collector's Club
Plant: Exploring the Botanical World, Phaidon editors, Phaidon
Amazing Rare Things, David Attenborough, Royal Collection Enterprises
Fruit: An Illustrated History, Peter Blackburne-Maze, Scriptum Editions
Forgotten Masters: Indian Painting for the East India Company, William Dalrymple,
    Philip Wilson Publishers
Botany for the Artist, Sarah Simblet, Dorling Kindersley
Treasures of Botanical Art, Shirley Sherwood and Martin Rix, Kew Publishing

Online resources

Carolyn Jenkins
www.carolynjenkins.co.uk
Instagram: @jenkinscarolyn

Helen Birch
Instagram: @helenbirch_drawdrawdraw
https://linktr.ee/helenbirch_drawdrawdraw

Botanical websites

Association of British Botanical Artists
www.britishbotanicalartists.com

American Society of Botanical Artists
www.asba-art.org

Botanical Art & Artists
www.botanicalartandartists.com

Society of Botanical Artists
www.soc-botanical-artists.org

Royal Horticultural Society
www.rhs.org.uk

Société Française d'Illustration Botanique
www.sfib.art

Botanical Art Society of Australia
www.botanicalartsocietyaustralia.com

The Japanese Association of Botanical Illustration
www.art-hana.com/english/

Dutch Society of Botanical Artists
www.botanischkunstenaarsnederland.nl

Natural History Museum Images
www.nhmimages.com

Kew Gardens
www.kew.org

Rory McEwen
www.rorymcewen.com

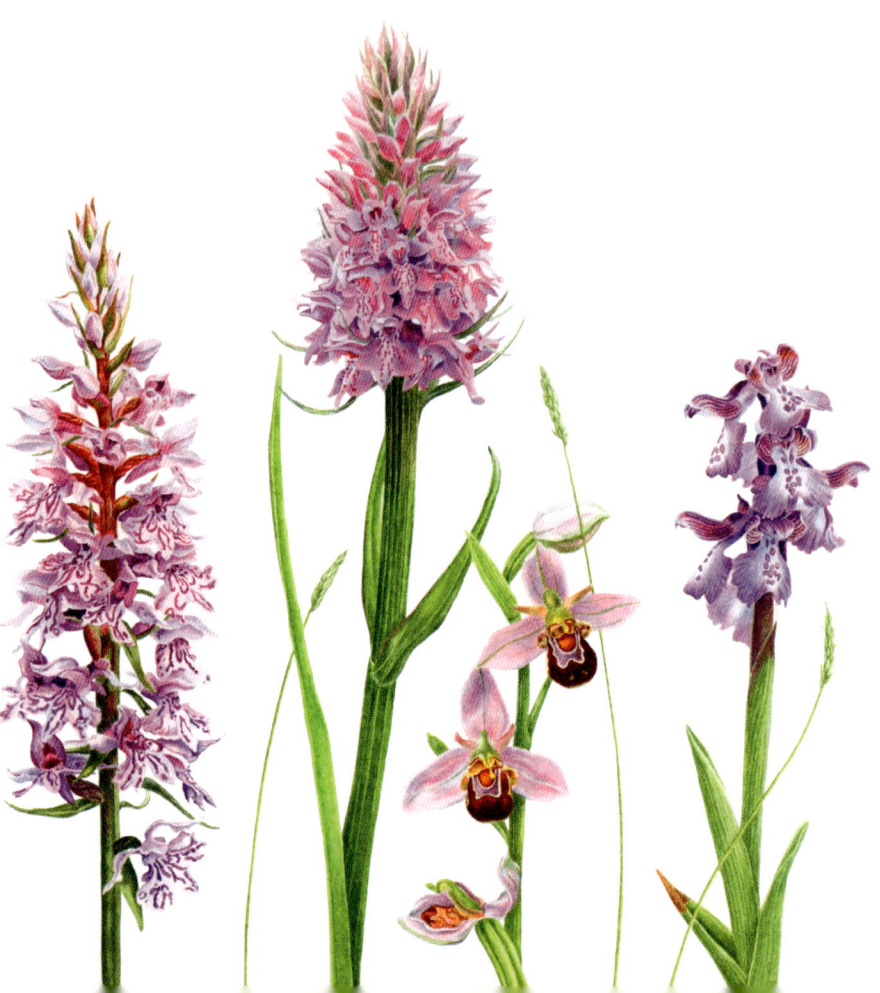

Right Wild Orchids. Southern marsh orchid (*Dactylorhiza praetermissa*); Common spotted orchid (*Dactylorhiza fuchsii*); Bee orchid (*Ophrys apifera*); Green-winged orchid (*Anacamptis morio*)

INDEX

References to illustrations are in *italics*.

ACKNOWLEDGEMENTS

CJ Thank you to Jemima Schlee for her invaluable help, honest opinions and criticisms during the initial stages of working out the compositions of my paintings. And thank you to everyone at my illustration agent, Folio Art, for all their hard work

HB A big thank you to Carolyn for inviting to me to participate on this book project with her. It's been a joy to get up close to such accomplished botanical paintings.

To all of my green-fingered friends and family – thank you to you too.

Illustration credits

The authors would also like to thank the following for their contribution to the illustrations:

First published in *Highgrove, A Garden Celebrated* by H.R.H. The Prince of Wales & Bunny Guinness. Weidenfeld & Nicolson, pages 1, 5 and 126. Matthew Axe, Creative Director, pages 2–3, 6–7, 22–23, 62 (above left), 63 (below), 64–65 (below), 68–69, 98–99, 116–117 (below), 119 (below), 123. © The Trustees of the Natural History Museum, London pages 24, 27 and 28 (above). Illustration for Superdrug beauty products, page 88 Anna Topalidou, designer of packaging, page 94.

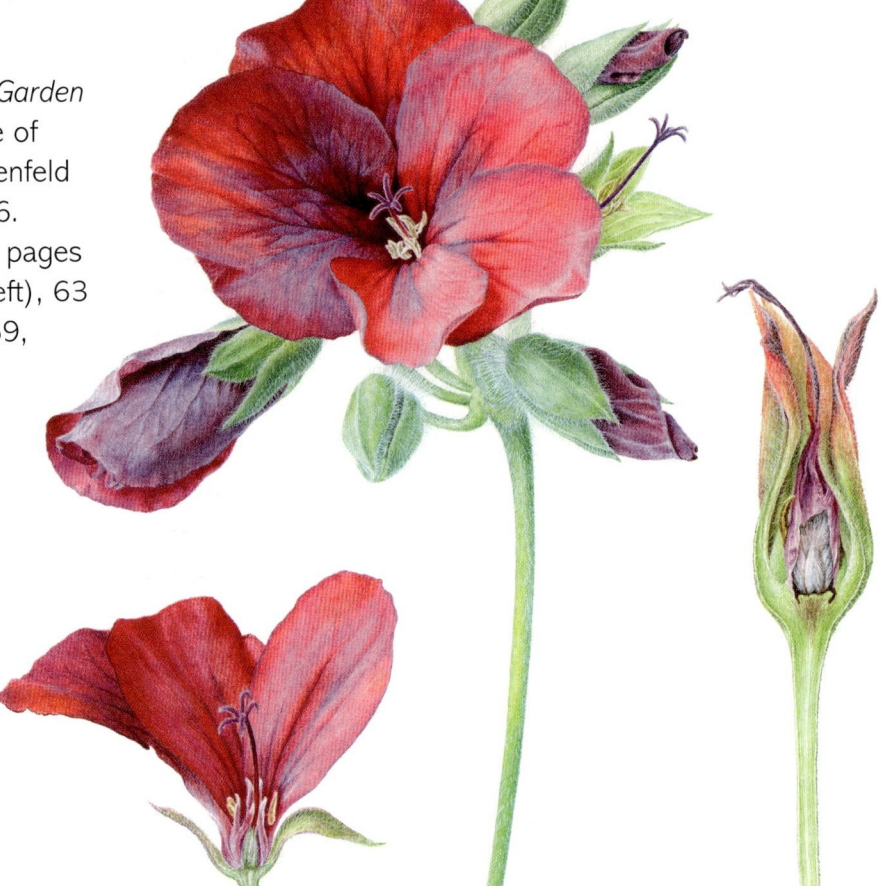

Right *Pelargonium* 'Mystery'.